高等学校**跨境电子商务**系列规划丛书

U0365804

跨境电商英语

徐珺　主编 / 夏蓉　张颖　孟庆丰　李依林　副主编

清华大学出版社
北　京

内容简介

本书根据跨境电商专业人才培养的客观需求编写,旨在响应"一带一路"倡议,为高校教学与企业项目融合搭建桥梁,培养出真正符合产业端需求的应用型跨境电商人才。

本书由 10 个单元构成,分别是"开启跨境电商之路、注册跨境电商账户、网店设置与商品选择、平台内营销、平台外营销、售前服务、售中服务、售后服务、商务沟通和商务合同"。注重跨境电商英语的语言文体特点,既有理论思辨,又注重理论联系实践。让学生能够在较短的时间内,在掌握跨境电商基础知识的基础上,掌握并灵活运用跨境电商英语,提升跨境电商"听、说、读、写、译"的技能与水平。

本书既适合作为跨境电子商务专业的教材,也适合高等院校英语专业、商务英语专业和高等院校国际金融专业、国际贸易专业使用,还可供企业培训以及社会培训机构使用。

图书在版编目(CIP)数据

跨境电商英语/徐珺主编.—北京:清华大学出版社,2020.9(2023.9重印)
(高等学校跨境电子商务系列规划丛书)
ISBN 978-7-302-55103-4

Ⅰ.①跨…　Ⅱ.①徐…　Ⅲ.①电子商务-英语-高等学校-教材　Ⅳ.①F713.36

中国版本图书馆 CIP 数据核字(2020)第 048216 号

责任编辑:张　民
封面设计:傅瑞学
责任校对:时翠兰
责任印制:沈　露

出版发行:清华大学出版社
　　　　　网　　　址:http://www.tup.com.cn,http://www.wqbook.com
　　　　　地　　　址:北京清华大学学研大厦 A 座　　　　　邮　　编:100084
　　　　　社 总 机:010-83470000　　　　　　　　　　　邮　　购:010-62786544
　　　　　投稿与读者服务:010-62776969, c-service@tup.tsinghua.edu.cn
　　　　　质量反馈:010-62772015, zhiliang@tup.tsinghua.edu.cn
　　　　　课件下载:http://www.tup.com.cn,010-83470236
印 装 者:三河市龙大印装有限公司
经　　销:全国新华书店
开　　本:185mm×260mm　　　　印　张:16.75　　　　字　数:383 千字
版　　次:2020 年 9 月第 1 版　　　　　　　　　　印　次:2023 年 9 月第 4 次印刷
定　　价:49.00 元

产品编号:082578-01

前　言

电子商务是伴随着计算机技术的发展,融计算机科学、市场营销学、管理学、经济学、法学和现代物流于一体的新型交叉学科。它是以信息网络技术为手段,以商品交换为中心的商务活动;也可理解为在互联网(Internet)、企业内部网(Intranet)和增值网(Value Added Network,VAN)上以电子交易方式进行交易和相关服务的活动,是传统商业活动各环节的电子化、网络化和信息化。2007—2008 年,我国试办电子商务专业;2011 年,电子商务专业正式纳入教育部的专业目录(专业代码为 110209)。

跨境电子商务是一个新型的概念,也是一个新生事物。跨境电子商务通常是指分属不同关境的交易主体,通过电子商务平台达成交易、进行支付结算,并通过跨境物流送达商品、完成交易的一种国际商业活动。跨境电子商务具有全球化(Globalization)、无形性(Intangibility)、匿名性(Anonymity)、即时性(Instantaniety)、无纸化(Paperlessness)和快速演进(Rapid Evolution)等特点。

随着科学技术的发展,尤其是计算机和网络技术的发展,电子商务已被广泛认可和接受。中国的发展离不开世界,世界的发展也离不开中国。我国拥有全球最多的网购用户,是世界第一大网络零售市场。伴随着"一带一路"倡议的实施,跨境电商迎来了更加广阔的舞台和千载难逢的发展机遇,因为"一带一路"沿线大多是新兴经济体和发展中国家,占全球总人口数的 63%,处于经济发展的上升期,具有巨大的市场潜力。据相关文献资料显示,我国已经与 14 个国家和地区签署了电商合作文件。2018 年 8 月《中华人民共和国电子商务法》的颁布,标志着我国企业开展跨境电商合作有了法律保障。

从上述简要分析可以看出,我国跨境电商前景广阔。然而,我国跨境电商处于发展初期,也存在着亟待解决的一系列问题:①传统中小型外贸企业转型升级、新兴的跨境电商经营企业高速发展都急需大量的相关人才,特别是兼具国际贸易和电子商务特征的跨境电商企业对人才的综合性需求较强,单一的专业人才培养无法满足跨境电商企业对人才的需求。②国内绝大多数高校尚未建立跨境电子商务专业,高校教学体系滞后,跨境电商企业很难直接招聘到满意的跨境电商英语人才,这在一定程度上制约了跨境电商的发展;③缺少跨境电子商务成套教材,无法满足目前跨境电商产业界的需求。这些问题的存在既

FOREWORD

不利于跨境电商专业人才的培养,也不利于相关学科体系建设。

2020 年 4 月,教育部高等学校外国语言文学类专业教学指导委员会发布了《普通高等学校本科外国语言文学类专业教学指南》(以下简称《指南》),其中的第三部分是普通高等学校本科商务英语专业教学指南,适用于国际商务、国际贸易、国际会计、国际金融、跨境电子商务等专业方向。

我们认真贯彻国务院关于推进产教融合的方针,积极落实《指南》的相关规定,响应“一带一路”倡议,为高校教学与企业项目融合搭建桥梁,致力于培养符合产业端需求的商务英语专业人才和应用型跨境电商人才,打造特色鲜明的《跨境电商英语》教材。

本教材具有以下特点:

(1) 定位科学、难易适度。在教学内容选择、知识结构选择、教学过程编排、教学方法设计和教学效果测试等方面进行了精心的论证和规划,有的放矢地编写了各个单元的跨境电商英语教学内容。

(2) 内容新颖、图文并茂。在教材编写过程中,紧扣跨境电商这个主题,紧密结合教学大纲的要求和学生的现实需求,选取鲜活的语料,佐以丰富的配图,灵活多样,由浅入深、循序渐进,有机融合课文学习与技能训练,有助于提升学生的“听、说、读、写、译”能力。

(3) 重点突出、结构合理。本教材系统地涵盖了跨境电商专业主干与核心课程的内容,共计 10 个单元,分别是开启跨境电商之路、注册跨境电商账户、网店设置与商品选择、平台内营销、平台外营销、售前服务、售中服务、售后服务、商务沟通和商务合同。注重跨境电商英语的语言文体特点,既有理论思辨,又注重理论联系实践。

(4) 讲练结合、学以致用。考虑学生多样的学习需求,以及学生的个体差异,倡导主动、探究、合作的教学理念与授课方式,以保障教学质量。具体体现在:①每个单元均配有主干课文,同时,提供丰富多样的课后练习。②每个单元还配有拓展阅读与练习,方便学生自学。拓展阅读与练习有助于开拓学生的视野,便于学生结合每个单元所学的内容,进行模拟测试,确保学习效果,可以起到举一反三的效果。

(5) 注重现代教育技术和辅助教学手段的运用。与纸质教材配套,合理地运用现代计算机和多媒体技术,给学生提供练习答案。这样,有助于充分调动学生的自主学习意识,提升学生主动学习的能力,从而提高教学质量。

综上所述,本教材编写组致力于满足“互联网+”时代大学生学习的新需求,为我国跨境电商不断发展提供教材支持和人才培养支持。本教材得到了对外经济贸易大学中央高校教育教学改革专项项目——教材项目(项目号 103-741903,2019)的支持。和对外经济贸易大学“一带一路”系列著作项目(“一带一路”视域下的语言服务跨学科研究,TS4-21)的支持。

　　本教材得以顺利完成是我们编写组成员数次会议、头脑风暴的结果，是我们夜以继日、辛勤耕耘的结果，是我们团结高效、通力合作的结果。在《跨境电商英语》教材提交出版社的今天，作为教材的主编，我要把最诚挚的感谢和祝福献给所有的编者以及家人，因为我们这个教材的编写，全部都是在周末、在节假日、在夜深人静的时候完成的！感谢我们全体编写人员家人的关心、理解和大力支持。同时，我也把感谢献给我的硕士生田玮同学，感谢她帮我们整理了相关的词汇。

　　本教材得以顺利出版，得益于国家服务外包人力资源研究院和清华大学出版社的支持。衷心感谢何雄老师、王娟老师的帮助、理解和大力支持！衷心感谢清华大学出版社领导和各位编辑老师给予我们的帮助、理解和大力支持！

　　本教材在编写过程中参考了大量的文献，对此，我们尽可能一一标注，但由于参考的书籍和文献多，跨度大，在析出文献标注时难免有所遗漏。如果疏漏了某些文献，恳望相关作者和出版机构在予以谅解的同时，通过电子邮件或者电话告诉我们，以便在再版时补充或更正，以利于后续研究与教学。在此，我们谨向所有相关作者和出版机构一并表示衷心的感谢。

　　简言之，本教材结合跨境电商人才的客观需要，让学生能够在较短的时间内，在掌握跨境电商基础知识的基础上，掌握并灵活运用跨境电商英语，提升跨境电商"听、说、读、写、译"的技能与水平。本书既适合作为跨境电子商务专业的教材，也适合高等院校英语专业、商务英语专业和高等院校国际金融专业、国际贸易专业使用，还可供企业培训以及社会培训机构使用。

　　囿于编著水平和编著时间，书中不当之处在所难免，敬请广大读者批评指正。

徐　珺

2020 年 5 月于对外经济贸易大学科研楼办公室

目 录

CONTENTS

CONTENTS

CONTENTS

CONTENTS

Unit 1

Getting Started for Cross-border E-commerce

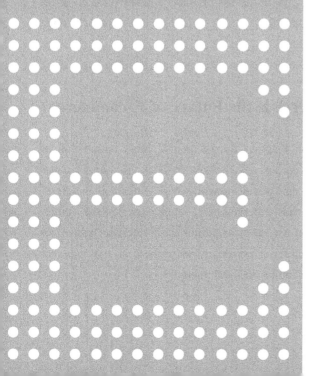

Learning Objectives

To realize the opportunities and challenges in the cross-border selling

To learn the primary E-commerce business models

To understand the need of localizing the cross-border selling

Warming up

1. Work in a group and share with each other your knowledge of or experiences with cross-border E-commerce platforms.

2. Read the words or phrases and their explanations. Then complete the following paragraph(s) with the words or phrases. Change the form when necessary.

border	the line that divides two countries or areas; the land near this line
location	a fixed place or position in space
payment	an act of paying money
shop	do one's shopping at; do business with; be a customer or client of
social media	interactive computer-mediated technologies that facilitate the creation and sharing of information, ideas, career interests and other forms of expression via virtual communities and networks

The Internet enables consumers to _____ globally, by purchasing products and services across their _____, driven by a common language, a common border, special offers, or simply because the product or service isn't available in the consumer's own region. The increasing popularity of tablets and smartphones, allows consumers worldwide to compare prices, connect with other consumers via _____, to discuss products and services, to select a web shop independent of its _____ and to transfer _____ via their PC, laptop, mobile phone or tablet at any place, anytime, anywhere.

(Adapted from http://www.crossborder-ecommerce.com/international-expansion)

Text: Why Cross-border E-commerce is the Future of E-commerce?

Cross-border E-commerce is a phenomenon that has quietly gained huge momentum as customers purchase products from outside their borders. In the last 2 years, E-commerce has seen distributed E-commerce (buy buttons on certain social networks — Twitter and Pinterest) and more recently conversational E-commerce has emerged as a contender for the future. Conversational E-commerce is seen as a potential use case for customer service which involves the usage of technology to help with communication. I personally view these as fads whereas cross-border E-commerce has potential to be the future of E-commerce.

What is cross-border E-commerce?

Cross-border E-commerce can refer to online trade between a business (retailer or brand) and a consumer (B2C), between two businesses, often brands or wholesalers (B2B), or between two private persons (C2C), e.g., via marketplace platforms, such as Amazon, Alibaba, or eBay.

What are the risks for cross-border E-commerce?

There are 3 main risks that influence cross-border E-commerce:

Fraud is arguably the biggest challenge faced by merchants who allow customers to purchase from them outside the borders of their country. Thus, picking a good payment service that is aware of local customer behavior is critical.

Logistics and reverse logistics are also just as important and can negatively impact the perception of your business by local customers. Consistent and predictable logistics is a requirement for a business that is wanting to capitalize on cross-border E-commerce.

Regulations — local government and taxation needs thorough examination and could potentially negatively impact your business.

How big is the size of the opportunity?

By 2020, over 2 billion e-shoppers, or 60 percent of target global population, would be transacting 13.5 percent of their overall retail consumptions online, equivalent to a market value of US $ 3.4 trillion (Global B2C GMV, growing at CAGR(Compound Annual Growth Rate) of 13.5 percent from 2014 to 2020) according to Accenture (see Figure 1-1).

Where are the opportunities for cross-border E-commerce?

China — Chinese cross-border E-commerce is worth $ 60 billion but legislation might impact it. The reason for the potential government interference is due to brands using cross-border E-commerce as a way to circumvent the regulations of their products with local agencies. Known as cross-border E-commerce, the booming backdoor avenue allows Chinese consumers to buy overseas-manufactured goods online and effectively circumvent the regulatory issues that have stymied access to consumer products from cosmetics to Cognac. Faced with pressure from conventional retailers at home, and the loss of tax revenue, the government is now looking at overhauling the legal loophole.

South East Asia — Singapore, Indonesia. Reports state that the E-commerce market in Southeast Asia will reach US $ 200 billion by 2025 with online sales growth at a CAGR of 32%. With 600 million consumers and 260 million people online, it is the largest market of Internet users in the world. It thus makes complete sense that both Amazon and Alibaba have increased their interest in this area.

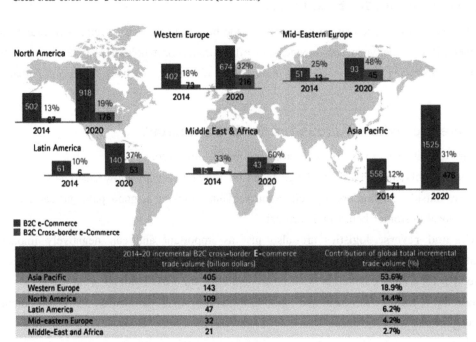

Global cross-border B2C E-commerce transaction value (US$ billion)

	2014-20 incremental B2C cross-border E-commerce trade volume (billion dollars)	Contribution of global total incremental trade volume (%)
Asia Pacific	405	53.6%
Western Europe	143	18.9%
North America	109	14.4%
Latin America	47	6.2%
Mid-eastern Europe	32	4.2%
Middle-East and Africa	21	2.7%

Figure 1-1

Australia — Australians like buying clothes from online businesses from outside their borders. Since March 2016, the Chinese authorities have published a series of regulations aimed at extending normal import tariffs and regulatory requirements to goods imported into China via cross-border E-commerce channels. But it is still hoped that goods imported into China via cross-border E-commerce can continue benefiting from the business-friendly policies and regulatory exemption.

France — The fastest growing E-commerce segment in France is cross-border purchases. Nearly half of all French consumers regularly buy from cross-border merchants and 19% of all online sales in 2016 were made on non-domestic websites, four point higher than the European average of 15%, most frequently Germany, the UK, Belgium, the US, and China. The major problem with French customers is that their transactions are relatively small in comparison to the countries mentioned before it.

Mexico — is a long-term market due to the staggering rate at which the market for E-commerce is growing at 21%. The growth is hampered by security concerns over payment. Amazon has partnered with a local retailer to ensure that customers can pay for their purchases with cash. The market has low competition and with the rate of growth, Mexico could in a long term become the most important market in Latin American E-commerce.

As mentioned earlier, cross-border payments are difficult and should be managed to ensure that customers are not surprised by additional government levies when items arrive at their final destination. Understanding local taxation and ensuring that the customer pays accordingly is crucial; otherwise, the purchase will be returned and create an aggravated customer, which will harm your business and brand.

In summary, cross-border E-commerce is here to stay and needs to be considered accordingly as a growth strategy for an E-commerce business. It needs investment (payment processing, staff and logistics) and should be done in a staged manner for maximum impact.

(Adapted from https://E-commerce-platforms.com/
articles/cross-border-E-commerce-future-E-commerce)

Words & Expressions

momentum	/məʊˈmɛntəm/	n.	the ability to keep increasing, developing, or being more successful 动力,势头
fad	/fæd/	n.	something that people like or do for a short time, or that is fashionable for a short time 一时的狂热;时尚,风尚
retailer	/ˈriːteɪlə/	n.	a person or business that sells goods to customers in a shop 零售商;零售商店
wholesaler	/həʊˈseilə/	n.	a person or business that sells items to retail stores that will then sell them to individual customers for a higher price 批发商
fraud	/frɔːd/	n.	the crime of deceiving people in order to gain something such as money or goods 欺诈;诈骗
merchant	/ˈmɜːtʃənt/	n.	someone who buys and sells goods in large quantities 商人;批发商
logistics	/ləˈdʒɪstɪks/	n.	the practical arrangements that are needed in order to make a plan that involves a lot of people and equipment successful 物流;组织工作
perception	/pəˈsɛpʃən/	n.	an idea, a belief or an image you have as a result of how you see or understand sth 看法;见解
taxation	/tækˈseɪʃən/		the system of charging taxes 征税;课税;税收(制度)
transact	/trænˈzækt/	v.	to do business with someone 办理(业务);交易
legislation	/ˌlɛdʒɪsˈleɪʃən/	n.	a law or set of laws 法规;法律
interference	/ˌɪntəˈfɪərəns/	n.	an act of interfering 干涉;干预;介入
circumvent	/ˌsɜːkəmˈvɛnt/	v.	to avoid a problem or rule that restricts you, especially in a clever or dishonest way — used to show disapproval(尤指巧妙或不诚实地)回避;规避

stymie	/ˈstaɪmɪ/	v.	find it very difficult to take action or to continue what you are doing.妨碍
cosmetics	/kɒzˈmɛtɪks/	n.	creams, powders etc. that you use on your face and body in order to look more attractive 化妆品；美容品
conventional	/kənˈvɛnʃənəl/	adj.	used for a long time and considered the usual type 传统的；常规的
revenue	/ˈrɛvɪˌnjuː/	n.	money that the government receives from tax(政府的) 财政收入
overhaul	/əʊvəˈhɔːl/	v.	to change a system or method in order to improve it 全面改革(制度或方法)
loophole	/ˈluːpˌhəʊl/	n.	a small mistake in a law that makes it possible to avoid doing something that the law is supposed to make you do (法律中的) 漏洞；空子
tariff	/ˈtærɪf/	n.	tax on imports or exports between sovereign states 关税
segment	/ˈsɛgmənt/	n.	a part of something that is different from or affected differently from the whole in some way 部分；段；片
exemption	/ɪgˈzempʃən/	n.	immunity from an obligation, or duty (义务等的) 免除；免(税)
staggering	/ˈstægərɪŋ/	adj.	extremely great or surprising 大得惊人的；令人吃惊的
hamper	/ˈhæmpə/	v.	to make it difficult for someone to do something 阻碍，妨碍；牵制
levy	/ˈlɛvɪ/	n.	a sum of money that you have to pay, for example, as a tax to the government 税款
aggravated	/ˈægrəˌveɪtɪd/	adj.	a serious crime that involves violence (罪行) 严重的
crucial	/ˈkruːʃəl/	adj.	extremely important, because everything else depends on it 至关重要的；关键性的
emerge as			成为；一跃成为
capitalize on sth.			充分利用
be aware of			意识到
make a complete sense			完全合情合理
be equivalent to			对等
partner with			做伙伴；与合作伙伴
in summary			总之；概括起来

Notes & Terms

cross-border E-commerce	international online trade, which entails the sale or purchase of products via online shops across national borders 跨境电商

conversational E-commerce	E-commerce via various means of conversation such as live chat on E-commerce websites or on messaging apps, or via voice assistants 会话式电子商务
market value	the price at which an asset would trade in a competitive auction setting 市场价值;市价
transaction value	a method which is used to determine the duty of imported goods based on the price payable 成交价格;交易金额
import tariff	a tax or duty imposed on imports and some exports by a country's customs authorities 进口关税
GMV	Gross Merchandise Volume 网站成交金额
CAGR	Compound Annual Growth Rate 复合年均增长率
B2B	Business to Business 企业与企业之间通过互联网进行产品、服务及信息的交换
C2C	Customer to Customer 消费者与消费者之间的电子商务
B2C	Business to Customer "商对客",是电子商务的一种模式,也就是直接面向消费者销售产品和服务的商业零售模式
Accenture	a global management consulting and professional services firm that provides strategy, consulting, digital, technology and operations services 埃森哲咨询公司
Cognac	a type of fine brandy made in the southwestern part of France 干邑白兰地(产于法国西南部)

Understanding the text

Ⅰ. Complete the following summary of the text.

Cross-border E-commerce, or international online trade, has been developing into a quickly growing ecosystem and becoming a great success story for many _____, such as brands, wholesalers, or manufacturers by selling their products over the _____ to retailers, or directly to _____. In spite of risks, including fraud, logistics, and local regulations etc., the size of opportunities, according to the report released by Accenture, is huge. The growth _____ can find its footprint in several countries and regions such as China, South East Asia, Australia, France and Mexico. Cross-border E-commerce needs to be considered as a growth strategy and investment on _____ management, staff and logistics should be made in a staged manner.

Ⅱ. Read the text and decide whether the following statements are true (T) or false (F).

(   ) 1 The author is optimistic about the future of cross-border E-commerce.

(   ) 2 Alibaba, Amazon and eBay are regular C2C marketplaces.

(   ) 3   Logistics constitutes to be the biggest challenge for the cross-border purchase.

(   ) 4   Reverse logistics can negatively impact the perception of your business because end consumers have to return the defective products.

(   ) 5   The author recommends that local regulations and taxation should be looked into thoroughly.

Ⅲ. Answer the following questions according to the text.

1. What is cross-border E-commerce?

2. What are the risks for cross-border E-commerce?

3. Why is cross-border E-commerce the future of E-commerce?

4. Where are the opportunities for cross-border E-commerce?

5. What should you take into consideration when you are planning an international online business?

Language Work

Ⅰ. Choose the best choice to complete each of the following sentences.

1. The growth _____ that cross-border E-commerce has gained yields unrivaled opportunities for retailers and manufacturers.

    A. moment   B. momentum   C. monument   D. omnipotent

2. Almost anyone involved in the E-commerce industry recognizes the _____ that China holds.

    A. potential   B. likeliness   C. popularity   D. technologies

3. Conversational E-commerce is seen as a use case for customer service which involves the usage of technology to help with _____.

    A. socializing   B. research and development

    C. manufacturing   D. communication

4. By 2020, over 2 billion e-shoppers will be _____ 13.5 percent of their overall retail consumptions online.

    A. transcending   B. transferring   C. transacting   D. transporting

5. Meanwhile, a 2017 report by _____ giant Visa estimated that the medical tourism industry was worth more than $100 billion a year, and continuing to grow in value by quarter every year.

    A. pay   B. paid   C. payments   D. paying

Ⅱ. Match the English words in the left column with the English explanations in the right column.

_____ 1. fad   A. take advantage of a situation

_____ 2. fraud   B. a rule put in place by some authority, such as a government

_____　3. capitalize　　C. something that deceives or tricks another person, usually to get their money

_____　4. tariff　　D. a kind of tax on goods a country imports or exports

_____　5. regulation　　E. an interest followed with exaggerated zeal

Ⅲ. Translate the following sentences from the text into Chinese.

1. Faced with pressure from conventional retailers at home, and the loss of tax revenue, the government is now looking at overhauling the legal loophole.

_____
_____.

2. With 600 million consumers and 260 million people online, it is the largest market of Internet users in the world.

_____
_____.

3. Mexico is a long-term market due to the staggering rate at which the market for E-commerce is growing at 21%.

_____
_____.

4. Understanding local taxation and ensuring that the customer pays accordingly is crucial; otherwise, the purchase will be returned and create an aggravated customer, which will harm your business and brand.

_____
_____.

5. In summary, cross-border E-commerce is here to stay and needs to be considered accordingly as a growth strategy for an E-commerce business.

_____
_____.

Ⅳ. Translate the following sentences into English using the proper forms of the words or expressions given in brackets.

1. 我国跨境电子商务主要有企业对企业(即 B2B)和企业对消费者(即 B2C)的贸易模式。(model)

_____
_____.

2. 阿里巴巴国际站、亚马逊、易趣等是跨境商务业务比较成熟的平台。(well-developed)

_____
_____.

3. 跨境电子商务在交易方式、货物运输、支付结算等方面与传统贸易方式差异较大。(differ from)

4. 随着消费水平的提升,我国消费者对进口商品的需求日益增强。(prompt)

5. 作为世界上最大的电子商务市场,我国 2017 年的网络销售达 7.2 万亿元人民币,比 2016 年增长近 32.2%。(increase)

Supplementary Reading: Localization — Keys to Cross-border Selling in B2B E-commerce

The 2018 B2B Cross-border Survey sheds light on the status of cross-border selling and the key challenges merchants face as they gear up to tackle the opportunities.

Research consultancy Forrester estimates that cross-border selling will make up 20 percent of E-commerce by 2022, and according to a 2018 whitepaper by logistics provider DHL Express, cross-border B2B transactions will reach $ 1.2 trillion within the next five years. To seize on the market opportunity, an accelerating number of B2B merchants are ramping up their E-commerce outreach to overseas customers.

However, successfully selling to an international audience requires more than just translating an existing online store into new languages. To get a better sense of how cross-border E-commerce is unfolding, Oro Inc., leaders in open-source business applications, recently polled its global community of B2B merchants and practitioners with a series of questions about their current and planned efforts internationally. The responses received in the 2018 B2B Cross-border Survey shed light on the status of cross-border selling and the key challenges merchants are facing as they gear up to tackle the opportunities.

Although an overwhelming majority (80 percent) of companies that participated in the survey had little experience selling to markets outside of their primary regions, that is clearly in the process of changing quickly. The survey made it clear that 75 percent of merchants are planning significant investments in international markets and consider them crucial to future growth. As important, most merchants felt that understanding local markets will be critical to succeeding in new areas, especially given crucial differences between markets in buying habits; logistics like shipping and customs requirements; and handling local policies, regulations and taxes.

The following provides specific guidance around the critical elements of selling overseas and looks at the need for localization in cross-border E-commerce initiatives.

Personalized User Experience

A recent report by Common Sense Advisory found that 87 percent of consumers who have trouble reading English refuse to buy at English-only websites. So, a crucial first step is to translate your B2B E-commerce site into the local languages — not just literal translations, but localization of an entire site's content in accordance with the vernacular the customer is accustomed to.

According to the survey, 66 percent of respondents identified personalization for local audiences as their greatest challenge in expanding internationally: the need to understand international buyers and local conventions relating to online user experience. For B2B E-commerce businesses to thrive, their online storefronts need to provide intuitive, personalized user interfaces: sites that allow buyers to complete the entire shopping process, from browsing products to completing the purchase, according to local norms. In industry terms, this is called "self-service functionality," and it has become a critical success factor in both consumer and B2B E-commerce. Gartner has predicted that by 2020 customers will complete 85 percent of their online transactions with zero human interaction.

That self-service functionality can be achieved internationally only with effective regional adaptation. Using local measuring standards, offering discounts for regional holidays, and designing convenient and locally appropriate user experiences for specific international markets can help B2B merchants streamline sales processes and compete effectively with in-country brands.

Shipping and Customs

Shipping and customs regulations vary hugely from country to country — even more so for merchants whose products, such as aerosols or volatile liquids, are complicated to ship and distribute. In the 2018 B2B Cross-border Survey, 41 percent of respondents said they think adapting to local shipping logistics and customs needs poses the biggest challenge to selling overseas.

Each foreign country and region has its own set of product classification systems for import tariffs. Failing to accurately describe the product category or affix the correct product code on international shipping containers can result in additional costs. It's important for B2B online sellers to not only offer multiple shipping options but also to provide overseas customers with transparency into the charges that may accrue during delivery.

Taxation

In the United States, sales tax is typically charged at the final point of sale, so resellers and wholesalers are exempt from those fees. But more than 160 other countries in the world, including most of Europe, charge value-added tax (VAT) rather than sales tax, where taxes accrue at each point in the supply chain. This means that tax fees must be added to product prices and either paid for by merchants or passed on to customers. U.S. B2B merchants, accustomed to displaying prices independent of tax, need to show tax-inclusive pricing on

European online storefronts. According to the survey, 45 percent of B2B merchants find VAT registration and filing in multiple countries to be their biggest challenge in terms of taxes and regulation.

B2B sellers often offer large and diverse product catalogs, presenting an even greater challenge to navigating complex tax codes and calculating individual tax rates for each product and service. Sellers need to regularly monitor tax rate changes, which can have a significant impact on product pricing and business bottom lines.

Local Law and Regulations

In the survey, 33 percent of respondents pointed to local laws and regulations as the biggest challenge for international B2B E-commerce. International markets and regions have variable rules and regulations governing product labeling, licensing and merchandising. For B2B merchants selling into regulated industries, such as medical devices or healthcare supplements, it is particularly important to check with a country's regulatory bodies to see if products need to be licensed to sell. Additionally, some B2B product categories, like construction materials, refrigeration appliances and machinery equipment, are required to have health and safety certification called "CE marking" in European Union countries.

Individual countries' trade protection policies can also affect businesses selling abroad. The government of Argentina, for instance, famously introduced new protective restrictions in 2014 limiting citizens to two purchases of goods from foreign E-commerce websites each year. When planning your international expansion strategy, it is crucial to study these local rules and regulations to avoid legal pitfalls and to select the right markets to target.

(Adapted from https://www.sdcexec.com/risk-compliance/blog/
21017848/localization-key-to-crossborder-selling-in-b2b-ecommerce)

Words & Expressions

tablet	/ˈtæblɪt/	n.	a small portable computer that accepts input directly onto its screen rather than via a keyboard or mouse 平板电脑
localization	/ˌləʊkəlaɪˈzeɪʃn/	n.	A determination of the place where something is 本地化
tackle	/ˈtækəl/	v.	to make a determined effort to deal with a difficult problem or situation 应付;处理;解决(难题或局面)
accelerate	/ækˈsɛləˌreɪt/	v.	to happen or to make sth happen faster or earlier than expected(使)加速;加快
outreach	/ɑʊtriːtʃ/	n.	the activity of an organization that provides a service or advice to people in the community, especially those

			who cannot or are unlikely to come to an office, a hospital, etc. for help 外展服务(在服务机构以外的场所提供的社区服务等)
poll	/pəʊl/	*n.*	the process of questioning people who are representative of a larger group in order to get information about the general opinion 民意测验;民意调查
practitioner	/præk'tɪʃənə/	*n.*	someone who regularly does a particular activity 从事者;实践者
overwhelming	/ˌəʊvə'welmɪŋ/	*adj.*	very large or greater, more important etc. than any other 巨大的;压倒性的
ship	/ʃɪp/	*v.*	to send goods somewhere by ship, plane, truck etc. (用船、飞机、卡车等)运送
vernacular	/və'nækjʊlə/	*n.*	a form of a language that ordinary people use, especially one that is not the official language (尤指非官方语言的)本国语;本地语;土话;方言
personalization	/'pə: sənəlaizeiʃn/	*n.*	the action of designing or producing something to meet someone's individual requirement 个性化
convention	/kən'venʃn/	*n.*	the way in which sth is done that most people in a society expect and consider to be polite or the right way to do it 习俗;常规;惯例
thrive	/θraɪv/	*v.*	to become, and continue to be, successful, strong, healthy, etc.兴旺发达;繁荣;蓬勃发展;旺盛
storefront	/'stɔːfrʌnt/	*n.*	a room at the front of a shop/store 店面;铺面
intuitive	/ɪn'tjuːɪtɪv/	*adj.*	able to understand situations without being told or having any proof about them 直觉的
interface	/'ɪntəfeɪs/	*n.*	the point where two subjects, systems, etc. meet and affect each other (两学科、体系等的)接合点,边缘区域
browse	/braʊz/	*v.*	to look at the goods in a shop without wanting to buy any particular thing (在商店里)随便看看
streamline	/'striːmlaɪn/	*v.*	to make something such as a business, organization etc. work more simply and effectively 精简(企业、组织等);简化……使效率更高
transparency	/træn'spærənsi/	*n.*	the quality of sth, such as a situation or an argument, that makes it easy to understand 易懂;清楚;透明度
accrue	/ə'kruː/	*v.*	to accumulate or to keep growing in value or size (价值、大小等)增长
reseller	/'ri: selə/	*n.*	a person who sells (a product or service) again after having bought it 中间商

respondent	/rɪˈspɒndənt/	*n.* a person who gives an answer 被调查者;被访谈者
shed light on		阐明;使……清楚地显出
gear up		促进;增加;准备好
make up		补足(某数量)
seize on		抓住;攫获
ramp up		增加;使增加
have trouble doing		做某事有困难
in accordance with		依照;与……一致
vary from		不同;各不相同
exempt from		豁免;免除
tax-inclusive pricing		含税的价格

Notes & Terms

DHL Express	an American-founded company which is now the international courier, parcel, and express mail division of the German logistics company Deutsche Post DHL, which is the worlds' largest logistics company DHL 国际快递
open-source business	a business model using a computer program in which the source code is available to the general public for use or modification from its original design 开源式商业模式
Forrester	an American market research company that provides advice on existing and potential impact of technology, to its clients and the public 福利斯特公司(市场调研与咨询公司)
Common Sense Advisory	an American company that provides independent research to companies in Europe, Asia and the Americas via several membership programs 常识咨询(研究与咨询公司)
self-service functionality	a type of software (or sites) which allows customers to complete the entire shopping process 自助服务功能
Gartner	a global research and advisory firm providing insights, advice, and tools 高德纳公司(研究与咨询公司)
value-added tax (VAT)	a type of tax that is assessed incrementally, based on the increase in value of a product or service at each stage of production or distribution 增值税
CE marking	a certification mark that indicates conformity with health, safety, and environmental protection standards for products sold within the European Economic Area (EEA) CE 标识(产品进入欧盟境内销售的通行证)

Text Comprehension

Choose the best answer to each of the following questions according to the text.

1. According to the passage, an overwhelming majority (80%) of companies that participated in the survey had little experience selling to markets outside of their primary regions _____.

    A. but the situation will change quickly.

    B. because they had no interest in the overseas market.

    C. because they thought it too risky to make investments in international markets.

    D. because they didn't regard the cross-border E-commerce as their growth strategy.

2. Which of the following statements is NOT TRUE according to the passage?_____

    A. Most of e-shoppers can read English and regard it as the lingua franca at cross-border E-commerce platforms.

    B. It's important to translate the entire E-commerce site's content into the local languages, not just literal translation.

    C. User interfaces should be localized in accordance with the vernacular, norms and habits of the local consumers.

    D. "Self-service functionality" means online transactions can be completed with zero human interaction.

3. In order to sell successfully overseas, it's important for merchants to do the following EXCEPT _____.

    A. to provide overseas customers with detailed shipment charges.

    B. to describe the product category and employ the correct product code.

    C. to offer multiple shipping options.

    D. to pay all the shipping charges.

4. Sales tax in _____ is charged at the final point of sales, with resellers and wholesalers exempt from those fees.

    A. China

    B. the United States

    C. the United Kingdom

    D. Germany

5. According to the survey, which constitutes the biggest challenge for the most respondents to expand their businesses internationally?_____

    A. Local law and regulations.

    B. Taxation.

    C. Personalization for local consumers.

    D. Shipping and customs.

Language Work

Fill in the following blanks with the words or phrases given below. Change the forms where necessary.

localize	logistics	challenge	initiative	accrue
transparency	exempt	streamline	inclusive	adapt

1. In addition to monitoring fraud, companies are _____ the way employees file expenses.
2. Two U. S. senators this month called on Indian Prime Minister Narendra Modi to soften India's stance on data _____, warning that measures requiring it represent "key trade barriers" between the two nations.
3. On Tuesday, associations representing the aluminum industry in all three countries sent a letter to Mr. Trump asking for their industry to be _____ from any tariff or quota.
4. A coordinated and collaborative approach between and among all stakeholders at the international, regional and national levels is vital to a safe, secure and sustainable achieving E-commerce environment, leading to a(n) _____ global trade system and increased economic growth.
5. China and France agree on the need for stronger global governance while stressing the China-proposed Belt and Road _____ will be a boon for the world.

Workshop

Discussion: Work in a group and make a checklist, including the key factors you would, or should put into consideration if you plan to start cross-border selling at an E-commerce platform. Please specify with more details the opportunities and challenges you might come across when you sell a specific product to a targeted marketplace.

References

[1] http://www.crossborder-ecommerce.com/international-expansion, retrieved on 2019-03-26.
[2] https://E-commerce-platforms. com/articles/cross-border-E-commerce-future-E-commerce, retrieved on 2019-03-26.
[3] https://www.sdcexec. com/risk-compliance/blog/21017848/localization-key-to-crossborder-selling-in-b2b-ecommerce, retrieved on 2019-03-26.
[4] https://en.wikipedia.org/wiki/.
[5] https://www.vocabulary.com/dictionary/.
[6] https://www.investopedia.com/terms/m/marketvalue.asp.
[7] https://www.investopedia.com/terms/i/import-duty.asp.

[8] https://www.ecommercewiki.org/topics/7/cross-border-ecommerce/articles/98/what-is-cross-border-ecommerce.

[9] https://en.wikipedia.org/wiki/Conversational_commerce.

[10] https://www.linkedin.com/pulse/what-transaction-value-morris-mukandi-mukandi.

[11] https://en.wikipedia.org/wiki/Gross_merchandise_volume.

[12] https://www.investopedia.com/terms/c/cagr.asp.

[13] https://en.wikipedia.org/wiki/Business-to-business.

[14] https://en.wikipedia.org/wiki/Customer_to_customer.

[15] https://www.shopify.com/encyclopedia/business-to-consumer-b2c.

[16] https://en.wikipedia.org/wiki/Accenture.

[17] https://en.wikipedia.org/wiki/Cognac.

[18] https://en.wikipedia.org/wiki/DHL.

[19] https://en.m.wikipedia.org/wiki/Open-source_model.

[20] https://en.wikipedia.org/wiki/Forrester_Research.

[21] https://www.crunchbase.com/organization/common-sense-advisory#section-overview.

[22] https://en.wikipedia.org/wiki/Self-service_software.

[23] https://en.wikipedia.org/wiki/Gartner.

[24] https://en.wikipedia.org/wiki/Value-added_tax.

[25] https://en.wikipedia.org/wiki/CE_marking.

Unit 2

Registering for an Account

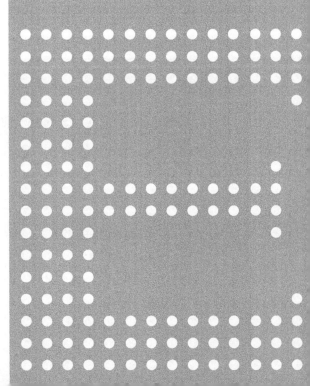

Learning Objectives

To learn how to register for an account on Alibaba and Amazon

To learn how to choose the right cross-border E-commerce platform for your E-commerce business

To learn how to get yourself ready to sell on cross-border E-commerce platforms

Warming up

1. Work in a group. Talk about the differences between Alibaba global and Amazon. Which is better for selling sourcing products globally?

2. Read the words or phrases and their explanations. Then complete the following paragraph(s) with the words or phrases. Change the form when necessary.

mailbox   a private box for delivery of mail

link   (computing) an instruction that connects one part of a program or an element on a list to another program or list

confirm   make sure something is set, or firm

tick   put a check mark on, or near, or next to

via   by means of, using

To register an account on Alibaba.com _____ laptop, please follow the steps below:

Step 1: Go to https://passport.alibaba.com/newlogin/icbuLogin.htm?return_url = http%3A% 2F%2F www.alibaba.com, click **Join Free** to register an account (see Figure 2-1).

Figure 2-1

Step 2: Enter your E-mail address, _____ the **Agreement** and **Next** (see Figure 2-2).

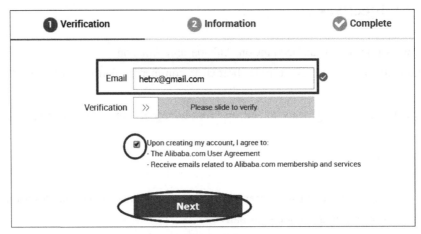

Figure 2-2

Step 3: A confirmation E-mail will be sent to your _____. Please click the _____ in the E-mail and fill in all the required information.

Step 4: If you do not have a business, you can fill the "Company name" field with your name.

Step 5: Click _____ after you fill in all the required field (see Figure 2-3).

Figure 2-3

(Adapted from https://passport.alibaba.com/newlogin/icbuLogin .htm?return url=http%3A% 2F% Fwww. alibaba. com)

Text: How to Sell Your Products on Alibaba

Alibaba may have started off as a modest B2B company in 1999, but today, the international commerce company's claims to fame includes a U.S. IPO that exceeds Google, Facebook and Twitter combined, and more than $ 7.6 billion in revenue for Q4 of 2016.

Alibaba can be a great channel to break into international markets and expand your global presence. Getting started is easy, but to make the most of your Alibaba engagement and see a boost to your bottom line, there are a few things to keep in mind as you register, set up and maintain your account.

If you're interested in selling your products on Alibaba, here's a quick walkthrough of what you'll need to get started.

1. Register for Your Account

First, you'll need to sign up for an Alibaba account. Registering for an account is pretty straightforward, and all you'll need is your name, a valid E-mail address and the name, location, and phone number of your company. At this time, you'll also have the opportunity to choose the type of account you'd like: a seller account, buyer account or a hybrid of both.

2. Establish Your Company Profile

After verifying your account via E-mail, you'll need to set up your company profile, also known as your company page. Keep in mind that this is the information that potential buyers (or sellers, if you're interested in becoming a buyer as well) will see, and so you'll want to be as thorough as possible. Generally speaking, you'll need to include the following information:

— Type of business

— Location

— Products you plan to sell

— Company size

— Target markets (where you hope to sell your products/services)

A thorough profile will instill confidence in potential partners, and taking the time to provide accurate information when you set up your profile can go a long way in securing future business.

Want to increase buyer confidence? Consider adding any product test results or certifications that you may have achieved. These can bode well for EU standards, which are typically stringent, and can place your product ahead of others, particularly when safety standards are part of the buying decision.

3. List Your Products

Obviously, to sell your products on Alibaba, you'll need to list them, and similar to providing complete business information, you'll also want to provide detailed descriptions and images of

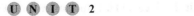

the products you choose to list. By providing accurate and thorough descriptions, you can increase product reach and attract potential buyers.

While the product listing itself is important, the number of products you list can also play a vital role in your success as an Alibaba seller. If your product page only includes 5-10 products, your page will appear empty or incomplete. Furthermore, the more products you have, the more likely you are to show up in product search results, which translate to more exposure and a higher chance at securing partners.

4. Be a Quality Communicator

If you haven't noticed yet, in many ways, perception is key to success. Creating a sense of integrity and confidence with regards to your brand is essential to maximizing any Alibaba partnerships. And while a stellar company page and detailed product descriptions can go a long way, they don't always close the deal.

As a seller in an international space, it's important that you respond and communicate with potential and existing buyers, maintaining healthy relationships that can grow your business. To help you do this, Alibaba provides a message center to manage communications. You can also install TradeManager, which is the Alibaba chat platform that lets you engage in real time with other Alibaba users.

5. Consider a Gold Membership

It's free to join Alibaba, but for those interested in really harnessing everything it offers, especially the customer base and site functionality, a Gold Membership may be worth considering. Currently, there are three different Gold Membership Levels: Basic, Standard and Premium.

Each of these levels offers members their own custom webpage; priority rankings in their search results; unlimited product postings (free memberships cap at 50); and the ability to quote buying requests. Additionally, each level has access to product showcases, which according to Alibaba, can translate into 100 times more product views.

As one might expect, Premium members receive preferential treatment and reap the benefits of 1st ranked product placements, 28 product showcases (Standard and Basic members receive 12 and 5, respectively), and they even receive their own personalized customer service.

6. Take Advantage of Alibaba Resources

Alibaba has a plethora of educational and training resources that can help business owners make the most of the tools and functionalities that they provide. From the basics of foreign trade and industry analysis to E-commerce and Alibaba basics, users who did into their learning center are bound to find information that can aid in increasing profits.

If you're interested in expanding your market or taking advantage of international sales opportunities, Alibaba can give your company the opportunity to do just that. Be sure to take the time to set up your account the right way and to use the tools and resources made available if you want to make the most of your role as an Alibaba seller.

(Adapted from https://www.nav.com/blog/sell-products-alibaba-22035/)

Words & Expressions

exceed	/ɪkˈsiːd/	*v.*	to be more than a particular number 超过;超出
walkthrough	/ˈwɔːkθruː/	*n.*	a step-by-step demonstration of a procedure or process or a step-by-step explanation of it as a novice attempts it 预排
straightforward	/streɪtˈfɔːwəd/	*adj.*	simple and easy to understand 简单的;易懂的
valid	/ˈvælɪd/	*adj.*	legally or officially acceptable 有效的;正式认可的
hybrid	/ˈhaɪbrɪd/	*n.*	something that is the product of mixing two or more different things (不同事物的)混合物,合成物
verify	/ˈverɪfaɪ/	*v.*	to check that sth is true or accurate 核实;查对;核准
profile	/ˈprəʊfaɪl/	*n.*	a description of sb/sth that gives useful information 概述;简介;传略
instill	/ɪnˈstɪl/	*v.*	to infuse slowly or gradually into the mind or feelings; insinuate; inject 逐步灌输
bode	/bəʊd/	*v.*	indicate by signs 预兆;预告
stringent	/ˈstrɪndʒənt/	*adj.*	very strict and that must be obeyed 严格的;严厉的
secure	/sɪˈkjʊə/	*v.*	get by special effort 获得
translate	/trænsˈleɪt/	*v.*	be equivalent in effect 转化
integrity	/ɪnˈtegrɪtɪ/	*n.*	the quality of being honest and having strong moral principles 诚实正直
maximize	/ˈmæksɪˌmaɪz/	*v.*	to increase sth as much as possible 使……增加到最大可能性
stellar	/ˈstelə/	*adj.*	outstanding, wonderful, better than everything else 优秀的;杰出的
harness	/ˈhaːnɪs/	*v.*	to control and use the force or strength of sth to produce power or to achieve sth 控制;利用
install	/ɪnˈstɔːl/	*n.*	to fix equipment or furniture into position so that it can be used 安装;设置
premium	/ˈpriːmɪəm/	*adj.*	of very high quality 优质的
showcase	/ˈʃəʊˌkeɪs/	*n.*	an event or situation that is designed to show the good qualities of a person, organization, product etc. 展示优点的场合(机会)
reap	/riːp/	*v.*	to get something, especially something good, as a result of what you have done 获得;取得(成果)

plethora	/ˈplɛθərə/	*n.*	(~ **of sth**) a very large number of something, usually more than you need 过多(过量)某事物
start off			以……开始
in revenue for			带来收益
set up			建立
break into			成功打入(某行业、某领域)
register for			注册;报名参加
as thorough as possible			尽可能地
with regard to			关于;至于
be worth doing			值得做
aid in			帮助;在……(方面)给予帮助

Notes & Terms

IPO	Initial Public Offerings, a process of offering shares in a private corporation to the public for the first time 首次公开募股
Google	an American multinational technology company that specializes in Internet-related services and products, which include online advertising technologies, search engine, cloud computing, software, and hardware 谷歌
Facebook	an American online social media and social networking service company based in Menlo Park, California 脸书
Twitter	an American online news and social networking service on which users post and interact with messages known as "tweets" 推特
bottom line	the profit or the amount of money that a business makes or loses (收益表的)底行;净利,净收益
target market	a market in which a company is trying to sell its products or services 目标市场
company page	a company's website homepage with a professional introduction of the business, aiming to inform the audience about its products and services 公司页面
potential buyer	a person who may have a reason or benefit to purchase your product 潜在买家;有意向的顾客
EU standards	European standards adopted by one of the three recognized European Standardization Organizations (ESOs): CEN, CENELEC or ETSI 欧洲标准
TradeManager	an online communication tool 阿里巴巴出口通或速卖通,用户与客户沟通的即时通信工具

Understanding the text

I . Complete the following summary of the text

Alibaba is a great channel by which you could break into international markets and expand your global presence. To get started, you will need to sign up for your _____, establish your company _____, and _____ your products. As a seller in a cross-border E-commerce platform, you are expected to respond to inquiries and _____ with potential and existing buyers. There are three different membership levels on Alibaba, with Premium members enjoying _____ treatment, and even more personalized customer service. In all, be sure to make full use of the tools and resources available if you want to make the most of your role as an Alibaba seller.

II . Read the text and decide whether the following statements are true (T) or false (F).

( )1 Only business-owners or manufacturers can register for an account on Alibaba.

( )2 In order to set up for an account, a valid E-mail address is a must.

( )3 Your company profile needs to be set up prior to the registration for an account.

( )4 The more products you have, the more profit your business is likely to receive.

( )5 It's important to make good use of the tools and resources available on Alibaba.

III . Answer the following questions according to the text.

1. What is needed in order to register for an account on Alibaba?

2. What types of account are available on Alibaba?

3. What information is required in order to establish your company profile?

4. What makes the product listings attractive?

5. How can you maintain good relationships with consumers?

Language Work

I . Choose the best choice to complete each of the following sentences.

1. They _____ that more and more bricks-and-mortar stores are closing down because of the challenges from E-commerce.

    A. acclaim   B. exclaim   C. claim   D. proclaim

2. He made such a _____ contribution to the university that it is naming one of the new building after him.

    A. modest   B. generous   C. minimum   D. genuine

3. The bigger collection of products you list on E-commerce, the more _____ to the product search.

    A. exposure   B. extension   C. expansion   D. exhibition

4. By sourcing products at Alibaba marketplace, you are _____ to enter cooperative business relations with Chinese suppliers.

    A. tied   B. involved   C. bound   D. associated

5. Ever since the rise of the Internet, education has been _____ towards producing innovative talents.

    A. harnessed   B. hatched   C. motivated   D. geared

Ⅱ. Match the English words in the left column with the English explanations in the right column.

_____ 1. maintain   A. a sign posted in a public place as an advertisement

_____ 2. profile   B. the act of putting something in words

_____ 3. description   C. an outline of something

_____ 4. functionality   D. keep the same; keep steady

_____ 5. posting   E. capability of serving a purpose well

Ⅲ. Translate the following sentences from the text into Chinese.

1. Alibaba can be a great channel to break into international markets and expand your global presence.

    _____

    _____.

2. Registering for an account is pretty straightforward, and all you'll need is your name, a valid E-mail address and the name, location, and phone number of your company.

    _____

    _____.

3. By providing accurate and thorough descriptions, you can increase product reach and attract potential buyers.

    _____

    _____.

4. Creating a sense of integrity and confidence with regards to your brand is essential to maximizing any Alibaba partnerships.

    _____

    _____.

5. Be sure to take the time to set up your account the right way and to use the tools and resources made available if you want to make the most of your role as an Alibaba seller.

    _____

    _____.

Ⅳ. Translate the following sentences into English using the proper forms of the words or expressions given in brackets.

1. 马云于 1999 年成立阿里巴巴,现拥有 2 万多名员工,网上销售占全国网上销售的 80% 以

上。(account for)

_____

_____ .

2. 在阿里巴巴国际站注册账号是一件很简单的事情,只需要按照步骤操作就可以。(register for)

_____

_____ .

3. 曝光率对网店来讲很重要,它可以促进交易。(facilitate)

_____

_____ .

4. 尽管消费全球化的概念盛行,中国消费者认为进口商品价格高,交货时间久。(prevail)

_____

_____ .

5. 对于跨境电商而言,了解中国受欢迎的电子商务应用程序对其在中国的品牌营销和市场拓展都是有利的。(advantageous)

_____

_____ .

Supplementary Reading: Amazon Seller Registration: Everything You Need to Know to Get Started

So you want to start an online business but aren't sure where to begin? Of course, there are tons of options out there, right? There's eBay and Etsy, blogging and Bitcoin. And of course, my favorite, Amazon. Yet, for new and aspiring entrepreneurs, setting up an online business can be intimidating. That's why I wanted to take a little time to break down the process of creating an Amazon business. This guide will cover the basics of Amazon as well as show you how to navigate Amazon seller registration.

Firstly, how do I start an Amazon business?

What's great about Amazon is that there's no one way to start an Amazon business. Even though it's been over five years since I went through the Amazon seller registration process, I keep learning cool new ways to do it. The one thing that I can't express enough, though, is how simple it is to sell on Amazon.

How to start an Amazon business in 3 easy steps.

1. *Choose what you plan to sell.* You don't have to go nuts and start your own private label (although, I highly recommend it once you're comfortable selling on Amazon). A lot of sellers get started selling their used stuff on Amazon. You can also sell books, both used and

those you write, wholesale goods, and even discounted products you can buy in department stores.

2. ***Go through Amazon seller registration***. Next, you'll need to register your "business" on Amazon. Remember, by business they don't mean that you're a big corporation. You can sell on Amazon as an individual.

3. ***List your products***. Once you're registered, you need to list your products. After that, all you have to do is wait for a sale. It's really that simple!

Next, how do I create a seller account on Amazon (Amazon seller registration)?

Once you've figured out what you plan on selling on Amazon, you'll need to go through the Amazon seller registration process, which is really quite simple.

1. Go to **https://services.amazon.com** (see Figure 2-4).

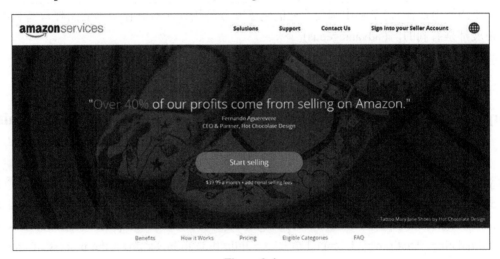

Figure 2-4

2. Scroll down the page below the heading "**Start Selling on Amazon today**." On the left side, look for the "**Selling on Amazon >**" button and click it. Note: this is if you want to sell as an individual seller to avoid the $39.99 a month professional seller subscription. If you want to sell as a professional (sell more than 40 products per month), then just click **the orange button** at the top (see Figure 2-5).

3. Choose which kind of seller account you'd like to start with. If you're going to sell more than 40 products per month, then sign up as a "**professional**." Even if you're doing it as a hobby and don't consider yourself a professional, this plan will help you save money. Otherwise, select "**individual**" (see Figure 2-6). You might also sell as an individual when you're starting out, especially if you're waiting on products to arrive or haven't yet built up enough inventory to sell 40+ products per month.

Figure 2-5

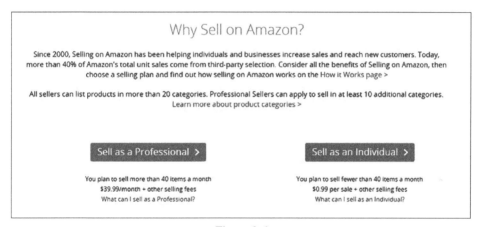

Figure 2-6

4. Enter your E-mail and select "**Create a New Account**" (see Figure 2-7).

5. Enter your personal information and create **a password** (see Figure 2-8).

6. Amazon seller **agreement** and **business information**. Now you'll need to enter the name of your business and agree to Amazon's terms of service. I've put LLC in the spot below, but you don't need to have a legal business entity to sell on Amazon (see Figure 2-9). If you're registering as an individual seller, you can list it under your given name.

7. Input your business's information and verify that you're not a bot. Next, you'll need to put all of your business's information in. Amazon will also ask for your **mobile number** so they can send you a text to verify that you're a real person and not a bot (see Figure 2-10).

8. Set up your **billing** and deposit methods. Amazon will need your credit card on file in case there's any advertising charge or you're registering as a professional seller. The bank account information is required, so they can deposit your funds once you make a sale (see Figure 2-11).

Figure 2-7

Figure 2-8

9. After that, you're in!

You may need to set up 2-step verification (to help protect your account), but once you've got all your ducks in row all you need to do is go to **https://sellercentral.amazon.com** to log in.

Thirdly, what else do I need to know about Amazon?

What is **the best seller ranking**? Amazon organizes all of its products with a Best Seller Ranking (BSR). The more popular an item is and the more it's sold, the higher the best seller ranking for the product is. Each department on Amazon has its own taxonomy of BSRs, as do the sub-categories.

What is **FBA**? FBA stands for Fulfillment by Amazon. It is a service offered by Amazon where they store your inventory for you in one of their fulfillment centers. Then, when you make a

Figure 2-9

Figure 2-10

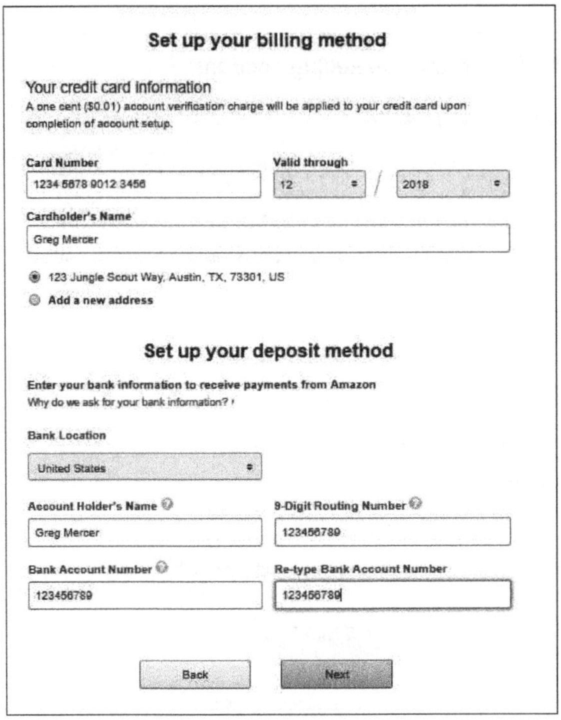

Figure 2-11

sale on Amazon, Amazon's staff (and robots!) actually pick, pack, ship, and handle customer service on your behalf.

How do I sell on **Amazon Prime**? If you sell through the Amazon FBA program and you have enough inventory to spread around through its fulfillment network, then your product will qualify for Amazon Prime. Amazon Prime items ship 2-3 days to customers. Plus, you get the "Amazon Prime" badge on your listing, which means you'll have a better chance of selling your product.

What is **private label**? Private label is a method of selling your own branded products on Amazon. It is, in my humble opinion, the most profitable way to make money on Amazon.

For more Amazon terms and lingo, check out our free Amazon Seller Glossary.

(Adapted from https://www.junglescout.com/blog/
amazon-seller-registration-create-account/)

Words & Expressions

aspiring	/əˈspaɪərɪŋ/	adj.	wanting to be successful in life 有抱负的；有志向的
entrepreneur	/ˌɒntrəprəˈnɜː/	n.	a person who makes money by starting or running businesses, especially when this involves taking financial risks 创业者；企业家(尤指涉及财务风险的)

intimidating	/ɪnˈtɪmɪˌdeɪtɪŋ/	*adj.*	**(for/to sb)** frightening in a way which makes a person feel less confident 吓人的;令人胆怯的
navigate	/ˈnævɪˌgeɪt/	*v.*	to find the right way to deal with a difficult or complicated situation 找到正确方法(对付困难复杂的情况)
corporation	/ˌkɔːpəˈreɪʃən/	*n.*	a group of people who are permitted by law to act as a single unit, esp. for the purpose of business, with rights and duties separate from those of its members 有限责任公司
subscription	/səbˈskrɪpʃən/	*n.*	an amount of money you pay regularly to be a member of an organization or to help its work, or the act of paying money for this 会(员)费;会(员)费的缴纳
inventory	/ˈɪnvəntərɪ/	*n.*	all the goods in a shop 存货;库存
input	/ˈɪnˌpʊt/	*v.*	the act of putting information into a computer 输入
bot	/bɒt/	*n.*	a computer program that performs a particular task again and again many times 自动程序;机器人程式
deposit	/dɪˈpɒzɪt/	*n.*	a sum of money that is paid into a bank account 存款
verification	/ˌverɪfɪˈkeɪʃən/	*n.*	the act or process of verifying 查证;核实
badge	/bædʒ/	*n.*	a small piece of metal or plastic, with a design or words on it, that a person wears to show that they belong to an organization, support sth, have achieved sth, have a particular rank, etc.徽章;奖章
humble	/ˈhʌmbəl/	*adj.*	modest; without excess of pride 谦逊的;卑微的
lingo	/ˈlɪŋgəʊ/	*n.*	expressions used by a particular group of people 行话;术语
out there			在那里
break down			细列(以便分析)
go nut			傻眼
highly recommend			高度推荐
figure out			想出;弄明白
scroll down			向下滚屏;滚动条向下滚动
get one's ducks in row			把某人的事情打理好

Notes & Terms

| eBay | | an American multinational E-commerce corporation based in San Jose, California that facilitates consumer-to-consumer and business-to-business sales through its website 易趣 |

Etsy	an E-commerce website (etsy.com) focused on handmade or vintage items and craft supplies 易集(手工艺品交易网站)
Bitcoin	a cryptocurrency, a form of electronic cash 比特币(BTC)
department store	a retail establishment offering a wide range of consumer goods in different categories known as "departments" 百货公司;百货商店;百货店
LLC	a limited liability company which is the US-specific form of a private limited company (美国)有限责任公司
best seller ranking (BSR)	a rank given to Amazon products based on the product's orders compared to other products in the same category within a given amount of time 畅销商品排行榜
fulfillment by Amazon (FBA)	an E-commerce service in which third-party vendors store their products in Amazon's fulfillment centers and the E-commerce giant picks, sorts, packs, ships, tracks and handles returns and refunds for these products 亚马逊物流
Amazon Prime	a paid subscription service offered by Amazon that gives users access to services that would otherwise be unavailable, or cost extra, to the typical Amazon customer (亚马逊平台上的)付费会员服务
private label	products manufactured by one company for sale under another company's brand 自有品牌;私有品牌
Amazon Seller Glossary	a complete guide to the top Amazon terminology, including common terms, jargon, and abbreviations 亚马逊销售术语表

Text Comprehension

Choose the best answer to each of the following questions according to the text.

1. According to the author, which of the following statements is TRUE?

   A. There is no one way to start business on Amazon because the formalities are bureaucratic.

   B. It might take 5 years to figure out how to register for an Amazon account.

   C. The complexity of Amazon is beyond words.

   D. It's cool to keep learning new tools on Amazon.

2. Which of the following is NOT mentioned in the text regarding the stuff you can sell on Amazon?

   A. Second-hand stuff.   B. Pets.

   C. Discounted products.   D. Wholesale goods.

3. What is free on Amazon?

   A. Registering for an individual account on Amazon.

B. Buying your own inventory.

C. Selling your used stuff.

D. Making sales.

4. Which fee ranges between 12% and 40% on Amazon?

   A. Registration fee.　　　　　　　B. Individual seller fee.

   C. Amazon referral fee.　　　　　　D. FBA.

5. Which is the most profitable way to sell on Amazon, according to the author?

   A. Selling through FBA program.

   B. Using "Amazon Prime" badge.

   C. Paying referral fee.

   D. Using private label.

Language Work

Fill in the following blanks with the words or phrases given below. Change the forms where necessary.

aspiring	break down	registration	launch	inventory
profitable	scare off	fulfillment	navigate	taxonomy

1. Are you _____ a new product at your online store recently?

2. It's important for _____ E-commerce entrepreneurs to avoid being trapped in the international regulatory maze.

3. E-commerce platforms selling non-luxury products often require volume in order to be _____.

4. When data analysts _____ the C2C E-commerce milk powder sales in China, they found Aptamil held a share of 4.1 percent of milk powder sales on C2C platforms in China during that time.

5. Volkswagen, the world's largest automaker by unit sales with 10.83 million vehicles sold last year, says that combining data from its 122 factories will allow it to standardize production planning and management of _____.

Workshop

Pair Work: Try with your partner to register for an account at a different cross-border E-commerce platform. Share with the class your registration experience by giving a presentation, illustrating the steps in the process and your findings as well.

References

[1] https://passport.alibaba.com/newlogin/icbuLogin.htm?returnurl=http%3A%2F%2Fwww.alibaba.com, retrieved on 2019-03-26.

[2] https://www.nav.com/blog/sell-products-alibaba-22035/, retrieved on 2019-03-26.

[3] https://www.junglescout.com/blog/amazon-seller-registration-create-account/, retrieved on 2019-03-26.

[4] https://en.wikipedia.org/wiki/.

[5] https://www.vocabulary.com/dictionary/.

[6] https://www.investopedia.com/terms/i/ipo.asp.

[7] https://en.wikipedia.org/wiki/Google.

[8] https://en.wikipedia.org/wiki/Facebook.

[9] https://en.wikipedia.org/wiki/Twitter.

[10] https://dictionary.cambridge.org/dictionary/english/bottom-line.

[11] https://www.shopify.com/encyclopedia/target-market.

[12] https://blog.udemy.com/company-profile-examples/.

[13] https://www.quora.com/What-is-a-potential-buyer-How-do-you-attract-them-to-a-business.

[14] https://www.cen.eu/work/products/ENs/Pages/default.aspx.

[15] https://service.alibaba.com/ensupplier/faq_detail/24226221.htm.

[16] https://en.wikipedia.org/wiki/EBay.

[17] https://en.wikipedia.org/wiki/Etsy.

[18] https://en.wikipedia.org/wiki/Bitcoin.

[19] https://en.wikipedia.org/wiki/Department_store.

[20] https://en.wikipedia.org/wiki/Limited_liability_company.

[21] https://www.sellerapp.com/amazon-best-seller-rank.html.

[22] https://feedvisor.com/university/fulfillment-by-amazon/.

[23] https://en.wikipedia.org/wiki/Amazon_Prime.

[24] https://en.wikipedia.org/wiki/Private_label.

[25] https://www.junglescout.com/amazon-seller-glossary/.

Unit 3

Store Design and
Product Selection

Learning Objectives

To know elements for design of a cross-border E-commerce store

To learn to select the products for an E-commerce store

To learn to integrate the store design and product selection principles to improve conversion rate

Warming up

1. Work in a group and discuss what are the basic elements of a cross-border E-commerce store and what is the necessary information for the online product description.

2. Read the words or phrases and their explanations. Then complete the following paragraph(s) with the words or phrases. Change the form when necessary.

revenue	the money that a government receives from taxes or that an organization, etc. receives from its business
legitimate	fair and acceptable
convert	to change or make sth change from one form, purpose, system, etc. to another
layout	the way in which the parts of sth such as the page of a book, a garden or a building are arranged
venture	a business project or activity, especially one that involves taking risks

Once you've chosen the right platform for your cross-border E-commerce operation, the next thing you need to consider is the design. Design is so important to the success or otherwise of your _____, beyond merely the aesthetics of the site. Pretty websites don't always _____ at the highest rate, and achieving any upwards tweak in your conversion rates can make a massive difference to your _____(and ultimately your bottom line).

At the same time, that doesn't mean you should be focusing solely on conversion rates, at the expense of a credible, professional-looking design. Your conversion rate will seriously suffer if your website looks untrustworthy, or anything less than _____ and credible. Simple things make a big difference here, so it really is worth finding a good freelance designer and pushing for a more attractive, conversion-focused _____.

(Adapted from https://ecommerceguide.com/guides/ecommerce-store-design/)

Text: E-commerce Website Design

To be successful in cross-border E-commerce business, it is imperative to be able to attract online customers and convince them to buy your products. Basically, this means that your E-commerce website design must be focused on the clients' specific needs. Every step of the shopping and buying process should be designed to give customers a great experience. In order to do so, some basic rules have to be followed.

Show visitors what products you are selling

Everything should be designed to make it as easy as possible to find the products visitors are looking for and to buy it. Therefore, it is essential to make it easy for them to see your catalog of products. Customers also want to be able to have all the information they need to make an informed decision before buying. So, provide as much information as you can on the product (see Figure 3-1).

Figure 3-1

Describe adequately every product you are selling to ensure that the client knows everything he would know if he was shopping in a store. Psychologically, it is better to use descriptive words when doing so than technical terms, since they unconsciously make the customer more likely to buy (see Figure 3-2).

Figure 3-2

Design and usability

A good design for your E-commerce website is not necessarily a design that will amaze the customers, but rather one that focuses on usability. The main feature of your website is to be easy for the customers to find what they want and to showcase your products properly. This includes related photos of the products as well as detailed descriptions providing every detail they might need (see Figure 3-3).

Figure 3-3

Showcase the products properly

It can be good to try to differentiate yourself from competition through an innovative website. However, some basic components should be present on any E-commerce website (see Figure 3-4).

Figure 3-4

1. Quality photos

Photos are the only way for online customers to see the products they are buying. It is worth investing in high-quality photos for every product displayed on your website so that clients can zoom in and take a closer look at every detail (see Figure 3-5).

Figure 3-5

It is also a good idea to display more than one picture for a product. In any case, the pictures displayed have to place the product in front display: use a neutral background and keep the picture simple (see Figure 3-6).

Figure 3-6

2. Reviews

Adding reviews to your website is a great way to gain credibility amongst your potential customers. If they can read what other independent clients really think about the products you are selling or about your customer service, they will believe it more than anything else you can

say on your website.

So, any positive review you get will help convert potential customers into actual buyers. If you get negative reviews, they can be used to either improve your product or service or to give your point of view on the subject at hand.

3. Layout

Some basic tools should be easy to find by the customer, no matter where he is on your website: the shopping cart, the information regarding shipping as well as the help they can get if desired. The shopping cart as well as the FAQ page and your contact information are often located at the top or right side of the page. Links to the FAQ and contact pages can also regularly be found at the bottom of the page. Overall, the important thing is the client should not have to search for them.

4. Navigation

Usually, potential clients need to check everything out before making their decision; that means browsing many pages of your website. You need to make that experience enjoyable for them, by making navigation easy and smooth. Customers should always be able to locate where they are on the website, which means your website must have a highly functional navigation menu (see Figure 3-7).

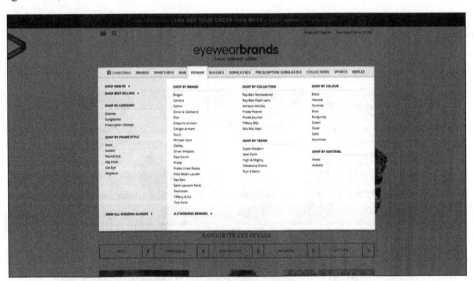

Figure 3-7

They should also be able to find anything they are looking for quickly, so your website needs a good search engine that works properly, as well as tabs and categories of items that can be chosen for navigation. If they have a registered account in your website, your clients should be able to leave your website and come back at a later time to find all their preferences saved.

5. Search

Your website should allow your potential clients to search by keywords what they are looking for, as well as through categories and by combining those two to get more precise results. Therefore, your E-commerce web design should have a good built-in search engine and you should consider using plugins to make it more efficient if required. Once they get results from a search, customers should be allowed to sort them the way they like: by price, popularity, date, etc.

For a search to provide good results, your catalog of products has to be well thought of. Before creating categories to display on your website, it is useful to carefully think about which ones are the most significant for the type of products you are selling. Once the best categories have been established, ensure that every product is associated with the right category (see Figure 3-8).

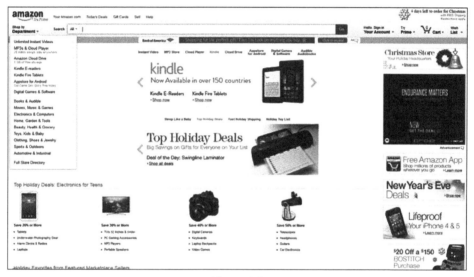

Figure 3-8

6. The shopping cart

A well-built shopping cart should give some basic functionalities. Your website should allow your customers to go back and forth without losing anything they have chosen. It should also keep track of the different tabs a customer can use while shopping.

Ideally, do not leave the page your client is on when he decides to use the shopping cart; it is better to have a pop-up window with the shopping cart functionalities so that he can always know where he is and move from there.

An easy-to-use shopping cart makes it easy to modify quantities of the products your potential customers have chosen, including removing a product if desired. Your shopping cart should remain transparent so that your customer does not feel like you hid fees or something else from him. For example, your shopping cart should allow viewing an estimate of the total price, including shipping and taxes, before beginning the check-out (see Figure 3-9).

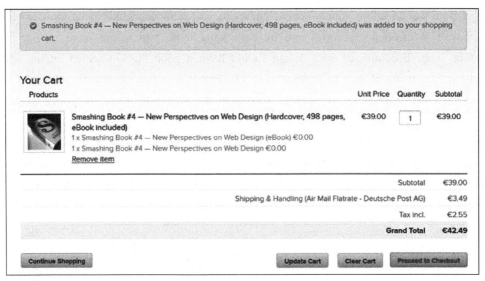

Figure 3-9

7. Related products

If some products are related to one a client is considering buying, they should be suggested to him and easy to choose from to add to the cart (see Figure 3-10).

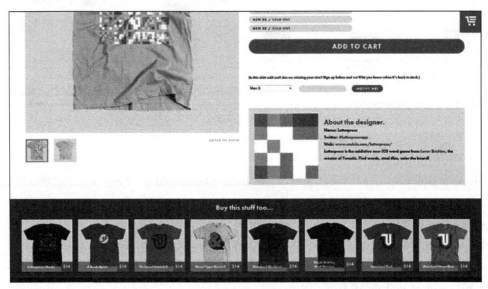

Figure 3-10

8. The check-out process

The check-out process should be easy to go through and give little possibility for the client to change his mind. Ideally, it should be composed of only two pages: the first one displaying the items chosen and the price and allowing the customer to enter the required information to proceed to the purchase, and the second allowing him to review and approve the purchase.

9. Contact information

Contact information should be easy to find no matter what page your customer is on. Ideally, provide more than one way a customer can ask their questions. This is even more important if you are selling high-value or highly technical items (see Figure 3-11).

Figure 3-11

10. Customer support

Make it easy for them to know where to ask any type of question they might have, including about returning items. A structured help request form provided on your website can be more reassuring for your customers, showing that you are a serious business. Quickly send an E-mail ensuring your client that you have received his enquiry and that it will be answered shortly. Make your FAQ as comprehensive as possible. Include all the details about your return policy, as well as replacing parts for your products if applicable.

11. Shipping rates

If you are using a major shipping company, it can most likely provide you with a tool that allows you to know how much shipping will cost. If not, you can use a fixed shipping charge that is high enough to ship any of your items. Whatever you do, ensure the information is always available to your customers (see Figure 3-12).

An account shouldn't be necessary to buy a product

Some customers might be reluctant to register a formal account with your company in order to buy something. It is recommended to make registering optional so that it will not discourage

Figure 3-12

anyone from buying.

Make available several payment options

The more payment options you have, the more likely your clients are going to trust at least one of them. Accept all major credit cards and make an instantaneous electronic check for their validity.

Conclusion

To have a successful E-commerce business, you clients' experience on your website should be your main preoccupation. You want them to have a great shopping experience and to find it easy to make their purchase once they have their heart set on a product. The easier it is for them to go through all that process on your website, the most likely they will buy and become loyal customers.

(Adapted from https://www.designyourway.net/blog/
inspiration/designing-E-commerce-websites-properly/)

Words & Expressions

imperative	/ɪmˈpɛrətɪv/	*adj.*	~ (**that...**) / ~ (**to do sth**) very important and needing immediate attention or action 重要紧急的；迫切的；急需处理的
convince	/kənˈvɪns/	*v.*	to persuade sb to do sth 说服，劝说(某人做某事)
psychologically	/ˌsaɪkəˈlɒdʒɪklɪ/	*adv.*	in terms of psychology 心理上
unconsciously	/ʌnˈkɑnʃəsli/	*adv.*	without being aware 无意地；不知不觉地
usability	/ˌjuːzəˈbɪləti/	*n.*	the quality of being able to provide good service 合用，可用；可用性

feature	/ˈfiːtʃə/	n.	something important, interesting or typical of a place or thing 特色;特征;特点
differentiate	/ˌdɪfəˈrenʃɪˌeɪt/	v.	recognize or show the difference between things 区分
component	/kəmˈpəʊnənt/	n.	one of several parts of which sth is made 组成部分; 成分;部件
neutral	/ˈnjuːtrəl/	adj.	not very bright or strong, such as grey or light brown 素净的;淡素的;不鲜艳的
review	/rɪˈvjuː/	n.	a report in the media in which someone gives their opinion of something such as a new book or movie 评价,评论
credibility	/ˌkredɪˈbɪlɪtɪ/	n.	the quality that sb/sth has that makes people believe or trust them 可信性;可靠性
navigation	/ˌnævɪˈgeɪʃən/	n.	the skill or the process of planning a route for a ship or other vehicle and taking it there 导航;领航
smooth	/smuːð/	adj.	happening or continuing without any problems 顺利的;平稳的
tab	/tæb/	n.	a small piece of cloth or paper that is attached to something, usually with information about that thing written on it 标签
category	/ˈkætɪgərɪ/	n.	a group of people or things with particular features in common 类别,种类
precise	/prɪˈsaɪs/	adj.	clear and accurate 准确的;精确的
sort	/sɔːt/	v.	~ sth (into sth) to arrange things in groups or in a particular order according to their type, etc.; to separate things of one type from others 整理;把……分类
catalog	/ˈkætəlɒg/	n.	a complete list of things, usually arranged systematically 目录
functionality	/ˌfʌŋkʃəˈnælɪtɪ/	n.	the range of functions that a computer or other electronic system can perform 功能
modify	/ˈmɒdɪfaɪ/	v.	to change sth slightly, especially in order to make it more suitable for a particular purpose 调整;修改
remove	/rɪˈmuːv/	v.	~ sth/sb (from sth/sb) to take sth/sb away from a place 移开;拿开;去掉
transparent	/trænˈspærənt/	adj.	allowing you to see the truth easily 显而易见的
estimate	/ˈestɪmeɪt/	n.	a judgement that you make without having the exact details or figures about the size, amount, cost, etc. of sth 估计;估价

proceed	/prəˈsiːd/	v.	to do sth next, after having done sth else first 接着做；继而做
approve	/əˈpruːv/	v.	~ (of sb/sth) to think that sb/sth is good, acceptable or suitable 赞成；同意
reassuring	/ˌriːəˈʃʊərɪŋ/	adj.	making you feel less worried or uncertain about sth 令人感到宽慰的；令人放心的
enquiry	/ɪnˈkwaɪəri/	n.	~ (from sb) (about sb/sth) a request for information about sb/sth; a question about sb/sth 询问；打听
comprehensive	/ˌkɒmprɪˈhensɪv/	adj.	including all, or almost all, the items, details, facts, information, etc., that may be concerned 全面的；综合的；详尽的
optional	/ˈɒpʃənəl/	adj.	that you can choose to do or have if you want to 可选择的
instantaneous	/ˌɪnstənˈteɪnɪəs/	adj.	happening immediately 立即的；立刻的；瞬间的
validity	/vəˈlɪdɪti/	n.	the state of being legally or officially acceptable 有效，合法性
preoccupation	/priːˌɒkjʊˈpeɪʃən/	n.	~ (with sth) a state of thinking about sth continuously; sth that you think about frequently or for a long time 盘算；思虑
not necessarily			未必；不一定
zoom in			放大
shopping cart			购物车；购物手推车
be associated with			与……有关
keep track of			记录；保持与……的联系；掌握……的线索
be related to			与……有关
go through			通过；完成
be composed of			由……组成
help request form			帮助请求表
be reluctant to			不愿意，不情愿

Notes & Terms

| FAQ | a list of frequently asked questions (FAQs) and answers on a particular topic (also known as Questions and Answers [Q&A] or Frequently Answered Questions) 常见问题；常见问题解答 |
| search engine | A web search engine or Internet search engine is a software system that is designed to carry out web search (Internet search), which means to search |

the World Wide Web in a systematic way for particular information specified in a web search query 搜索引擎

plugin　　　　　a software component that adds a specific feature to an existing computer program(计算机)插件

pop-up window　　a graphical user interface (GUI) display area, usually a small window, that suddenly appears ("pops up") in the foreground of the visual interface 弹出视窗;弹出式窗口

Understanding the text

Ⅰ. Complete the following summary of the text.

It is important to design the E-commerce store to guarantee the customers a great shopping experience on your site. First, it is necessary to clearly show them the _____ of your products. Then, the store design should focus on the _____ of information for the customers. To showcase the products properly, some basic _____ should be incorporated into the store design, including the quality photos, reviews, layout, navigation, search, the shopping cart, adding related products, the checkout process, contact information, customer support, and shipping rates. However, it is better not to require the customers to register a formal _____ to make a purchase on the site. Last, it is suggested to offer several _____ choices for the clients.

Ⅱ. Read the text and decide whether the following statements are true (T) or false (F).

(　　)1　The design of E-commerce store should be based on the owner's rules because it is difficult to predict the customers' preferences.

(　　)2　When we provide information of the products, we'd better use technical words to make professional description for the clients.

(　　)3　The negative reviews on products or service from the customers are harmful and useless to the E-commerce store.

(　　)4　To provide good search results to the customers, it is helpful to think about the catalog and categories of the products.

(　　)5　The information on the shipping rates should be clearly given to the customers.

Ⅲ. Answer the following questions according to the text.

1. Why is it important to provide as much information as possible on the products?

2. What should be the main feature of the E-commerce store design?

3. Why is it necessary to add the review function to the store?

4. Where are the basic tools of shopping cart, FAQ and contact pages usually located on the site?

5. What functions should the shopping cart have?

Language Work

Ⅰ. Choose the best choice to complete each of the following sentences.

1. Needless to say, an open line of communication between the designer and the client is _____ at this stage for the final success.

    A. impressive   B. implicit   C. imperative   D. impartial

2. Organizations do not have to evaluate each product, _____ or raw material input to control the cost.

    A. innocent   B. component   C. companion   D. opponent

3. The newly released annual report _____ any doubts about the company's future.

    A. improved   B. evolved   C. approved   D. removed

4. The high quality and unique design of our new products have received extensive and positive _____ from the users.

    A. reviews   B. interviews   C. previews   D. purviews

5. Money management needs to be able to _____ sales and profits at any given time from the moment the tickets go on sale.

    A. keep track of   B. keep away from

    C. keep back from   D. keep out of

Ⅱ. Match the English words in the left column with the English explanations in the right column.

_____ 1. feature   A. clear and easy to see or understand

_____ 2. credibility   B. to continue to do something that has already been planned or started

_____ 3. transparent   C. an interesting or important part or characteristic of something

_____ 4. proceed   D. a question you ask in order to get some information

_____ 5. enquiry   E. the quality of being believable or trustworthy

Ⅲ. Translate the following sentences from the text into Chinese.

1. It is worth investing in high-quality photos for every product displayed on your website so that clients can zoom in and take a closer look at every detail.

    _____

    _____.

2. Customers should always be able to locate where they are on the website, which means your website must have a highly functional navigation menu.

    _____

    _____.

3. The check-out process should be easy to go through and give little possibility for the client to change his mind.

_____

_____.

4. A structured help request form provided on your website can be more reassuring for your customers, showing that you are a serious business.

_____

_____.

5. The easier it is for them to go through all that process on your website, the most likely they will buy and become loyal customers.

_____

_____.

Ⅳ. Translate the following sentences into English using the proper forms of the words or expressions given in brackets.

1. 董事会将于下周开会讨论是否通过这项并购提议。(approve)

_____

_____.

2. 根据政府部门的保守估计，未来 5 年，跨境电商规模有望翻番。(optimize)

_____

_____.

3. 在面试中，求职者需要尽最大的努力来说服面试官自己就是最合适的人选。(convince)

_____

_____.

4. 他们并不一定是要解散管理层，只是在表达他们对公司的糟糕业绩失望到了何种程度。(not necessarily)

_____

_____.

5. 全球贸易量的规模与世界经济周期的变化紧密相关。(be associated with)

_____

_____.

Supplementary Reading: How to Choose the Perfect Product for Your E-commerce Store

You can have all the E-commerce knowledge and expertise possible, but without an amazing product to sell, your E-commerce store will be heading nowhere. Picking the right product is probably the most important decision you'll make in starting your E-commerce business, and you should take the time and care to make the right choice.

You'll want to pick a product that sits in a growing market, as well as one that you're incredibly passionate about. After all, this will be the basis of your E-commerce business for the foreseeable future.

Here's how to pick the perfect product for your E-commerce store:

Follow Your Passion

Perhaps the simplest way to pick a product for your new E-commerce store is to opt for something that you're passionate about. Choosing a product about which you're passionate will make the day-to-day running of your business so much easier, thanks to the extra motivation that comes with doing something you love.

If you're choosing an industry or sector in which you have experience, then you'll be able to more easily understand the needs of your customers, as well as target your marketing campaigns effectively. Having a good understanding of the market you're entering, as well as any legal and technical requirements will make getting off the ground a whole lot easier.

Identify a Niche

For a new E-commerce business, trying to jump right in at the deep end with a mass market product offering can be tough. Instead, think about a product that fits a smaller niche. You want to be able to target a specific market and address their concerns really effectively. Starting with a smaller niche market means you'll likely have less competition, and won't have your prices instantly driven down by competitors.

Spot a Trend

Spotting an emerging market trend is a great way of picking out a product with fantastic growth potential. If you can capitalize on a developing trend and be one of the first to market, you'll immediately have the jump on competing E-commerce stores. If you can identify a growing market for your E-commerce store and pick the right product, you'll have a fantastic opportunity to take advantage of growing demand from customers. Spotting the right trend can get your E-commerce business off to a flying start.

Pick Something Unique

Think carefully about picking a product that isn't easy to replicate. If you are able to offer a product that is truly unique, you're immediately adding value to customers.

Differentiating your product selection enough means you won't be in direct competition with much larger brands right away. Perhaps most importantly, you won't be so susceptible to having your prices driven down by the likes of Amazon. Huge brands like this could otherwise run similar products as loss leaders to squeeze you out of the market.

Think About Repeat Customers

With the long-term success of your E-commerce business in mind, it's vital that you consider repeat customers when choosing your products. Unless you're selling an incredibly high value item, you'll need to keep customers coming back to make a success of your store. It's much cheaper to retain your existing customers than just attract new ones, so think about how often your customer will have to make repeat purchases. Are your products of choice consumable or will it run out of use often? Perhaps you could run a subscription model to maintain a steady stream of customers?

Consider Storage & Shipping

While it may not be your first consideration, how easy your products are to store and ship can have a big impact on the viability of your E-commerce business. If possible, pick products that can either be stored for long periods, or produced and shipped quickly. You need to make the most of the storage space available to you, and you don't want too much capital tied up in stock.

You should also think about choosing a product that is easy to store and ship. A product that can be packaged easily and won't break in transit will incur lower shipping costs, allowing you to pass these savings on to customers.

In Summary

Picking a product to sell is a momentous moment for your E-commerce store. It will define the shape of your business for years to come, and picking the right one can be the difference between success and failure.

A great product is unique, captures a growing trend and is something you truly care about. If you can find a product for your E-commerce store that ticks these boxes, you're a long way to finding success.

> (Adapted from https://www.statementagency.com/blog/2017/06/how-to-choose-the-
> perfect-product-for-your-ecommerce-store?from=groupmessage&isappinstalled=0)

Words & Expressions

target	/ˈtɑːgɪt/	v.	to try to have an effect on a particular group of people 面向,把……对准(某群体)
niche	/niːʃ; nɪtʃ/	n.	an opportunity to sell a particular product to a particular group of people 利基
spot	/spɒt/	v.	to see or notice a person or thing, especially suddenly or when it is not easy to do so 看见;看出;注意到;发现

replicate	/ˈrɛplɪkeɪt/	v.	to copy sth exactly 复制;(精确地)仿制
susceptible	/səˈsɛptəbəl/	adj.	very likely to be influenced, harmed or affected by sb/sth 易受影响;敏感
viability	/ˌvaɪəˈbɪlətɪ/	n.	ability to work successfully 可行性;生存能力
incur	/ɪnˈkɜː/	v.	to become subject to (something unwelcome unpleasant) as a result of one's own behavior or actions 招致;引起
momentous	/məʊˈmɛntəs/	adj.	very important or serious, especially because there may be important results 关键的;重要的;重大的
make decision in			在某方面做决定
sit in			出席;参与
passionate about			热衷于某事
the foreseeable future			不久;很快
opt for			选择
day-to-day running			日常运行
get off the ground			起飞;成功运行
address concerns			解决问题

Notes & Terms

add value	increase the value of sth 增加(利用)价值
repeat customer	someone who buys again what they have purchased before 回头客
existing customer	regular customer 常惠顾客

Text Comprehension

Choose the best answer to each of the following questions according to the text.

1. Which of the following is highlighted in the text?

   A. The importance of the E-commerce knowledge.

   B. The importance of the product selection.

   C. The importance of presales.

   D. The importance of the platform.

2. Which of the following is NOT mentioned by the author regarding the advantages of choosing a product you are passionate about?

   A. It will make your daily operation easier.

   B. You're more motivated to do what you have a desire to do.

   C. You will have better understanding of the customer needs and product requirements.

   D. You will be able to sell the product at a more competitive price.

3. What does the author say about choosing an E-commerce niche product?

   A. You will have fewer competitors.

   B. You will have fewer customers.

   C. Only a small group of people can afford to purchase it.

   D. It will be difficult to expand your business.

4. Which of the following is most important for a quick success of an E-commerce business?

   A. Securing storage space.

   B. Identifying the market trend.

   C. Offering shipping solutions.

   D. Locating a market niche.

5. Which of the following is most important for a long-term success of an E-commerce business?

   A. To retain customers.

   B. To find a unique product.

   C. To follow your passion.

   D. To have E-commerce expertise.

Language Work

Fill in the following blanks with the words or phrases given below. Change the forms where necessary.

spot	storage	repeat	niche	replicate
unique	passion	viability	incur	pick

1. Media is _____, downloaded, backed up and stored.

2. Some sites focus mostly on selling a wide range of products while some specialize in selling products based on more in-depth analysis and their expertise about product _____.

3. Do you want to know what it takes to successfully increase customer satisfaction and generate _____ sales?

4. I recently came across a tutorial which explained how to _____ fraud.

5. To start an E-commerce business, you need a sales process and _____ methods that meet the demands and high expectations of your customers.

Workshop

Presentation: Work in a group and discuss the selection of a product that you agree to sell on your cross-border E-commerce web site, taking into account what you have learned from this unit. And make a presentation in the class to explain your ideas.

References

[1] https://ecommerceguide.com/guides/ecommerce-store-design/, retrieved on 2019-03-22.

[2] https://www.designyourway.net/blog/inspiration/designing-E-commerce-websites-properly/, retrieved on 2019-03-29.

[3] https://www.statementagency.com/blog/2017/06/how-to-choose-the-perfect-product-for-your-ecommerce-store?from=groupmessage&isappinstalled=0, retrieved on 2019-04-13.

[4] https://en.wikipedia.org/wiki/FAQ.

[5] https://en.wikipedia.org/wiki/Web_search_engine.

[6] https://en.wikipedia.org/wiki/Plug-in_(computing).

[7] https://en.wikipedia.org/wiki/Pop-up_ad.

[8] https://en.wikipedia.org/wiki/.

[9] http://www.youdao.com/.

Unit 4

Inside-platform Marketing

Learning Objectives

To understand the definition and importance of marketing.

To get familiar with common marketing techniques for E-commerce.

To learn to plan marketing strategies for cross-border E-commerce.

Warming up

1. Work in a group and discuss how you usually get the product information on the online shopping platforms (such as through E-mail, via WeChat messages, by viewing the ads, etc.)
2. Read the words or phrases and their explanations. Then complete the following paragraph(s) with the words or phrases. Change the form when necessary.

brand   particular make of goods or their trade mark

retain   to keep or continue to have in possession or use

loyalty   being true and faithful

promotional   of or relating to advertising or other activity intended to increase the sales of a product

purchase   (action of) buying sth.

Cross-border E-commerce marketing is the practice of using _____ tactics to drive overseas traffic to your online store, converting that traffic into paying customers, and _____ those customers after _____. A holistic E-commerce marketing strategy is made up of marketing tactics both on and off your website. A sound marketing strategy can help you build _____ awareness, drive customer _____, and ultimately increase online sales. You can use E-commerce marketing to promote your online store as a whole or to drive more sales for specific products.

(Adapted from www.shopify.com)

Text: Marketing for E-commerce

Marketing is defined by the American Marketing Association as "the activity, set of institutions, and processes for creating, communicating, delivering, and exchanging offerings that have value for customers, clients, partners, and society at large." The term developed from the original meaning which referred literally to going to market with goods for sale. From a sales process perspective, marketing is "a set of processes that are interconnected and interdependent with other functions" of a business aimed at achieving customer interest and satisfaction.

The process of marketing is that of bringing a product to market, which includes these steps: broad market research; market targeting and market segmentation; determining distribution, pricing and promotion strategies; developing a communications strategy; budgeting; and visioning long-term market development goals. Many parts of the marketing process (e. g. product design, art director, brand management, advertising, copywriting, etc.) involve use of the creative arts.

Marketing for E-commerce means the marketing strategies and techniques that are used for buying and selling products or services through the Internet or any other electronic network like tablets, mobiles. It can also be referred to as online marketing or Internet marketing.

E-commerce marketing can bring a variety of benefits as follows:

- As one of the most inexpensive ways of marketing of recent times, E-commerce marketing strategy is cheaper than any other offline advertising method, which proves to be beneficial to any small-scale business. At the same time, the customer requires no investment to visit. To view a product requires only one click.

- Carried on a large scale, it helps in attracting multiple customers at a time at global level. It has the ability to target the customers from any corner of the world. Therefore, you can earn more profit in minimal time.

- It helps in building healthy customer relationship. The services offered by E-commerce online marketing are more effective. E-commerce marketing not only deals with selling products but also gathers customer feedback, which helps the dealer to improve the flaws in the product if any.

The most important goal of E-commerce marketing is to increase the traffic. Every marketing strategy deals with understanding of customers. Only attracting to your site is not enough. The targeted audience should also buy your product and then your marketing cycle gets completed.

The following are some techniques to do marketing for E-commerce stores and products:

Advertising: To publish your ads or banners on the E-commerce platform or other targeted websites or media helps attract the customers and increase the web traffic to your E-commerce store and your products or service. In online display advertising, display ads generate awareness quickly. Unlike search, which requires someone to be aware of a need, display advertising can drive awareness of something new and without previous knowledge. Display works well for direct response. Display is not only used for generating awareness, but it's used for direct response campaigns that link to a landing page with a clear "call to action".

Video marketing: It means creating a promotional video of the product and displaying it as an advertisement in a particular website. It has become the most popular way to attract the customers. Normally you visit any online video sites such as YouTube, and the E-commerce websites display their product video as an advertisement before the actual video you want to view. This helps in gaining a lot of traffic.

Promotion: In E-commerce marketing, promotion refers to any type of digital marketing communication used to inform or persuade target audiences of the relative merits of a product, service, brand or issue. The aim of promotion is to increase awareness, create interest, generate sales or create brand loyalty. The online store owners can achieve these goals by providing some "special offers", like discounts, coupons, freebies, loss leaders, premiums, prizes, product samples, and rebates to attract the potential online shoppers and stimulate their demand for the product. They can also join in the promotional campaigns on the E-commerce platform on some special celebrations or events to stimulate product interest, trial, or purchase, like "double 11 shopping festival", "black Friday", or "Mother's Day", etc.

E-mail marketing: It refers to sending advertisements, requesting business, or soliciting sales by using E-mails with the purpose of enhancing a merchant's relationship with current or previous customers, encouraging customer loyalty and repeat business, acquiring new customers or convincing current customers to purchase something immediately. E-mail marketing can be carried out through different types of E-mail: transactional E-mail and direct E-mail. The former is usually triggered based on a customer's action with a company. To be qualified as transactional or relationship messages, these communications' primary purpose must be "to facilitate, complete, or confirm a commercial transaction that the recipient has previously agreed to enter into with the sender" along with a few other narrow definitions of transactional messaging. Triggered transactional messages include dropped basket messages, password reset E-mails, purchase or order confirmation E-mails, order status E-mails, reorder E-mails, and receipt E-mails. The latter involves sending an E-mail solely to communicate a promotional message (for example, a special offer or a product catalog). Companies usually collect a list of customer E-mail addresses to send direct promotional messages by encouraging the customers to register with their E-mail address, or they rent a list of E-mail addresses from service companies.

Mobile marketing: It is a multi-channel online marketing technique focused on reaching a specific audience on their smartphones, tablets, or any other related devices through websites, E-mail, SMS (Short Message Service) and MMS (Multimedia Message Service), social media or mobile applications. Mobile marketing can provide customers with time and location sensitive, personalized information that promotes goods, services and ideas.

With the strong growth in the use of smartphones, app usage has also greatly increased. Therefore, mobile marketers have increasingly taken advantage of smartphone apps as a marketing resource.

The APP-based mobile marketing may include the following modes:

1. Advertisement implantation mode is a common marketing mode in most applications. Through banner ads, consumer announcements, or in-screen advertising, users will jump to the specified page which displays the advertising content when users click. This mode is more intuitive, and can attract users' attention quickly.

2. User participation mode is mainly applied to website transplantation and brand app. The company publishes its own brand app to the app store for users to download, so that users can intuitively understand the enterprise or product information better. As a practical tool, this app

brings great convenience to users' life.

3. The shopping website embedded mode means the electronic business offering platforms in the mobile app, which is convenient for users to browse commodity information anytime and anywhere, place an order, and track an order. This mode has promoted the transformation of traditional E-commerce enterprises from shopping websites to mobile Internet channels, which is a necessary way to use mobile app for online and offline interactive development, such as Amazon, eBay, and so on.

The other types of E-commerce marketing are affiliate marketing, social media marketing, search engine marketing and search engine optimization (SEO), etc.

(Adapted from http://www.cheasyy.com/marketing-E-commerce/,

https://en.wikipedia.org/wiki/Marketing)

Words & Expressions

define	/dɪˈfaɪn/	v.	~ **sth** (**as sth**) to state precisely the meaning of (e.g., words) 给(词语等)下定义
distribution	/ˌdɪstrɪˈbjuːʃən/	n.	the system of transporting and delivering goods(商品) 运销,经销,分销
promotion	/prəˈməʊʃən/	n.	advertising or other activity intended to increase the sales of a product (为推销商品而作的)广告宣传,促销活动
budgeting	/ˈbʌdʒɪtɪŋ/	n.	planning of how money will be spent over a period of time, in relation to the amount of money available 编制预算
multiple	/ˈmʌltɪpəl/	adj.	many in number; involving many different people or things 数量多的;多种多样的
minimal	/ˈmɪnɪməl/	adj.	very small in size or amount; as small as possible 极小的;极少的;最小的
banner	/ˈbænə/	n.	a long piece of cloth with a message on it that is carried between two poles or hung in a public place to show support for sth 横幅
coupon	/ˈkuːpɒn/	n.	a small piece of ticket or document that you can exchange for sth or that gives you the right to buy sth at a cheaper price than normal 配给券;(购物)票证;(购物)优惠券
freebie	/ˈfriːbɪ/	n.	something that is given to sb without payment, usually by a company (常指公司提供的)免费品
rebate	/ˈriːbeɪt/	n.	an amount of money that is paid back to you because

			you have paid too much 退款,返款
solicit	/səˈlɪsɪt/	v.	~ **sth (from sb)** / ~ **(sb) (for sth)** to ask sb for sth, such as support, money, or information; to try to get sth or persuade sb to do sth　索求；征求；筹集
trigger	/ˈtrɪɡə/	v.	to make sth happen suddenly 发动；引起；触发
implantation	/ˌɪmplɑːnˈteɪʃən/	n.	the act of implanting or the state of being implanted 植入
participation	/pɑːˌtɪsɪˈpeɪʃn/	n.	~ **(in sth)** the act of taking part in an activity or event 参加；参与
embed	/ɪmˈbɛd/	v.	~ **sth (in sth)** to fix sth firmly into a substance or solid object　嵌入
transformation	/ˌtrænsfəˈmeɪʃn/	n.	~ **(from sth) (to/into sth)** a complete change in sb/sth (彻底的)变化,转变
at large			整个,普遍
refer to			指的是
from a/an...perspective			从……角度来看
as follows			如下
loss leader			亏本促销商品
take advantage of			利用

Notes & Terms

the American Marketing Association (AMA)	a professional association for marketing professionals with over 30,000 members. It has 76 professional chapters and 250 collegiate chapters across the United States 美国市场营销协会
market targeting	the process of actually determining the select markets and planning the advertising media used to make the segment appealing 目标市场选择
market segmentation	the activity of dividing a broad consumer or business market, normally consisting of existing and potential customers, into sub-groups of consumers (known as *segments*) based on some type of shared characteristics 市场细分
call to action	a marketing term used extensively in advertising and selling. It most often refers to the use of words or phrases that can be incorporated into sales scripts, advertising messages or web pages that encourage consumers to take prompt action, usually using an imperative verb such as "call now", "find out more" or "visit a store today" 行动呼吁；行动号召

double 11 shopping festival	a shopping holiday popular among young Chinese people that has become the largest offline and online shopping day in the world, with Alibaba shoppers exceeding 168.2 billion yuan (US $25.4 billion) in spending during the 2017 celebration 双十一购物节
black Friday	an informal name for the Friday following Thanksgiving Day in the United States, which is celebrated on the fourth Thursday of November. The day after Thanksgiving has been regarded as the beginning of America's Christmas shopping season since 1952. 黑色星期五
Mother's Day	a celebration honoring the mother of the family, as well as motherhood, maternal bonds, and the influence of mothers in society. It is celebrated on various days in many parts of the world, most commonly in the months of March or May. In the US, it is on the second Sunday in May. 母亲节
SMS (Short Message Service)	a text messaging service component of most telephone, Internet, and mobile-device systems 短信服务
MMS (Multimedia Message Service)	a standard way to send messages that include multimedia content to and from a mobile phone over a cellular network 多媒体信息服务
affiliate marketing	a type of performance-based marketing in which a business rewards one or more affiliates for each visitor or customer brought by the affiliate's own marketing efforts 联盟营销
social media marketing	the use of social media platforms and websites to promote a product or service 社交媒体营销
search engine marketing	a form of Internet marketing that involves the promotion of websites by increasing their visibility in search engine results pages (SERPs) primarily through paid advertising 搜索引擎营销

Understanding the text

Ⅰ. Complete the following summary of the text.

E-commerce marketing, refers to the marketing strategies and techniques for selling on the _____ or the other electronic devices. It can bring the following benefits: 1) reducing the cost in marketing; 2) attracting targeted _____ ; 3) building good _____ with customers; and increasing _____ to the site, etc. The commonly applied marketing techniques for E-commerce include: 1) advertising on the E-commerce platform or the other websites; 2) video marketing; 3) online promotional campaigns; 4) E-mail marketing; and 5) mobile marketing, especially _____ mobile marketing.

II. Read the text and decide whether the following statements are true (T) or false (F).

( )1   Marketing is actually composed of a series of interconnected processes.

( )2   Compared with the offline marketing strategy, E-commerce marketing tends to be more expensive.

( )3   The completion of the marketing cycle is marked by attracting customers to the site.

( )4   Display advertising can stimulate viewers' direct response without their awareness of their need.

( )5   A transactional E-mail is sent only to communicate a promotional message.

III. Answer the following questions according to the text.

1. What are the major steps of the marketing process?

2. What is marketing for E-commerce?

3. What benefits can E-commerce marketing bring?

4. What are the common techniques to do marketing for E-commerce stores and products?

5. Would you place order on the things advertised on Wechat? Why or why not?

Language Work

I. Choose the best choice to complete each of the following sentences.

1. The tourism ads not only focus on the _____ of the tourism products but also have to compete with those ads from their rivals.

   A. persuasion   B. participation   C. promotion   D. preservation

2. They were planning to _____ funds from a number of organizations for the launch of new products into the market.

   A. solicit   B. substitute   C. secure   D. signify

3. At the core of every successful business leader is an _____ understanding of the relationships among the important elements.

   A. interesting   B. infinite   C. intricate   D. intuitive

4. In the world market _____, there is a sharp rise in cross-border electronic transactions.

   A. at all   B. at large   C. by all means   D. in all

5. There is no cost for this advertising program and every store on the platform can _____ it.

   A. make fun of   B. make sense of

   C. take advantage of   D. take advice of

II. Match the English words in the left column with the English explanations in the right column.

_____   1. distribution   A. having or involving many individuals, items or types

_____   2. multiple   B. to cause something to happen or work

_____   3. coupon   C. a thorough or dramatic change in form or appearance

_____   4. trigger   D. a piece of printed paper which allows you to pay less
                                    money than usual for a product, or to get it free

_____   5. transformation   E. the act of process of supplying goods to shops or
                                    businesses

Ⅲ. Translate the following sentences from the text into Chinese.

1. From a sales process perspective, marketing is "a set of processes that are interconnected and interdependent with other functions" of a business aimed at achieving customer interest and satisfaction.

_____

_____.

2. E-commerce marketing not only deals with selling products but also gathers customer feedback, which helps the dealer to improve the flaws in the product if any.

_____

_____.

3. Unlike search, which requires someone to be aware of a need, display advertising can drive awareness of something new and without previous knowledge.

_____

_____.

4. Mobile marketing can provide customers with time and location sensitive, personalized information that promotes goods, services and ideas.

_____

_____.

5. This mode has promoted the transformation of traditional E-commerce enterprises from shopping websites to mobile Internet channels, which is a necessary way to use mobile app for online and offline interactive development, such as Amazon, eBay, and so on.

_____

_____.

Ⅳ. Translate the following sentences into English using the proper forms of the words or expressions given in brackets.

1. 很难给跨境电商概念下一个精确的定义。(define)

_____

_____.

2. 我们需要尽一切可能将汇率对业务的影响降到最低程度。(minimal)

_____

_____.

3. 应该鼓励国内企业通过创造、创新积极参与国际市场竞争。(participate)

_____

_____.

4. 从实际角度而言,营销即满足顾客的各种需求。(from a/an...perspective)

5. 任何从事跨境电商的企业都要了解并遵守目标市场的法律法规。(be aware of)

Supplementary Reading: E-commerce Marketing Ideas to Drive More Sales

Every online store wants to increase traffic and conversions. But even after you've put together a basic strategy it can still be challenging to decide on which marketing tactics you should try. That's why we put together an overview of effective marketing tactics and E-commerce tools along with ideas to help you implement each approach as follows.

1. Upsell your products

Most of us have heard some variation of the saying, "Would you like to supersize your order?" It's an example of upselling, or the approach of selling a slightly more premium product than the one the customer was originally considering.

For many businesses, upselling can be more effective than acquiring a new customer. Sometimes your customers don't know that a premium product is available, or they may simply need more evidence to understand how an upgrade (or package) is a better fit for their needs.

There are two main considerations when using upselling to increase sales:

1) Make sure your upsells are related to the original product

2) Be sensitive to the anticipated price range of your customers

Your product has to fit the customer's original needs, and they may not be enthusiastic about a higher price point once they have an anchor price in mind. An anchor price is often the first number a customer sees, and it's the number against which they compare other price points. The new product must be a discernibly better fit than the original for it to be worth the additional cost.

2. Reduce abandoned carts

Harsh truth: You're losing money every time a visitor abandons their cart without purchasing.

This phenomenon is well-studied. Visitors add items to their carts, but abandon their carts during the checkout process. According to the Baymard Institute, 69.23% of shopping carts are abandoned.

One simple and effective E-commerce marketing idea to reduce the frequency of abandoned carts is an E-mail recovery campaign, which can convince your visitors to make a return visit and complete their original purchase. Perhaps they could have been persuaded with a discount or free shipping, for example.

Craft an E-mail that entices your visitors to return to their carts by reminding them of what they considered purchasing in the first place, and why.

3. Capture more E-mail subscribers

Dollar for dollar, E-mail marketing is one of the most effective channels at your disposal for making sales and generating repeat customers. Roughly 17% of digital marketing cost happens in E-mail, but it contributes 24% of revenue, according to a study by Forrester Research.

There are too many tweets and Facebook posts for us to keep up with, and E-mail can offer a more intimate interaction. People are still more protective of messages sent to their personal inboxes versus their social feeds. Plus, E-mail gives you the space to say things that can't fit into a social media post.

To get started with E-mail marketing, actively promote your newsletter, blog and any other E-mail capture efforts to get as many subscribers as you can.

4. Improve your E-mail campaigns

It's not enough to simply capture a bunch of E-mail addresses. You then need to send regular, valuable E-mails for the channel to be an effective E-commerce marketing activity.

There are many occasions that are perfect for sending E-mails that your subscribers will actually appreciate:

- Send a welcome E-mail as soon as a customer makes a purchase.
- Provide exclusive promo codes and free gifts.
- Send regular newsletters to alert subscribers of new discount offers, product tips, and, when appropriate, company news.
- Share relevant content to help customers get the most out of their recently purchased items.
- Run a BOGO campaign in time for the holidays to promote self-gifting during the season, too.
- Thank your highest-value customers. Send a personal note expressing your appreciation for their business.
- Solicit feedback. If someone visits your site but doesn't make a purchase, ask about their experience and how you can improve it.

5. Send wishlist reminder E-mails

One final type of E-mail to add to your list of E-commerce marketing ideas: the wishlist reminder E-mail. The wishlist reminder E-mail is closely related to the abandoned cart E-mail. Both are designed to convince shoppers to take the final step in purchasing the products they have shown intent to buy.

Has it been a while since someone checked in on their wishlist? Have an item on sale that's been put on a lot of wishlists? Is it selling out? Send out an E-mail to let your customers know.

6. Make it easy for your customers to get what they want

If your store is poorly designed, then you're losing customers. But what exactly does a poorly designed store look like?

Besides appearing untrustworthy, the store could be suffering from some combination of the following: lacking a clear value proposition, hard-to-read font, or confusing navigation.

Even when you've improved the dimensions above, you could still be making a few design mistakes. Are you properly segmenting your products or are you putting too many products on a single page? Have you figured out the right balance between text and visuals? These are just a few of the many things that you should consider. If your theme isn't converting well, consider some of the other great themes available.

7. Engage online store visitors with live chat

There are other high-impact ways to engage with site visitors and customers outside of E-mail. For example, you could use live chat to engage with shoppers on your site.

Many live chat tools let you target browsers on certain pages, after they've been on your site for a certain length of time, or even after they've arrived on your site through an E-mail newsletter. Live chat also enables you to have direct conversations with your customers so you can answer and address customer concerns right while they're planning to buy.

8. Embrace personalization

Personalization is another effective marketing tactic to drive online sales. Using behavioral data, personalized experiences are served to the visitor, according to their past actions and preferences.

You can also account for location in personalization to create an experience catered to where your customers are in the world. Someone in southern California may be looking for bathing suits in October, while your Maine customers probably need coats, for example.

9. Leverage user-generated content

User-generated content (UGC) is a great way to generate social proof. When prospective customers see that people just like them are regularly purchasing your products, they'll feel more confident in doing the same.

According to Salesforce, 54% of consumers trust information from online reviews and recommendations from their peers, compared to the 20% who trust the brand itself.

UGC can take many forms. Technically, even product reviews are UGC. One of the most effective types of UGC is pictures of customers actually using your products.

10. Optimize your product pages

Conversion rate optimization (CRO) is the practice of optimizing your website for on-site conversions and increased sales. Practicing CRO helps you identify problem areas on your site. Where are you losing sales? Who's dropping off and why? What can you do to capture those missed opportunities? This process is done through both qualitative and quantitative research, so you get a holistic and unbiased view of how conversion-oriented your site is.

Once you've conducted your research to identify challenges and opportunities, you can develop hypotheses and tests to see which approaches generate the most sales.

11. Reward your loyal customers

Focusing on customer retention is a cost-effective way to increase online sales. Return customers account for 22% of a retailer's revenue, while making up just 11% of the total customer base, according to statistics. They also spend 15% more over the course of a year.

One way to reward loyal customers and big spenders is through a customer loyalty program. There are many ways both your customers and you can benefit from a loyalty program. They give customers extra incentive to make a purchase and they keep your brand top-of-mind through automated reminders.

You choose how to reward customers, how frequently and for what actions. For instance, you might have a point-based program, which has its own point-based currency that can be redeemed for discounts, free shipping or free gifts.

(Adapted from https://www.shopify.com/blog/ecommerce-marketing)

Words & Expressions

variation	/ˌvɛərɪˈeɪʃən/	*n.*	~ (**in/of sth**) a change, especially in the amount or level of sth (数量、水平等的)变化,变更,变异
original	/əˈrɪdʒɪnəl/	*adj.*	existing at the beginning of a particular period, process or activity 原来的;起初的;雏形的
anticipated	/ænˈtɪsəˌpeɪtɪd/	*adj.*	expected to be good, exciting, or interesting 预期的;期望的
discernibly	/dɪˈsɜːnɪblɪ/	*adv.*	recognizably 可辨别的;可识别的
harsh	/hɑːʃ/	*adj.*	cruel, severe and unkind 残酷的;严酷的;严厉的
entice	/ɪnˈtaɪs/	*v.*	~ **sb** (**into doing sth**) to persuade sb/sth to go somewhere or to do sth, usually by offering them sth 诱使;引诱
tweet	/twiːt/	*n.*	a post made on the Tweeter online message service 推文
intent	/ɪnˈtɛnt/	*n.*	intention to do something 意图
proposition	/ˌprɒpəˈzɪʃən/	*n.*	a statement that expresses an opinion 见解;主张;观点
dimension	/dɪˈmɛnʃən/	*n.*	an aspect, or way of looking at or thinking about sth 方面;维度
tactic	/ˈtæktɪk/	*n.*	the particular method you use to achieve sth 策略;手段;招数

leverage	/ˈliːvərɪdʒ/	v.	to spread or use sth 利用
prospective	/prəˈspɛktɪv/	adj.	expected to do sth or to become sth 可能的；预期的
optimize	/ˈɒptɪˌmaɪz/	v.	to make sth as good as it can be; to use sth in the best possible way 使最优化；充分利用
qualitative	/ˈkwɒlɪtətɪv/	adj.	connected with how good sth is, rather than with how much of it there is 定性的；质性的
quantitative	/ˈkwɒntɪtətɪv/	adj.	connected with the amount or number of sth rather than with how good it is 量化的；定量性的
holistic	/həʊˈlɪstɪk/	adj.	considering a whole thing or being to be more than a collection of parts 整体的；全面的
unbiased	/ʌnˈbaɪəst/	adj.	fair and not influenced by your own or sb else's opinions, desires, etc. 公正的；不偏不倚的；无偏见的
hypothesis	/haɪˈpɒθɪsɪs/	n.	(*pl.* **hypotheses**) an idea or explanation of sth that is based on a few known facts but that has not yet been proved to be true or correct 假说，假设
retention	/rɪˈtɛnʃən/	n.	the action of keeping sth rather than losing it or stopping it 保持；维持；保留
incentive	/ɪnˈsɛntɪv/	n.	~ (for/to sb/sth) (to do sth) something that encourages you to do sth 激励；刺激；鼓励
premium product			优质产品，高级产品
be sensitive to			对……敏感
be enthusiastic about			热衷于，对……充满热情
anchor price			锚定价格
at one's disposal			由……做主；由……随意支配
keep up with...			赶得上……
exclusive promo code			独家优惠码
live chat			在线聊天；即时聊天
engage with			与……接洽
cater to			迎合；为……服务

Notes & Terms

Baymard Institute	an independent web usability research institute that conducts original large-scale research studies on all aspects of the E-commerce user experience — from form fields to the entire mobile experience 一家独立网络研究机构
BOGO	or BOGOF, an initialism for "buy one, get one free", a common form of sales promotion 买一送一

California	a state in the Pacific Region of the United States 加利福尼亚州 (美国州名)
Maine	a state in the New England region of the northeastern United States 缅因州(美国州名)
user-generated content (UGC)	alternatively known as user-created content (UCC), is any form of content, such as images, videos, text and audio, that have been posted by users on online platforms such as social media and wikis 用户生成内容
Conversion rate optimization (CRO)	In Internet marketing, conversion optimization, or conversion rate optimization (CRO) is a system for increasing the percentage of visitors to a website that convert into customers, or more generally, take any desired action on a webpage 转化率优化
customer loyalty program	a structured marketing strategy designed by merchants to encourage customers to continue to shop at or use the services of businesses associated with each program 客户忠诚计划

Text Comprehension

Choose the best answer to each of the following questions according to the text.

1. According to the passage, which of the following is a case of upselling?

   A. Selling a product to upper-class customers.

   B. Selling a product of better quality.

   C. Selling a product with a discount.

   D. Selling a product at a lower price.

2. Compared with social media posting, E-mails do NOT have the advantage in _____.

   A. bringing closer interaction with customers

   B. sending more personal messages

   C. giving particular space for some information

   D. advertising the product

3. Which is considered a part of poor design of online store?

   A. Trustworthy appearance.   B. A clear value statement.

   C. Easy-to-read font.   D. Messy navigation.

4. According to the text, which of the following does NOT belong to UGC?

   A. Consumers' online reviews.

   B. Recommendations from peers.

   C. Trust in brand.

   D. Pictures of customers using the products.

5. Which of the following best concludes the main idea of the passage?

A. Some effective marketing strategies for the promotion of online sales.

B. E-mail marketing techniques.

C. Customer relationship management.

D. E-commerce advertising campaigns.

Language Work

Fill in the following blanks with the words or phrases given below. Change the forms where necessary.

variation	dimension	prospective	original	convince
optimize	holistic	incentive	be related to	be sensitive to

1. If you have an idea at work, or want to get a raise, or want to _____ your kids to read a book, then there is something applicable from the marketing world.

2. Consumers have to have some _____ to share their thoughts, opinions and experiences on an online store.

3. We should first look into investment requirements to see whether the _____ investor can meet these requirements.

4. The board meeting ended with the decision that our company should go back to the _____ plan.

5. Any business engaged in fast moving consumer goods must _____ the emerging changes among the young people.

Workshop

Presentation: Work in a group and decide on a certain product (for example, a smartwatch, a pair of sport jeans, a type of herbal facial cream, a local handcraft, etc.) to sell online, then make a PowerPoint presentation on the marketing plan for this product.

References

[1] https://www.shopify.com/blog/ecommerce-marketing, retrieved on 2019/02/02.

[2] https://en.wikipedia.org/wiki/Marketing.

[3] https://en.wikipedia.org/wiki/E-mail_marketing.

[4] https://en.wikipedia.org/wiki/Advertising#New_media_and_advertising_approaches.

[5] https://en.wikipedia.org/wiki/Mobile_marketing.

[6] http://www.cheasyy.com/marketing-E-commerce/.

[7] https://www.shopify.com/blog/ecommerce-marketing.

[8] www.shopify.com, retrieved on 2019-02-02.

[9]　http: //www.cheasyy.com/marketing-E-commerce/, retrieved on 2019-02-02.

[10]　https: //en.wikipedia.org/wiki/Marketing, retrieved on 2019-02-02.

[11]　https: //en.wikipedia.org/wiki/American_Marketing_Association.

[12]　https: //en.wikipedia.org/wiki/Target_market.

[13]　https: //en.wikipedia.org/wiki/Market_segmentation.

[14]　https: //en.wikipedia.org/wiki/Call_to_action_(marketing) .

[15]　https: //en.wikipedia.org/wiki/Singles%27_Day.

[16]　https: //en.wikipedia.org/wiki/Black_Friday_(shopping) .

[17]　https: //en.wikipedia.org/wiki/Mother%27s_Day.

[18]　https: //en.wikipedia.org/wiki/Multimedia_Messaging_Service.

[19]　https: //en.wikipedia.org/wiki/Affiliate_marketing.

[20]　https: //en.wikipedia.org/wiki/Social_media_marketing.

[21]　https: //en.wikipedia.org/wiki/Search_engine_marketing.

[22]　https: //baymard.com/about.

[23]　https: //en.wikipedia.org/wiki/Forrester_Research.

[24]　https: //en.wikipedia.org/wiki/Facebook.

[25]　https: //en.wikipedia.org/wiki/User-generated_content.

[26]　https: //en.wikipedia.org/wiki/Conversion_rate_optimization.

[27]　https: //en.wikipedia.org/wiki/Loyalty_program.

Unit 5

Outside-platform
Marketing

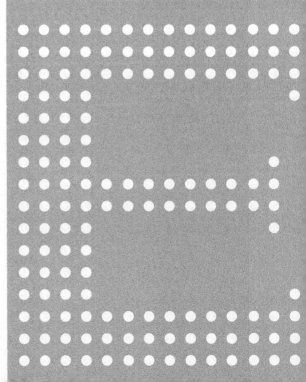

Learning Objectives

To know how to use social media marketing for E-commerce

To understand search engine marketing for E-commerce

To integrate effective marketing strategies for cross-border E-commerce

Warming up

1. Which social media do you often use (such as QQ, Wechat, Weibo, DingTalk, etc.)? What are their typical features? How do you compare their advantages and disadvantages?

2. Read the words or phrases and their explanations. Then complete the following paragraph(s) with the words or phrases. Change the form when necessary.

comment	something that you say or write which gives an opinion on or explains sb/sth
outbound	moving away from a place rather than arriving in it
traffic	the movement of messages and signals through an electronic communication system
community	a group of people who share the same religion, race, job, etc.
interact	to communicate with sb, especially while you work, play or spend time with them

Social networking websites allow individuals, businesses and other organizations to interact with one another and build relationships and _____ online. When companies join these social channels, consumers can _____ with them directly. That interaction can be more personal to users than traditional methods of _____ marketing and advertising. Social networking sites act as word of mouth or more precisely, e-word of mouth. The Internet's ability to reach billions across the globe has given online word of mouth a powerful voice and far reach. The ability to rapidly change buying patterns and product or service acquisition and activity to a growing number of consumers is defined as an influence network. Social networking sites and blogs allow followers to "retweet" or "repost" _____ made by others about a product being promoted, which occurs quite frequently on some social media sites. By repeating the message, the user's connections are able to see the message, therefore reaching more people. Because the information about the product is being put out there and is getting repeated, more _____ is brought to the product/company.

(Adapted from https://en.wikipedia.org/wiki/Social_media_marketing)

Text: Social Media Marketing for E-commerce

by Kelly Mason

Studies show that 74% of customers rely on social media to help guide their purchasing decisions. Social media platforms such as Facebook, Instagram, Twitter, and Pinterest can help retailers market to larger audiences by meeting customers where they already hang out online and allowing customers to easily access their brand.

Integrating a social media strategy into your company's overall marketing efforts (such as Pay Per Click advertising, SEO, E-mail marketing, and blogging — just to name a few) can help to drive traffic and conversions to your store, increase customer engagement and loyalty, and improve brand awareness.

Let's take a look at how to get started with social media marketing for your E-commerce business:

Set Goals

You should have goals in mind for every new marketing endeavor your business starts — you need to know what your benchmarks are for success. Try to be specific and set measurable goals. For example, if your goal is to increase brand awareness, you may want to measure the number of social media followers you have. If you want to use social media to drive sales, you may want to measure the amount of traffic to your site from social media and the number of conversions that come from a lead on social media. Most social media platforms have analytics built in that allows you to see increases in followers, post reach and more. Google Analytics lets you easily track visitors that have come to your site from a social source (see Figure 5-1).

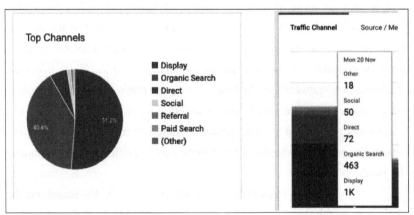

You can easily track traffic from a number of sources, including social media, through Google Analytics

Figure 5-1

Choose Your Platforms

There are TONS of social media networks and social sharing services — from Facebook, Twitter, LinkedIn, Instagram, Pinterest, YouTube, Snapchat, and beyond into lesser-known networks such as Reddit, Periscope, and Tumblr.

There are hundreds of platforms out there — **you don't need to be on all of them, but you do need to find the ones that are relevant** to your business and where your target audience hangs out.

Share the Right Content

Your success on social media is directly related to the creating and sharing of interesting and relevant content. To grab a user's attention on social media, you have to appeal to what they are interested in, not just what you want them to be interested in.

Grabbing your customer's attention on social media can be as simple as posting some photos of new products you are carrying on your Facebook, to tweeting out a link to your latest blog post, to creating Pinterest boards that showcase your products, to sharing user-created content on your Instagram. You want to create and share content that shows your expertise and exemplifies your brand voice (see Figure 5-2).

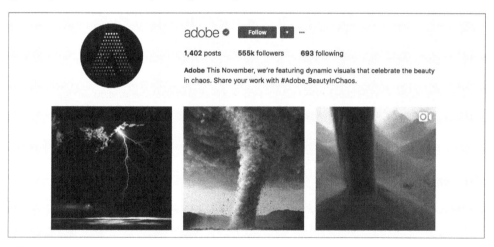

The Adobe Instagram does a great job at grabbing your attention with creative imagery that is all user-created (with the help of Adobe software, of course).

Figure 5-2

Optimize Content

Once you know which platforms you want to post on, and what type of content works for your audience, you need to make sure your content is optimized for each platform you plan to post on. **Not all of your content needs to be shared everywhere**, and not all content is going to work the same on every social media platform. Every platform is going to have a slightly different user-base with different expectations of the content on that platform. While you want to push the same messaging across your social media platforms, how you do it will be different.

For example, Facebook is a great platform for sharing video — if you own a home decorating business you could share a video walkthrough of your latest home renovation project, whereas on Twitter you are much more limited in characters and user's attention span, so you might want to tweet out a photo of your recent project with a poll where users can interact and express their feelings (see Figure 5-3).

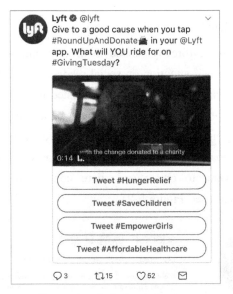

Example of a Twitter poll posted by Lyft that both promotes use of their service, while engaging customers through asking which charity they want to support.

Figure 5-3

Social Sharing Buttons

It's important to share things on your social media accounts, but do you have a way for customers to share items from your site onto THEIR accounts? **By including social sharing buttons on your website, you allow your customers to share the things they find interesting**, allowing your content to reach larger and new audiences in an organic way.

Social sharing buttons come in all shapes, sizes, colors, and configurations. You will need to find what works best for your individual store. On the Customer Paradigm blog, we have buttons configured in a menu on the left-hand side of the page, they move and expand as you interact with them (see Figure 5-4).

Interact with Followers

Social media is meant for interaction; it gives customers and companies unique access to each

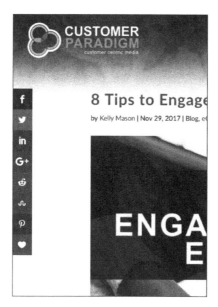

The social sharing buttons on the Customer Paradigm blog — they animate as viewers interact with them and make sharing articles easy.

Figure 5-4

other. Social media is the perfect space to interact with customers and let them know what makes your brand stand out. Some ways to interact with your followers on your social media platforms include:

- **Customer Support:** Many companies have begun using their social media as an outlet for customer support. With the familiarity of the platforms to users, many users have begun to reach out to companies to voice questions, comments, concerns, and complaints. For example, Southwest Airlines responds to all of their customer's questions, comments, concerns, and more (see Figure 5-5).

Southwest regularly responds to comments, concerns, and questions as well as offers customer support through their Twitter account.

Figure 5-5

- **Reviews:** You can use your social media platform as another outlet where customers can leave reviews. Reviews are a crucial factor in purchasing decisions. Having customers leave reviews on your social media platforms is a powerful tool in influencing how other customers view your business.

- **Groups:** Connect with your audience through groups. Sites like Facebook and LinkedIn have a "groups" feature where you can join or start a group on just about any topic. Chances are there are already groups that fit your niche — find them and join in the conversation. For example, I spend a lot of time talking with others in the Magento and E-commerce world through Facebook groups — it's a great way to keep up with what is going on in your community and have a presence (see Figure 5-6).

Figure 5-6

- **Live Chat:** Host a Twitter live chat — or "tweet chat". Hosting a live chat event on Twitter is a great way to start a scheduled, focused conversation with your customers. Typically, you would use a single hashtag to filter your Twitter chat out from the rest of Twitter. You will typically want to announce the date, time, and topic beforehand so that customers will know when to tune in. A live chat between you and your customers is a great way to break down the business/customer barrier. For example, social media software company Buffer hosts a weekly chat where they ask followers different opinion-based questions about social media, marketing, and more (see Figure 5-7):

Figure 5-7

Be Consistent

It can take months to really get the hang of social media and get a consistent stream of content going. Posting your content on a regular, consistent basis is key to improving your social media engagement. People like regularity — they want to know what to expect and when to expect it. While posting frequency is going to vary based on social media platform and what is right for your industry, we suggest creating a posting calendar to keep yourself on track. There are a number of marketing automation tools (many that are free, or have free trials available!) out there that allow you to schedule posts in advance, making it easier to post consistently and saving you valuable time.

Closing Thoughts

Social media can be a powerful tool for E-commerce businesses — if used correctly, social media can grow your audience, influence sales, and promote your brand.

(Adapted from https://www.customerparadigm.com/social-media-for-ecommerce/)

Words & Expressions

access	/ˈæksɛs/	v.	to reach, enter or use sth 到达;进入;使用
		n.	~ (to sth) the opportunity or right to use sth or to see sb/sth (使用或见到的)机会,权利
integrate	/ˈɪntɪˌɡreɪt/	v.	~ (A) (into/with B)/~ A and B to combine two or more things so that they work together; to combine with sth else in this way (使)合并,成为一体
conversion	/kənˈvɜːʃən/	n.	~ (from sth) (into/to sth) the act or process of changing sth from one form, use or system to another 转变;转换;转化
endeavor	/ɪnˈdɛvə/	n.	a purposeful or industrious undertaking (especially one that requires effort or boldness) 努力;尽力
benchmark	/ˈbɛntʃˌmɑːk/	n.	something which can be measured and used as a standard that other things can be compared with 基准
analytics	/ˌænəˈlɪtɪks/	n.	discovery and communication of meaningful patterns in data 解析法
lesser-known	/ˈlɛsə ˈnəʊn/	adj.	barely known 鲜为人知的,不为人知的
relevant	/ˈrɛlɪvənt/	adj.	closely connected with the subject you are discussing or the situation you are thinking about 相关的;切题的
expertise	/ˌɛkspɜːˈtiːz/	n.	~ (in sth/in doing sth) expert knowledge or skill in a particular subject, activity or job 专门知识;专门技能;专长
exemplify	/ɪɡˈzɛmplɪfaɪ/	v.	to give an example in order to make sth clearer 举例说明;例证;例示

renovation	/ˌrenəˈveɪʃn/	n.	the act of improving by renewing and restoring 翻修,改造
charity	/ˈtʃærɪtɪ/	n.	the aim of giving money, food, help, etc. to people who are in need 慈善;赈济;施舍
configuration	/kənˌfɪgəˈreɪʃən/	n.	an arrangement of the parts of sth or a group of things; the form or shape that this arrangement produces 布局;结构
animate	/ˈænɪmeɪt/	v.	to make sth more lively or full of energy 使具活力;使生气勃勃
outlet	/ˈaʊtlet/	n.	a way of expressing or making good use of strong feelings, ideas or energy(感情、思想、精力发泄的)出路;表现机会
familiarity	/fəˌmɪlɪˈærɪtɪ/	n.	~ (with sth) / ~ (to sb) the state of knowing sb/sth well; the state of recognizing sb/sth 熟悉;通晓;认识
typically	/ˈtɪpɪkəlɪ/	adv.	used to say that sth usually happens in the way that you are stating 通常;一般
hashtag	/ˈhæʃtæg/	n.	a word or a phrase prefixed with the symbol #标签
filter	/ˈfɪltə/	v.	~ (sth out) to remove sb/sth that you do not want from a large number of people or things using a special system, device, etc. (用专门的系统、装置等)过滤掉,筛除,淘汰掉
barrier	/ˈbærɪə/	n.	~ (between A and B) / ~ (against sth) something that exists between one thing or person and another and keeps them separate 分界线;屏障;隔阂
consistent	/kənˈsɪstənt/	adj.	happening in the same way and continuing for a period of time 连续的;持续的
regularity	/ˌregjʊˈlærɪtɪ/	n.	the fact that the same thing happens again and again, and usually with the same length of time between each time it happens 规律性;经常性
automation	/ˌɔːtəˈmeɪʃən/	n.	the condition of being automatically operated or controlled 自动化;自动操作

rely on	依靠,依赖
hang out	挂出;闲逛
just to name a few	仅举几例
have … in mind	考虑;想到
appeal to	激发
tweet out	推送(推文)
attention span	注意广度;注意力的持续时间

stand out	突出;脱颖而出
respond to	响应;回应;回答
Chances are …	有可能……
tune in	收听;调入
get the hang of	得知……的窍门;熟悉某物的用法;理解某事
keep … on track	使……走上正轨;保持……正常进行

Notes & Terms

Instagram	(also known as **IG** or **insta**) a photo and video-sharing social networking service owned by Facebook, Inc.　照片墙(一款图片分享应用)
Pinterest	a social media web and mobile application company that operates a software system designed to discover information on the World Wide Web, mainly using images and, on a smaller scale, GIFs and videos 拼趣网
Google Analytics	a web analytics service offered by Google that tracks and reports website traffic, currently as a platform inside the Google Marketing Platform brand 谷歌分析(互联网公司 Google 为网站提供的数据统计服务)
YouTube	an American video-sharing website headquartered in San Bruno, California. YouTube allows users to upload, view, rate, share, add to favorites, report, comment on videos, and subscribe to other users. It offers a wide variety of user-generated and corporate media videos 视频网站(可以让用户免费上传、观赏、分享视频短片的热门视频共享网站)
Snapchat	an American technology and camera company, founded on September 16, 2011, by Evan Spiegel and Bobby Murphy and based in Santa Monica, California 色拉布(照片分享平台,支持照片阅后即焚)
Reddit	(stylized in its logo as reddit) an American social news aggregation, web content rating, and discussion website.一个新闻网站
Periscope	a live video streaming app for Android and iOS developed by Kayvon Beykpour and Joe Bernstein and acquired by Twitter before launch in 2015 潜望镜(一个视频直播应用程序)
Tumblr	(stylized as **tumblr**) a microblogging and social networking website founded by David Karp in 2007 and owned by Verizon Media 微博客(一个社交网站)
Lyft	an on-demand transportation company primarily providing ride-hailing services and based in San Francisco, California. It develops, markets, and operates the Lyft car transportation mobile app 来福车(一款打车应用软件)

Customer Paradigm	a full-service interactive media, ecommerce, *custom* software, and Internet marketing agency 一家互联网营销咨询机构
Magento	an open-source E-commerce platform written in PHP. The software was originally developed by Varien, Inc, a US private company headquartered in Culver City, California, with assistance from volunteers.麦进斗(电子商务网站应用程序)
Buffer	a company that creates the software application Buffer for the web and mobile, designed to manage accounts in social networks, by providing the means for a user to schedule posts to Twitter, Facebook, Instagram, and Linkedin, as well as analyze their results and engage with their community 一家社交网站
Pay Per Click	also known as cost per click (CPC), is an Internet advertising model used to drive traffic to websites, in which an advertiser pays a publisher (typically a search engine, website owner, or a network of websites) when the ad is clicked 按点击付费

Understanding the text

Ⅰ. Complete the following summary of the text.

To use social media marketing strategy for E-commerce, the online store should start with setting specific and attainable _____. Then it is important to decide on suitable social media _____ for the business. It is not enough to share the proper content on them; it is necessary to _____ it on each of them. In this case, don't forget to add the social media sharing buttons for the convenience to the customers. Furthermore, it is necessary to _____ with the followers on the social media in ways of customer support, reviews, groups and live chat, etc., and by regularly and _____ updating the posting.

Ⅱ. Read the text and decide whether the following statements are true (T) or false (F).

(   )1   According to studies, most customers make their shopping decisions on the basis of social media.

(   )2   To reach more potential customers, it is necessary to make presence for the E-commerce store on all the social media platforms.

(   )3   To attract the customers' attention on social media, the E-commerce store must depend on what it uses to interest them.

(   )4   It will be helpful for the customers to share things interesting to them to include social sharing buttons.

(   )5   It is suggested by the author to post content on the social media casually and randomly.

Ⅲ. Answer the following questions according to the text.

1. Why is it necessary to use social media marketing?

2. What kind of goals should be set?

3. What kind of content is right to post on social media?

4. How can the E-commerce store interact with the followers on social media?

5. Can you share your experience in interacting with your favorite brand on social media?

Language Work

Ⅰ. Choose the best choice to complete each of the following sentences.

1. Within each store, we would make every _____ to have separate shops with merchandise from China.

   A. favor   B. endeavor   C. labor   D. flavor

2. In microeconomics, production is the _____ of inputs into outputs.

   A. convention   B. conversation   C. concession   D. conversion

3. Housing prices should include the cost of housing construction and _____ costs of components, which should be identified in the contract.

   A. invention   B. renovation   C. innovation   D. reservation

4. With the implementation of the new policy, this country is witnessing a pattern of _____ growth in the economy.

   A. assistant   B. resistant   C. consistent   D. existent

5. This requires us to understand and _____ customer needs and requirements better than any other wholesale company.

   A. respond to   B. recede to   C. refer to   D. resort to

Ⅱ. Match the English words in the left column with the English explanations in the right column.

_____	1. integrate	A. special skill or knowledge that is acquired by training, study, or practice
_____	2. benchmark	B. something such as a rule, law, or policy that makes it difficult or impossible for something to happen or be achieved
_____	3. expertise	C. to form, coordinate, or blend into a functioning or unified whole
_____	4. configuration	D. something whose quality or quantity is known and which can therefore be used as a standard with which other things can be compared
_____	5. barrier	E. the shape or arrangement of the parts of something

Ⅲ. Translate the following sentences from the text into Chinese.

1. Once you know which platforms you want to post on, and what type of content works for your audience, you need to make sure your content is optimized for each platform you plan to post on.

_____

_____ .

2. Social sharing buttons come in all shapes, sizes, colors, and configurations.

_____

_____ .

3. Social media is meant for interaction; it gives customers and companies unique access to each other.

_____

_____ .

4. Posting your content on a regular, consistent basis is key to improving your social media engagement.

_____

_____ .

5. While posting frequency is going to vary based on social media platform and what is right for your industry, we suggest creating a posting calendar to keep yourself on track.

_____

_____ .

Ⅳ. Translate the following sentences into English using the proper forms of the words or expressions given in brackets.

1. 只有高级管理层才有权查阅这些文件。(access)

_____

_____ .

2. 我们必须充分利用手上的资源来改进产品的设计。(optimize)

_____

_____ .

3. 我们需要收集所有与客户消费习惯有关的数据。(related to)

_____

_____ .

4. 慈善机构的运营很大程度上依靠公众捐赠。(rely on)

_____

_____ .

5. 如果能为顾客提供极好的产品或者好的服务,那么他们很可能会回购更多并且告诉他们的朋友。(chances are...)

Supplementary Reading: Search Engine Marketing

Search engine marketing (SEM) is a form of Internet marketing that involves the promotion of websites by increasing their visibility in search engine results pages (SERPs) primarily through paid advertising. SEM may incorporate search engine optimization (SEO), which adjusts or rewrites website content and site architecture to achieve a higher ranking in search engine results pages to enhance pay per click (PPC) listings.

Methods and metrics

Search engine marketing uses at least five methods and metrics to optimize websites.

1. **Keyword research and analysis** involves three "steps": ensuring the site can be indexed in the search engines, finding the most relevant and popular keywords for the site and its products, and using those keywords on the site in a way that will generate and convert traffic. A follow-on effect of keyword analysis and research is the search perception impact. Search perception impact describes the identified impact of a brand's search results on consumer perception, including title and meta tags, site indexing, and keyword focus. As online searching is often the first step for potential consumers/customers, the search perception impact shapes the brand impression for each individual.

2. **Website saturation and popularity**, or how much presence a website has on search engines, can be analyzed through the number of pages of the site that are indexed by search engines (saturation) and how many backlinks the site has (popularity). It requires pages to contain keywords people are looking for and ensure that they rank high enough in search engine rankings. Most search engines include some form of link popularity in their ranking algorithms. The following are major tools measuring various aspects of saturation and link popularity: Link Popularity, Top 10 Google Analysis, and Marketleap's Link Popularity and Search Engine Saturation.

3. **Back end tools**, including Web analytic tools and HTML validators, provide data on a website and its visitors and allow the success of a website to be measured. They range from simple traffic counters to tools that work with log files and to more sophisticated tools that are based on page tagging (putting JavaScript or an image on a page to track actions). These tools can deliver conversion-related information.

4. **Whois tools** reveal the owners of various websites and can provide valuable information relating to copyright and trademark issues.

5. **Google Mobile-Friendly Website Checker**: This test will analyze a URL and report if the page has a mobile-friendly design.

Search engine marketing is a way to create and edit a website so that search engines rank it higher than other pages. It should be also focused on keyword marketing or pay-per-click advertising (PPC). The technology enables advertisers to bid on specific keywords or phrases and ensures ads appear with the results of search engines.

With the development of this system, the price is growing under the high level of competition. Many advertisers prefer to expand their activities, including increasing search engines and adding more keywords. The more advertisers are willing to pay for clicks, the higher the ranking for advertising, which leads to higher traffic. PPC comes at a cost. The higher position is likely to cost $5 for a given keyword, and $4.50 for a third location. A third advertiser earns 10% less than the top advertiser, while reducing traffic by 50%. The investors must consider their return on investment and then determine whether the increase in traffic is worth the increase.

There are many reasons explaining why advertisers choose the SEM strategy. First, creating a SEM account is easy and can build traffic quickly based on the degree of competition. The shopper who uses the search engine to find information tends to trust and focus on the links showed in the results pages. However, a large number of online sellers do not buy search engine optimization to obtain higher ranking lists of search results, but prefer paid links. A growing number of online publishers are allowing search engines such as Google to crawl content on their pages and place relevant ads on it. From an online seller's point of view, this is an extension of the payment settlement and an additional incentive to invest in paid advertising projects. Therefore, it is virtually impossible for advertisers with limited budgets to maintain the highest rankings in the increasingly competitive search market.

Google's search engine marketing is one of the western world's marketing leaders, while its search engine marketing is its biggest source of profit. Google's search engine providers are clearly ahead of the Yahoo! and Bing network. The display of unknown search results is free, while advertisers are willing to pay for each click of the ad in the sponsored search results.

Paid inclusion

Paid inclusion involves a search engine company charging fees for the inclusion of a website in their results pages. Also known as sponsored listings, paid inclusion products are provided by most search engine companies either in the main results area or as a separately identified advertising area.

The fee structure is both a filter against superfluous submissions and a revenue generator. Typically, the fee covers an annual subscription for one webpage, which will automatically be catalogued on a regular basis. However, some companies are experimenting with non-subscription based fee structures where purchased listings are displayed permanently. A per-click fee may also apply. Each search engine is different. Some sites allow only paid inclusion, although these have had little success. More frequently, many search engines, like Yahoo!, mix paid inclusion (per-page and per-click fee) with results from web crawling. Others, like Google, do not let webmasters pay to be in their search engine listing.

Some detractors of paid inclusion allege that it causes searches to return results based more on the economic standing of the interests of a web site, and less on the relevancy of that site to end-users.

Often the line between pay per click advertising and paid inclusion is debatable. Some have lobbied for any paid listings to be labeled as an advertisement, while defenders insist they are not actually ads since the webmasters do not control the content of the listing, its ranking, or even whether it is shown to any users. Another advantage of paid inclusion is that it allows site owners to specify particular schedules for crawling pages. In the general case, one has no control as to when their page will be crawled or added to a search engine index. Paid inclusion proves to be particularly useful for cases where pages are dynamically generated and frequently modified.

Paid inclusion is a search engine marketing method in itself, but also a tool of search engine optimization, since experts and firms can test out different approaches to improving ranking and see the results often within a couple of days, instead of waiting weeks or months. Knowledge gained this way can be used to optimize other web pages, without paying the search engine company.

Comparison with SEO

SEM is the wider discipline that incorporates SEO. SEM includes both paid search results (using tools like Google Adwords or Bing Ads, formerly known as Microsoft adCenter) and organic search results (SEO). SEM uses paid advertising with AdWords or Bing Ads, pay per click (particularly beneficial for local providers as it enables potential consumers to contact a company directly with one click), article submissions, advertising and making sure SEO has been done. A keyword analysis is performed for both SEO and SEM, but not necessarily at the same time. SEM and SEO both need to be monitored and updated frequently to reflect evolving best practice.

In some contexts, the term SEM is used exclusively to mean pay per click advertising, particularly in the commercial advertising and marketing communities which have a vested interest in this narrow definition. Such usage excludes the wider search marketing community that is engaged in other forms of SEM such as search engine optimization and search retargeting. Creating the link between SEO and PPC represents an integral part of the SEM concept. Sometimes, especially when separate teams work on SEO and PPC and the efforts are not synced, positive results of aligning their strategies can be lost. The aim of both SEO and PPC is maximizing the visibility in search and thus, their actions to achieve it should be centrally coordinated. Both teams can benefit from setting shared goals and combined metrics, evaluating data together to determine future strategy or discuss which of the tools works better to get the traffic for selected keywords in the national and local search results. Thanks to this, the search visibility can be increased along with optimizing both conversions and costs.

SEO & SEM are two pillars of one marketing job and they both run side by side to produce much better results than focusing on only one pillar.

(Adapted from https://en.wikipedia.org/wiki/Search_engine_marketing)

Words & Expressions

involve	/ɪnˈvɒlv/	v.	to include sth as a part or affect someone or something 包含;牵涉
visibility	/ˌvɪzɪˈbɪlɪtɪ/	n.	the fact or state of being easy to see 可见性;明显性
incorporate	/ɪnˈkɔːpəˌreɪt/	v.	**~ sth (in/into/within sth)** to include sth so that it forms a part of sth 包含;使并入
architecture	/ˈɑːkɪˌtɛktʃə/	n.	the structure of something 结构
enhance	/ɪnˈhɑːns/	v.	to increase or further improve the good quality, value or status of sb/sth 提高;增强;增进
metrics	/ˈmɛtrɪks/	n.	a system or standard of measurement 计量体系;衡量标准
index	/ˈɪndɛks/	v.	to make an index of documents, the contents of a book, etc.; to add sth to a list of this type 为……编索引;将……编入索引
generate	/ˈdʒɛnəˌreɪt/	v.	to produce or create sth 产生;引起
saturation	/ˌsætʃəˈreɪʃən/	n.	the state or process that happens when no more of sth can be accepted or added because there is already too much of it or too many of them 饱和;饱和状态
algorithm	/ˈælgəˌrɪðəm/	n.	a set of rules that must be followed when solving a particular problem 算法;计算程序
validator	/ˈvaliˌdeitə/	n.	a computer program used to check the validity or syntactical correctness of a fragment of code or document 验证器;验证程序
competition	/ˌkɒmplˈtɪʃən/	n.	**~ (between/with sb) ~ (for sth)** a situation in which people or organizations compete with each other for sth that not everyone can have 竞争;角逐
sponsor	/ˈspɒnsə/	v.	to pay the costs of a particular event, programme, etc. as a way of advertising 赞助(活动、节目等)
superfluous	/suːˈpɜːfluəs/	adj.	more than is needed or wanted 多余的,过剩的,不必要的
catalogue	/ˈkætəlɒg/	v.	to make a complete list of all the things in a group 为……编目录,把……列入目录中
detractor	/dɪˈtræktə/	n.	a person who tries to make sb/sth seem less good or

			valuable by criticizing it 诋毁者；贬低者；恶意批评者
allege	/əˈlɛdʒ/	v.	to state sth as a fact but without giving proof（未提出证据）断言，指称，声称
relevancy	/ˈrɛləvənsiː/	n.	the relation of something to the matter at hand 关联；恰当
debatable	/dɪˈbeɪtəbəl/	adj.	not certain because people can have different ideas and opinions about the thing being discussed 可争辩的；有争议的
lobby	/ˈlɒbɪ/	n.	~ (sb) (for/against sth) to try to influence a politician or the government and, for example, persuade them to support or oppose a change in the law 游说（从政者或政府）
specify	/ˈspɛsɪˌfaɪ/	v.	to state sth, especially by giving an exact measurement, time, exact instructions, etc. 具体说明；明确规定；详述；详列
approach	/əˈprəʊtʃ/	n.	~ (to sth) a way of dealing with sb/sth; a way of doing or thinking about sth such as a problem or a task（待人接物或思考问题的）方式，方法，态度
integral	/ˈɪntɪɡrəl/	adj.	~ (to sth) being an essential part of sth 必需的；不可或缺的
synced	/sɪŋkt/	adj.	in agreement with sb/sth; working well with sb/sth 一致；协调
align	/əˈlaɪn/	v.	~ sth (with/to sth) to change sth slightly so that it is in the correct relationship to sth else 使一致
coordinate	/kəʊˈɔːdɪneɪt/		to organize the different parts of an activity and the people involved in it so that it works well 使协调；使相配合
pillar	/ˈpɪlə/	n.	a basic part or feature of a system, organization, belief, etc.（组织、制度、信仰等的）核心，基础，支柱
from one's point of view			从……的观点看
as to			关于；至于
vested interest			既得利益，既定利益
back end tool			后端工具

Notes & Terms

Yahoo!	a web services provider headquartered in Sunnyvale, California and owned by Verizon Media 美国雅虎公司
Bing	a web search engine owned and operated by Microsoft. The service has its origins in Microsoft's previous search engines: MSN Search, Windows Live Search and later Live Search. Bing provides a variety of

	search services, including web, video, image and map search products. 必应搜索(微软公司的搜索引擎产品)
Google Adwords	Google Ads now, is an online advertising platform developed by Google, where advertisers pay to display brief advertisements, service offerings, product listings, video content, and generate mobile application installs within the Google ad network to web users.谷歌关键字广告
Bing Ads	(formerly Microsoft adCenter and MSN adCenter) is a service that provides pay per click advertising on both the Bing and Yahoo! search engines. 必应广告
Link Popularity	the number and quality of inbound links to a webpage with the goal of increasing the search engine rankings of that page or website 链接广泛度
search engine results page (SERPs)	the pages displayed by search engines in response to a query by a searcher. The main component of the SERP is the listing of results that are returned by the search engine in response to a keyword query, although the pages may also contain other results such as advertisements.搜索引擎结果页面
meta tags	tags used in HTML and XHTML documents to provide structured metadata about a Web page.元标记,元标签
HTML	Hypertext Markup Language, the standard markup language for creating web pages and web applications 超文本标记语言
log file	a file that records either events that occur in an operating system or other software runs, or messages between different users of a communication software 日志文件
JavaScript	a high-level, interpreted programming language that conforms to the ECMAScript specification. It is a programming language that is characterized as dynamic, weakly typed, prototype-based and multi-paradigm. Java 描述语言(一种基于对象和事件驱动的客户端脚本语言)
Whois	a query and response protocol that is widely used for querying databases that store the registered users or assignees of an Internet resource, such as a domain name, an IP address block or an autonomous system, but is also used for a wider range of other information 域名查询服务
URL	Uniform Resource Locator, colloquially termed a web address, is a reference to a web resource that specifies its location on a computer network and a mechanism for retrieving it.统一资源定位器

Text Comprehension

Choose the best answer to each of the following questions according to the text.

1. According to the passage, which of the following is NOT a step in the keyword research and analysis?

   A. Adjusting and rewriting website content and site architecture.

   B. Getting the site indexed in the search engines.

   C. Identifying proper keywords the website and products.

   D. Applying the keywords to bring more traffic.

2. Which of the following can offer information about the copyright and trademark issues?

   A. Website saturation and popularity.

   B. Back end tool.

   C. Whois tools.

   D. Google Mobile-Friendly Website Checker.

3. Which is the reason for advertisers to choose the SEM strategy?

   A. It avoids competition.

   B. It is an effective way to bring traffic quickly.

   C. It can design attractive webpages for the products.

   D. It reduces the cost for the advertisers.

4. Which of the following is a criticism on paid inclusion?

   A. It allows site owners to specify particular schedules for crawling pages.

   B. It is not effective when pages are dynamically generated.

   C. The shoppers do not trust the links showed in the results pages.

   D. The returned search results tend to be based on the economic interests of the website instead of the relevancy to the end-users.

5. Which of the following statements is NOT true for the relationship between SEM and SEO?

   A. SEO is included in the discipline of SEM.

   B. Both SEM and SEO should be often monitored and updated.

   C. SEO and SEM are different digital marketing practices and should be adopted alternatively.

   D. SEM and SEO can work together to generate better effect.

Language Work

Fill in the following blanks with the words or phrases given below. Change the forms where necessary.

involve	generate	perception	competition	sponsor
superfluous	allege	integral	specify	modify

1. The list in this section allows you to _____ up to 20 products for your bundle offer.
2. In this meeting, we will briefly discuss possible ways of reducing the costs and risks _____ in this investment.
3. In many cases, we can not achieve anything if there is only _____ but no cooperation.
4. "The lawsuits _____ that certain of Toyota's cars and trucks have a defect that causes sudden uncontrolled acceleration to speeds of up to 100 mph or more," the Los Angeles Times reported Monday.
5. If you lack the courage to sell or destroy your _____ belongings, you can put them in storage.

Workshop

Case study: Work in a group and do a case study on a brand or product advertised on Baidu, write a group report on the analysis of the marketing strategy and approaches as well as the evaluation of effect.

References

[1] https://en.wikipedia.org/wiki/Social_media_marketing, retrieved on 2019/03/02.

[2] https://www.customerparadigm.com/social-media-for-ecommerce/, retrieved on 2019/03/02.

[3] https://en.wikipedia.org/wiki/Search_engine_marketing, retrieved on 2019/03/02.

[4] https://en.wikipedia.org/wiki/Facebook.

[5] https://en.wikipedia.org/wiki/Instagram.

[6] https://en.wikipedia.org/wiki/Twitter.

[7] https://en.wikipedia.org/wiki/Pinterest.

[8] https://en.wikipedia.org/wiki/Google_Analytics.

[9] https://en.wikipedia.org/wiki/YouTube.

[10] https://en.wikipedia.org/wiki/Snap_Inc.

[11] https://en.wikipedia.org/wiki/Reddit.

[12] https://en.wikipedia.org/wiki/Periscope_(app).

[13] https://en.wikipedia.org/wiki/Tumblr.

[14] https://en.wikipedia.org/wiki/Lyft.

[15] https://www.customerparadigm.com/.

[16] https://en.wikipedia.org/wiki/Magento.

[17] https://en.wikipedia.org/wiki/Buffer_(application).

[18] https://en.wikipedia.org/wiki/Pay-per-click.

[19] https://en.wikipedia.org/wiki/Yahoo!.

[20] https://en.wikipedia.org/wiki/Bing_Ads.

[21] https://en.wikipedia.org/wiki/Link_building#Link_popularity.

[22] https://en.wikipedia.org/wiki/Search_engine_results_page.

[23] https://en.wikipedia.org/wiki/Meta_element.

[24] https://en.wikipedia.org/wiki/HTML.

[25] https://en.wikipedia.org/wiki/Log_file.

[26] https://en.wikipedia.org/wiki/JavaScript.

Unit 6

Pre-sale Services of Cross-border E-commerce

Learning Objectives

To learn how to price the products to sell on the E-commerce platform

To learn how to describe products for an E-commerce store

To learn the tactics that E-commerce businesses can use to increase sales

Warming up

1. Work in a group and share your experiences of buying things online. Discuss with your partners the factors that influence a customer's purchase decision and increase customer loyalty.

2. Read the words or phrases and their explanations. Then complete the following paragraph(s) with the words or phrases. Change the form when necessary.

field	answer adequately and successfully
funnel	a customer focused market model which illustrates the customer journey towards the purchase or sale of a product or service
one-on-one	directly between two individuals
SAAS	software-as-a-service
solution	a method of solving a problem

In B2C sales, pre-sales support is essential to educating consumers about the product, service or _____ offering they are interested in. This means _____ questions or explaining features in a _____ conversation with a consumer, to help the person make a decision and move forward in the sales _____. In more complex B2B sales, since presales support engineers have a deep understanding of the client and their needs, they can help the sales team propose the ideal _____. Beyond that, they can answer technical questions from prospective stakeholders regarding the RFP or implementation, which the sales person may not be able to answer.

(Adapted fromhttps://www.simplr.ai/learn/benefits-of-pre-sales-support)

Text: Pricing Strategy for E-commerce

by Burc Tanir

A good pricing strategy is essential for your E-commerce success. It helps you understand the pricing point at which you can maximize your profits on the sale of your products or services. For those who are new to the concept, it may seem like an intimidating one at first, but by considering the right factors you'll be able to make the right pricing decisions for your products in no time.

What is a Pricing Strategy for E-commerce?

A Pricing Strategy refers to the method a company uses to price their products or services. By applying various pricing approaches, your business will be more efficient, profitable, and sustainable in the long term.

If you don't base your pricing on any strategy, you might set it too high or too low. You'll lose customers if you price your products too high, as they will stop buying the products, whereas if you price too low, your profit margins will decline and you might end up leaving the impression that your products are poor quality.

Pricing strategy for E-commerce: First approach — cost-based

Cost-based pricing is a pricing method in which a fixed quantity or a percentage of the total cost is added to the cost of the product to determine its selling price. It is known to be one of the most intuitive ways to set a price. The logic is simple. After calculating the costs of a product for your company, you just have to apply the profit margin you want to achieve. That way, if the cost of product "A" is 50 and the margin you desire is 100%, you have to price it at 100. To do cost-based pricing, there are two main things you need to consider — the costs and the margins. Any type of cost-based pricing strategy begins with calculating the costs attached to the product. In order to calculate the costs of the products, you need to include the costs of production, promotion, and dropshipping. Luckily, with dropshipping you don't have to worry about the production costs, as you won't be coming in contact with the product. To achieve accuracy with cost-based pricing, you have to make sure that you are not ignoring any type of costs attached to the product. You need to consider the amount you are spending on your management expertise, or any other labor you are hiring, as well as any rent or land costs, or capital equipment that must also be valued.

Now, let's take a look at margins. How do you really know how much you should earn? Ideally a lot, but you have to keep it interesting for buyers, which takes us to our second approach.

A useful and sustainable way to enrich your pricing strategy is setting smart prices by defining repricing rules through competitor pricing intelligence software. With these tools, you're able to set ecommerce pricing rules by targeting certain profit margins and competitive pricing positions and can receive the smart price recommendations as an outcome (see Figure 6-1).

Pricing strategy for E-commerce: Second approach — market-oriented

Market-oriented pricing is a pricing strategy based on the market conditions and competition. This means that you compare the prices with similar products that are being offered on the market. That's why, this pricing strategy is sometimes referred to as competition-based pricing. In order to do market-oriented pricing, you need to know how you compare against your competitors. To find out, you can take advantage of a price tracking tool which will give you data about your competitors' prices and assortment, without needing to visit all their product pages every day. With this tool you will know if you are setting your prices among the most expensive online shops or among the cheapest. If you have set your prices way too low, you can make your margins bigger and keep your competitiveness. If on the other hand, you discover you are pricing too high, you may decide to lower your prices to start to get more visitors from price comparison engines and higher conversion rates. Also, you will know when your competitors are out of stock. When it happens, you can try to boost your sales with extra effort in advertising campaigns.

Figure 6-1 An example of the set of rules to figure out the smart price

If this is your first E-commerce experience, one thing you should focus on understanding is whether your Unique Selling Proposition (USP) is price-oriented or value-oriented. An understanding of your USP will help you figure out where you stand in comparison to your competitors, and where you aim to stand in the future.

It's always a good idea to understand what your competitors offer, and at what price. After researching your competitors, you now have a bigger and better picture, which makes it easier for you to determine your own pricing. You can, for instance, make an assessment based on the competition and in turn raise or lower your prices, or stick to what your competitors are offering. Penetration pricing, is another market-oriented pricing model where companies use very low prices in comparison to their competitors, as an advantage in order to enter a new market. Once they have successfully entered a market and gained market share, then they slowly start raising the price. This method can be of potential use to certain industries, however can also discourage customer groups that are more focused on pricing in comparison to the availability of the product.

Pricing strategy for E-commerce: Third approach — consumer-oriented

Consumer-oriented pricing, also known as value-based pricing, is a pricing strategy which sets prices according to the perceived or estimated value of the product or service to the customer. To benefit from the consumer-oriented pricing strategy, you need to have an understanding of your customers. Your customer groups might not all be the same. There may be some customers that carry out Internet research before selecting their preferred store. Or, there might be some customers who are looking for coupons or discount sales only. These customers might be of great potential to your E-commerce store as there's a great chance that they're willing to contribute data like their E-mail address for further reductions and discounts, which can be beneficial for your E-mail marketing.

So, for this approach to work well, we can determine that you need to know your customers well, which means you have to know who they are and what they value about your product and what your USP is. The truth is most of today's customers are deal-hunters. But there are still a proportion of customers that don't care much about the price. This is possible in luxury products. If your customers are among these last ones, you don't have to force your customers' attention to the price. What you have to do is focus on improving your brand, set a fixed valuable price and don't move it if it's not necessary.

You can use some Neuromarketing tips to optimize your pricing strategy:

- 99 is better than 100. The biggest E-commerce companies use it, so why wouldn't you? It's shorter, and it looks smaller.
- The same logic goes for pronunciations. A price that is pronounced shorter seems lower than a price pronounced longer. Thirty-six-twenty-eight dollars ($ 36.28) is worse than thirty-seven-one dollars ($ 37.01).
- If your buyers are experts, try to set prices as precisely as possible. They know the small differences between your products, and they will understand why one costs $ 36 and other $ 38. However, if they are not experts, do not make things difficult and just set it at $ 39.
- I guess you don't like paying, right? Nor do your customers. Price has to be visible, and don't oversize it, as nobody likes that.

Pricing Strategy for E-commerce Should Involve the Full Organization

As you have seen, pricing is a decision that has a lot of factors to take into consideration. The company itself, competitors and customers are the three top areas to think about. If you nail your pricing strategy for E-commerce, your conversion rates will rise, and your company will be more efficient. Besides, you will have a better knowledge of your business. Mix the approaches mentioned above and set the prices as they should be set. Also, you will see the effects of fine-tuned pricing strategies in your marketing results.

(Adapted from https://www.oberlo.com/blog/pricing-strategy-for-ecommerce)

Words & Expressions

essential /ɪˈsenʃəl/ *adj.* ~ (to/for sth) / ~ (to do sth) / ~ (that...) completely necessary; extremely important in a particular situation or for a particular activity 完全必要的;必不可少的;极其重

要的

maximize	/ˈmæksɪˌmaɪz/	v.	to increase sth as much as possible 使最大化;使增加到最大限度
efficient	/ɪˈfɪʃənt/	adj.	doing sth well and thoroughly with no waste of time, money, or energy 效率高的;有能力的
profitable	/ˈprɒfɪtəbəl/	adj.	that makes or is likely to make money 有利可图的;赚钱的
sustainable	/səˈsteɪnəbəl/	adj.	that can continue or be continued for a long time 可持续的
decline	/dɪˈklaɪn/	v.	to become smaller, fewer, weaker, etc. 减少;下降;衰弱;衰退
calculate	/ˈkælkjʊˌleɪt/	v.	to use numbers to find out a total number, amount, distance, etc. 计算;核算
attach	/əˈtætʃ/	v.	~ sth (to sth) to fasten or join one thing to another 把……固定,把……附(在……上)
accuracy	/ˈækjʊrəsɪ/	n.	the state of being exact or correct; the ability to do sth skillfully without making mistakes 准确(性);精确(程度)
oriented	/ˈɔːrɪɛntɪd/	adj.	functionally or intellectually directed or concerned 以……为导向的
assortment	/əˈsɔːtmənt/	n.	the act of distributing things into classes or categories of the same type 分类
boost	/buːst/	v.	to make sth increase, or become better or more successful 使增长;使兴旺
assessment	/əˈsɛsmənt/	n.	an opinion or a judgement about sb/sth that has been thought about very carefully 评价;估价;评估
availability	/əˌveɪləˈbɪlətɪ/	n.	the quality of being at hand when needed 可用性;有效性;可获得性
come in contact with			接触
be referred to as			被称为
out of stock			脱销;缺货
focus on			集中于;聚焦于
in comparison to			与……相比

Notes & Terms

profit margin	the difference between the selling price of a product and the cost of producing and marketing it 利润空间

dropshipping	Drop shipping is a supply chain management method in which the retailer does not keep goods in stock but instead transfers the customer orders and shipment details to either the manufacturer, another retailer, or a wholesaler, who then ships the goods directly to the customer. 代发货;制造商直接出货;转运配送
capital equipment	资本设备;固定设备
competitor pricing intelligence software	竞争对手定价情报软件
price comparison engine	比价引擎
Unique Selling Proposition(USP)	The unique selling proposition (USP) or unique selling point is a marketing concept first proposed as a theory to explain a pattern in successful advertising campaigns of the early 1940s. The USP states that such campaigns made unique propositions to customers that convinced them to switch brands. The term has been used to describe one's "personal brand" in the marketplace. Today, the term is used in other fields or just casually to refer to any aspect of an object that differentiates it from similar objects. 独特销售主张;独特卖点
Penetration pricing	Penetration pricing is a pricing strategy where the price of a product is initially set low to rapidly reach a wide fraction of the market and initiate word of mouth. The strategy works on the expectation that customers will switch to the new brand because of the lower price. Penetration pricing is most commonly associated with marketing objectives of enlarging market share and exploiting economies of scale or experience. 渗透定价
Neuromarketing	Neuromarketing is a commercial marketing communication field that applies neuropsychology to marketing research, studying consumers' sensorimotor, cognitive, and affective response to marketing stimuli. Neuromarketing seeks to understand the rationale behind how consumers make purchasing decisions and their responses to marketing stimuli in order to apply those learnings in the marketing realm. 神经营销学

Understanding the text

Ⅰ. Complete the following summary of the text.

A pricing strategy is very important for the success of an E-commerce business and it involves the consideration of a series of factors. There are mainly three _____ to the pricing strategy for E-commerce. The first is a cost-based pricing strategy where both the costs and the _____ should be considered. The second is a market-oriented pricing strategy where you need to understand how you compare against your _____. The third is a consumer-oriented pricing strategy where you need to know your _____ well. In all, pricing strategy for E-commerce should involve the full _____.

Ⅱ. Read the text and decide whether the following statements are true (T) or false (F).

(   ) 1   If your cross-border E-commerce business involves dropshipping, you don't need to consider the factor of production costs.

(   ) 2   According to the passage, the cost-based pricing strategy is also known as competition-based pricing.

(   ) 3   Penetration pricing is always attractive and effective to the customers who are more concerned about the price of product.

(   ) 4   For the customers who care little about price, we should pay more attention to improving the brand than driving their interest in price.

(   ) 5   Based on the principles of Neuromarketing, it is a better choice to set a price for a product at $33.68 than at $34, as the former is lower and more attractive to the customers.

Ⅲ. Answer the following questions according to the text.

1. Why is it necessary to adopt a pricing strategy?

2. What is a pricing strategy for E-commerce?

3. What is cost-based pricing and how to do it?

4. What is the key to the application of market-oriented pricing?

5. Can you give some real-life examples to illustrate the use of Neuromarketing tips in pricing?

Language Work

Ⅰ. Choose the best choice to complete each of the following sentences.

1. I do agree that insurance is _____ for my people with children, and that is one of the main reasons I keep offering it as a part of welfare to them.
   A. potential   B. financial   C. essential   D. substantial

2. The firm has decided to adopt a different _____ to the issue of low production efficiency.
   A. approach   B. approval   C. appraisal   D. application

3. They have _____ a number of conditions to the agreement.
   A. attended   B. attacked   C. attached   D. attempted

4. The government hopes that the new policy will _____ the exports of airplanes, machinery, technology and other products.
   A. burst   B. burden   C. boast   D. boost

5. It took the sales team about one month to _____ how to promote the new product.

    A. put out   B. figure out   C. draw out   D. leave out

II. Match the English words in the left column with the English explanations in the right column.

_____ 1. sustainable   A. consideration of someone or something and a judgment about them

_____ 2. maximize   B. to become less in quantity, importance, or strength

_____ 3. accuracy   C. to make sth as great in amount or importance as you can

_____ 4. assessment   D. able to continue at the same rate or level of activity without any problems

_____ 5. decline   E. the quality of being true or correct, even in small details

III. Translate the following sentences from the text into Chinese.

1. You'll lose customers if you price your products too high, as they will stop buying the products; whereas if you price too low, your profit margins will decline and you might end up leaving the impression that your products are poor quality.

_____

_____.

2. A useful and sustainable way to enrich your pricing strategy is setting smart prices by defining repricing rules through competitor pricing intelligence software.

_____

_____.

3. After researching your competitors, you now have a bigger and better picture, which makes it easier for you to determine your own pricing.

_____

_____.

4. These customers might be of great potential to your E-commerce store as there's a great chance that they're willing to contribute data like their E-mail address for further reductions and discounts, which can be beneficial for your E-mail marketing.

_____

_____.

5. If you nail your pricing strategy for E-commerce, your conversion rates will rise, and your company will be more efficient.

_____

_____.

IV. Translate the following sentences into English using the proper forms of the words or expressions given in brackets.

1. 这座城市的改革重点是要致力于发展服务导向型经济。(oriented)

_____

_____ .

2. 我学会了从自己读过的所有书中和接触过的所有人身上来获取灵感。(come in contact with)

_____

_____ .

3. 亚当·斯密通常被称为现代经济学的第一理论家。(be referred to as)

_____

_____ .

4. 管理人员应该学会利用能获得的所有资源来提高经营业绩。(take advantage of)

_____

_____ .

5. 虽然不能保证你们的营销活动一定能成功,但内容好、能让人记住的视频很有可能会帮助你的初创公司增加成功的机会。(there is a great chance that...)

_____

_____ .

Supplementary Reading: Tips for E-commerce Product Page Copy

by Graham Charlton

Great copywriting for E-commerce can make a big difference for conversions and can play a role in your customers' on-site experience, evoking emotion, instilling a feeling of confidence, and helping push them to complete a purchase.

It isn't as simple as listing products and using the manufacturer's product description. Attention should be paid to ensure that the copy works hard to increase search visibility as well as persuading customers to buy. Here are some key pointers.

Don't Use the Basic Manufacturer's Product Description

These product descriptions are used by lots of sites that sell the same products, and it seriously affects the product's ability to rank well on search engines. It also looks less genuine to shoppers.

For example, Walmart uses the manufacturer's description for this LG TV(see Figure 6-2).

And so does Dell (see Figure 6-3).

Ultimately neither site ranks highly on a search for this product. This could be due to a number of reasons, but this certainly doesn't help. Instead the manufacturer is top, followed by lots of reviews, sites, videos, and Amazon.

From a customer perspective, original copy works better and is more useful to customers than the generic product description. Phrases like "motion clarity index" may seem like meaningless sales jargon to many, indicating to consumers that the people behind the website don't have any knowledge about the product.

Compare the previous examples of product descriptions to that of AO.com — this is another LG model, but this product description is definitely more original (see Figure 6-4).

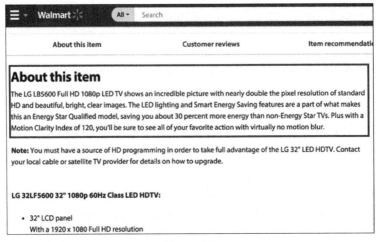

Figure 6-2

Figure 6-3

Figure 6-4

This version is more organic. By explaining the features without resorting to jargon, this gives the impression that the person writing the copy has actually used the product. Moreover, this is unique content that the search engines can index.

Use Search Data to Inform Copywriting

Search keyword referral data is now very rare, but e-tailers can use site search data to gain valuable insight into the kinds of terms and language customers use to describe and search for products. The keywords that people use to search within your website for products or information are very likely to be the same keywords they use when they are searching on Google, Bing, or other search engines. Then this can be incorporated into the product's meta data and the product descriptions, so that the copy can also reflect how customers are likely to search for products.

Highlight Key Features and Benefits

Web users like to scan pages and won't necessarily delve into the text of product descriptions to pick out key features. This is why it helps to display the key points clearly.

Note how Best Buy lists and explains the features of a drone in a way that makes it easier for users to scan quickly (see Figure 6-5).

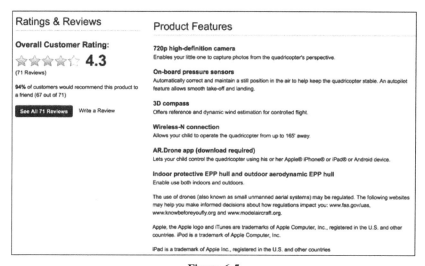

Figure 6-5

Technical Specifications

Products like laptops and cameras require the display of lots of detail — memory size, processing power, zoom, and so forth. This must be displayed in a way that makes it easy for customers to understand.

Formatting is important here, as customers should be able to scan to see the features and specifications that matter to them. Here, Newegg presents the specifications for a laptop (see Figure 6-6).

Learn more about the ASUS F554LA-WS71	
Model	
Brand	ASUS
Model	F554LA-WS71
Quick Info	
Color	Black
Operating System	Windows 8.1 64-Bit
CPU	Intel Core i7-5500U 2.4 GHz
Screen	15.6"
Memory	8 GB DDR3L
Storage	1 TB
Optical Drive	DL DVD+-RW/CD-RW
Graphics Card	Intel HD Graphics 5500
Video Memory	Shared memory
Communication	Gigabit LAN and WLAN
Dimensions (W x D x H)	15" x 10.1" x 1.0"
Weight	4.9 lbs.
CPU	
CPU Type	Intel Core i7

Figure 6-6

Another useful feature is the ability to compare different products and their specifications side-by-side, as demonstrated here on PC World (see Figure 6-7).

Figure 6-7

Different Products Require Varying Levels of Detail

The type of product, price points, and complexity should be taken into account when considering how much information the customer is likely to need in order to make a purchase. For instance, a simple product such as a tie requires very little detail.

Ties.com presents information on color, size, and material. The rest is left to the product imagery (see Figure 6-8).

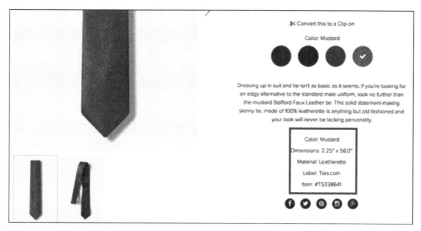

Figure 6-8

Answer the Questions Visitors Are Likely to Have About the Product

Anticipate and deal with likely questions. Use data from customer service and sales teams to provide the most important data prominently. Some sites have user-generated Q&A sections that allow customers to answer each other's questions. Here's an example from Newegg (see Figure 6-9).

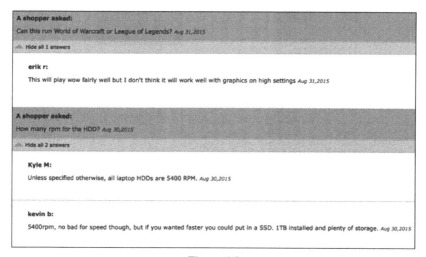

Figure 6-9

These user-generated Q&A sections should also help to tell retailers more about consumers' concerns and help improve product copy in future.

Let Customers Write Some of Your Copy

If your products are popular, your service is great and customers are saying so. Make sure people see this on your product pages. Reviews are the most obvious example of social proof. They essentially allow users to wax lyrical about your products if they're happy with them. Here's a great example from Modcloth on one of its product pages (see Figure 6-10).

Figure 6-10

Ensure That Copy Has the Correct Tone of Voice

Product copy should reflect the company's tone of voice, as well as being appropriate to the product sold. Copywriters should be able to adapt their writing style easily to suit the company's tone of voice, while ensuring that SEO objectives are taken care of.

You can always rely on J. Peterman for quirky and original product copy, which perfectly matches the brand. It's also pretty entertaining (see Figure 6-11).

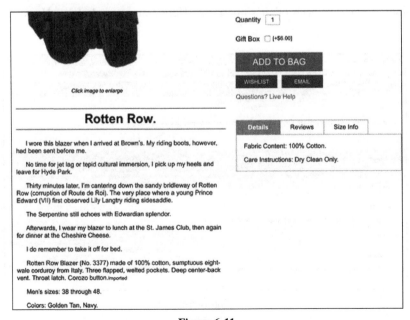

Figure 6-11

Test Positioning of Product Copy

This is something to test as the relative importance of various product page elements will differ between sites, products, and audiences. Many sites tend to prioritize product imagery over all else.

Jimmy Choo does so here, with the description one of the less prominent features on the page (see Figure 6-12).

Figure 6-12

However, some sites work a little harder for big ticket items. For example, this chair from Crate & Barrel is $1,600, and some customers need the copy to explain why it costs this much (see Figure 6-13).

Figure 6-13

Therefore, the copy emphasizes the quality of the material and the processes and the longevity of the product.

In Summary

There's no magic formula for great product page copy, but there are certainly some key mistakes to avoid, such as using generic descriptions for products. The copy must be compelling and persuasive and spell out the key features of products, while remaining close to the brand tone of voice.

After that, presentation of the copy is very important. Users scan pages for key details so it's important to highlight the key features of products for such users.

(Adapted from https://www.clickz.com/9-valuable-tips-for-your-E-commerce-product-page-copy/24622/)

Words & Expressions

copywriting	/ˈkɔpiˌraitiŋ/	n.	the act of writing copy (text) for the purpose of advertising or marketing a product, business, person, opinion or idea 文案策划;文案写作
evoke	/ɪˈvəʊk/	v.	to bring a feeling, a memory or an image into your mind 引起,唤起
generic	/dʒɪˈnɛrɪk/	adj.	shared by, including or typical of a whole group of things; not specific 一般的;普通的;通用的
jargon	/ˈdʒɑːgən/	n.	words or expressions that are used by a particular profession or group of people, and are difficult for others to understand 行话;黑话;行业术语
indicate	/ˈɪndɪˌkeɪt/	v.	to be a sign of sth; to show that sth is possible or likely 象征;暗示
organic	/ɔːˈgænɪk/	adj.	consisting of different parts that are all connected to each other 有机的;统一的;关联的
insight	/ˈɪnsaɪt/	n.	~ (into sth) an understanding of what sth is like 洞悉;了解
drone	/drəʊn/	n.	an aircraft without a pilot, controlled from the ground 无人驾驶飞机
specification	/ˌspɛsɪfɪˈkeɪʃən/	n.	a detailed description of how sth is, or should be, designed or made 规格;规范;明细单;说明书
formatting	/fɔːˈmeɪtiŋ/	n.	the organization of information according to preset specifications (usually for computer processing) 格式化
demonstrate	/ˈdɛmənˌstreɪt/	v.	~ sth (to sb) to show and explain how sth works or how to do sth 示范;演示

complexity	/kəmˈplɛksɪtɪ/	n.	the state of being formed of many parts; the state of being difficult to understand 复杂性;难懂
anticipate	/ænˈtɪsɪˌpeɪt/	v.	to see what might happen in the future and take action to prepare for it 预见,预计
prominently	/ˈprɒmɪnəntlɪ/	adv.	in a clear and prominent way 显著地;突出地
concern	/kənˈsɜːn/	n.	~ (about/for/over sth/sb) / ~ (that...) a feeling of worry, especially one that is shared by many people 担心,忧虑
quirky	/ˈkwɜːkɪ/	adj.	unusual, especially in an interesting way 离奇的,古怪的;奇特的
entertaining	/ˌɛntəˈteɪnɪŋ/	adj.	interesting and amusing 有趣的;娱乐的;使人愉快的
relative	/ˈrɛlətɪv/	adj.	considered and judged by being compared with sth else 相比较而言的;比较的
prioritize	/praɪˈɒrɪtaɪz/	v.	to treat sth as being more important than other things 优先处理
longevity	/lɒnˈdʒɛvɪtɪ/	n.	long life; the fact of lasting a long time 长寿;长命;持久
formula	/ˈfɔːmjʊlə/	n.	a series of letters, numbers or symbols that represent a rule or law 公式;方程式;计算式
compelling	/kəmˈpɛlɪŋ/	adj.	very interesting or exciting, so that you have to pay attention 极为有趣的;令人激动的;引人入胜的
presentation	/ˌprɛzənˈteɪʃən/	n.	the way in which something is said, offered, shown, or explained to others 讲述,描绘;显示;呈现;表现
highlight	/ˈhaɪlaɪt/	v.	to emphasize sth, especially so that people give it more attention 突出;强调

product page			产品说明页
make a difference			有影响;有关系
play a role in			在……中起作用;在……扮演一个角色
from...perspective			从……的角度来看
motion clarity index			运动清晰度指数
search keyword referral data			搜索关键字查询数据
resort to			采取;诉诸于
delve into			深入研究;钻研
take...into account			考虑;重视;体谅
wax lyrical about			热情洋溢地谈论
tone of voice			口吻;说话的语气
spell out			清楚地说出;清楚地说明

Notes & Terms

Walmart	an American multinational retail corporation that operates a chain of hypermarkets, discount department stores, and grocery stores 沃尔玛(世界连锁零售企业)
LG	a South Korean multinational conglomerate corporation 韩国 LG 公司
Dell	an American multinational computer technology company based in Round Rock, Texas, United States, that develops, sells, repairs, and supports computers and related products and services 美国戴尔公司
AO.com	an online-only retailer operating in the UK (AO.com), Germany (AO.de) and the Netherlands (AO. nl). It specializes in household appliances and electricals.一家纯网络零售连锁店
Best Buy	an American multinational consumer electronics retailer headquartered in Richfield, Minnesota 百思买集团
Newegg	an online retailer of items including computer hardware and consumer electronics 新蛋公司(美国 IT 数码产品网上零售商)
PC World	one of the United Kingdom's largest retail chains of mass market computer megastores 英国一家大型计算机销售商
Ties.com	an online company focused on menswear in Orange County, California 美国一家男士服饰网络专营店
Modcloth	an American online retailer of indie and vintage-inspired women's clothing 美国一家复古女装在线零售商
J. Peterman	The J. Peterman Company, an American catalog and retail enterprise from Lexington, Kentucky 美国一家目录和零售企业
Jimmy Choo	a British high fashion house specializing in shoes, handbags, accessories and fragrances 周仰杰(一家英国高级时装公司)
Crate & Barrel	a 105+ chain of retail stores in US and Canada, based in Northbrook, Illinois, specializing in housewares, furniture (indoor and out), and home accessories 美国著名家居品牌
e-tailer	(electronic retailer) a business that sells products or services on the Internet, instead of in a shop 网上零售商

Text Comprehension

Choose the best answer to each of the following questions according to the text.

1. Good E-commerce copywriting can influence the following aspects of customers' experience EXCEPT _____.

A. changing shopping habits

B. arousing their emotion

C. infusing a sense of confidence

D. encouraging them to make a purchase

2. Why is it suggested not to use the manufacturer's production description for the E-commerce product page copy?

A. Because they are too often used by different sites to sell the same thing.

B. Because it may greatly impact the ranking on search engines.

C. Because it may not sound reliable enough.

D. All of the above.

3. Which of the following can the site use to inform copywriting?

A. Generic description.

B. Jargon.

C. Search keyword referral data.

D. Site search data.

4. Which of the following is the most obvious example of social proof of products sold on the site?

A. Key features and benefits of the products.

B. Detailed technical specifications.

C. Reviews from the customers on the products.

D. The correct tone of voice.

5. Among the various product page elements, which one do many sites emphasize the most?

A. Shopping cart.   B. Product imagery.

C. Cost control.   D. Level of profitability.

Language Work

Fill in the following blanks with the words or phrases given below. Change the forms where necessary.

evoke	original	indicate	organic	insight
complexity	concern	prioritize	entertaining	presentation

1. The report expressed _____ over continuing currency inflation.

2. Last year witnessed record profits in the retail market, _____ a boom in the economy.

3. This company maintained its leading position in the market based on the continuous launch of _____ and high-quality products to win the hearts of customers.

4. The article gives us a real _____ into the causes of the present economic crisis.

5. In order to maintain social stability, the government decided to _____ the problem of

unemployment.

Workshop

Presentation: Work in a group and design a page copy for a certain product that you agree to sell on your cross-border E-commerce site, taking into account what you have learned from the two texts in this unit. And make a PowerPoint presentation in the class to explain your design ideas.

References

[1] https://www.simplr.ai/learn/benefits-of-pre-sales-support.

[2] https://en.wikipedia.org/wiki/.

[3] https://www.vocabulary.com/dictionary/.

[4] https://www.oberlo.com/blog/pricing-strategy-for-ecommerce, retrieved on 2019-04-12..

[5] https://en.wikipedia.org/wiki/Drop_shipping.

[6] https://en.wikipedia.org/wiki/Walmart.

[7] https://en.wikipedia.org/wiki/LG_Corporation.

[8] https://en.wikipedia.org/wiki/Dell.

[9] https://en.wikipedia.org/wiki/AO_World.

[10] https://en.wikipedia.org/wiki/Google.

[11] https://en.wikipedia.org/wiki/Bing_(search_engine).

[12] https://en.wikipedia.org/wiki/Best_Buy.

[13] https://en.wikipedia.org/wiki/Newegg.

[14] https://en.wikipedia.org/wiki/PC_World_(retailer).

[15] https://www.ties.com/about.

[16] https://en.wikipedia.org/wiki/John_Peterman#The_J._Peterman_Company.

[17] https://en.wikipedia.org/wiki/Jimmy_Choo_Ltd.

[18] https://en.wikipedia.org/wiki/Crate_%26_Barrel.

[19] https://en.wikipedia.org/wiki/Q%26A.

[20] https://en.wikipedia.org/wiki/Search_engine_optimization.

[21] https://www.clickz.com/9-valuable-tips-for-your-E-commerce-product-page-copy/24622/, retrieved on 2019-03-29.

[22] www.youdao.com.

Unit 7

On-sale Services of Cross-border E-commerce

Learning Objectives

To learn how to get acquainted with order processing on cross-border E-commerce platforms

To learn the process of delivery and logistics on cross-border E-commerce platforms

To learn useful expressions of order processing, delivery and logistics

Warming up

1. Work in a group and discuss problems you have come across when ordering a product online. Tell your partners how much you know about domestic delivery companies (such as SF Express, YTO Express, ZTO Express, STO Express, and Yunda Express, Best Express etc.) and give reasons for your preferences for any of them.

2. Read the words or phrases and their explanations. Then complete the following paragraph(s) with the words or phrases. Change the form when necessary.

data   information or facts

facilitate   to make an action or process easier or more likely to happen, especially one that you would like to happen

key   very important or necessary

means   a way of doing or achieving something

reduce   to make something smaller or less in size, amount, or price

Order processing systems, in one form or another, have been a part of doing business for ages, and have developed alongside technology to provide powerful _____ of capturing, tracking and shipping customers' orders. Advanced order processing systems can span multiple continents to track and _____ international orders, shipments and returns for a wide range of product lines and consumer segments. An order processing system captures order data from customer service employees or from customers directly, stores the _____ in a central database and sends order information to the accounting and shipping departments, if applicable. Order processing systems provide tracking data on orders and inventory for every step of the way. Customer satisfaction is _____ to long-term success in business, and fulfilling customer orders reliably and accurately is key to customer satisfaction. Order processing systems help ensure that all of your customers' orders are filled on time, since automated systems can _____ errors in order processing. This can enhance the customer experience and maximize your company's profitability.

(Adapted from https://smallbusiness.chron.com/
definition-order-processing-systems-3197.html)

Text: How to Get E-commerce Order Fulfillment Right

Order fulfillment is the process of storing inventory, picking and packing products, and shipping online orders to customers. This process can be completed in-house by an E-commerce company or outsourced to a third-party logistics (3PL) provider. E-commerce order fulfillment applies to both business-to-business (B2B) orders — where large quantities of product are shipped to big-box retailers — as well as business-to-consumer (B2C) orders that are shipped directly to a single shopper's home. For B2C orders, the end consumer may place the order on the merchant's website or through an online marketplace. After the customer completes their purchase, the fulfillment process begins.

Planning Your Order Fulfillment Strategy

E-commerce order fulfillment requires a sound strategy behind it — especially if you plan to grow your business. Good planning is necessary to secure the infrastructure, systems, processes, and team you'll need for success.

1. Location is everything.

Even if you don't operate a brick-and-mortar store, physical location still matters in E-commerce. Aside from the size of your storage space, where you fulfill orders from is one of the most important factors in meeting customer expectations around delivery costs and speeds. Since both affordable and fast shipping options are important to consumers, optimizing your fulfillment operation based on where your customers reside will help you reach the most people in the most cost-efficient manner.

Reducing shipping zones, or the distance packages travel, will typically reduce the cost of shipping and time in transit. Urban fulfillment centers are on the rise as they allow merchants to quickly and affordably ship to customers in big cities with large populations.

Another strategic step in optimizing fulfillment is to distribute inventory to multiple locations that are within close proximity of your customers. The more fulfillment locations near common shipping destinations, the more ground shipping can be leveraged, which is significantly cheaper than expedited air and faster than shipping from a greater distance.

2. Technology integrations.

Software that integrates seamlessly with E-commerce platforms and online marketplaces can help manage orders across sales channels without requiring any manual uploads or duplicate data entry.

This means that as soon as an order is placed online, fulfillment staff can quickly be alerted to pick, pack, and ship the items to the customer. Tracking information can then be sent back to the platform or marketplace and shared with the customer.

Another important piece of the fulfillment puzzle is visibility into inventory quantities on hand across fulfillment locations. This helps online retailers understand when to proactively order more inventory to prevent stockouts. E-commerce businesses need to leverage their integrations to connect the upstream activities of purchasing and manufacturing to the downstream activities of sales and product demand to make more accurate purchasing and production decisions.

3. Free 2-day shipping.

With fast shipping speeds like 2-day and even same-day becoming more prevalent, keeping transit times down and costs low will appeal to customers. However, pricing your shipping can be challenging as there is no one-size-fits-all approach or magic formula. And shipping is expensive — and certainly not free — for the merchant.

Offering free 2-day shipping helps lessen cart abandonment rates and get more shoppers to your checkout page in the first place; but the goal is to do this without increasing your returns rate. For inexpensive products, absorbing the cost of shipping will make you lose money, while increasing your product price may turn visitors elsewhere. A free 2-day shipping strategy often works best for more expensive products or stores with shoppers that generally spend more on average.

Deciding Which E-commerce Order Fulfillment Model to Use

Making the right choice for how you fulfill orders will depend on several factors, including your order volume, your products, what you're willing to manage yourself, and more. There are three common methods of order fulfillment — see which might be the best for you.

1. In-house order fulfillment.

In-house order fulfillment, also known as self-fulfillment(see Figure 7-1), occurs when the merchant completes each step of the fulfillment process internally, without the help of a dropshipper or third-party logistics provider. This model ranges from small order volumes fulfilled from home to investments in a larger scale operation and more extensive facility. It's common for merchants that are just starting out to manage inventory and pack orders in their home.

In-house fulfillment at this stage typically takes up a lot of valuable time that could otherwise be spent on acquiring more customers, developing new products, and launching marketing campaigns. Once merchants grow to a certain point and can no longer manage fulfillment alone, they are faced with either outsourcing fulfillment or building out the fulfillment infrastructure themselves.

The DIY(Do It Yourself) route entails:

- Securing warehouse space.
- Recruiting and staffing it.
- Purchasing the necessary equipment.

- Licensing warehouse management software.
- Getting workers' comp and liability insurance.
- And more.

The Self-Fulfillment Model

Figure 7-1

Advantages:

- It offers 100% control of inventory and the pick, pack, and ship process.
- It can be low-cost when the business is small because you are just paying for shipping (and doing the work yourself).
- Anyone can do it. You don't need any contacts (as long as you have space to store products, address labels, and packing resources such as packing slips).
- For businesses shipping significant volume, negotiated shipping rates through FedEx, UPS, and/or USPS can become a competitive advantage.

Disadvantages:

- It is time-consuming. Packing all of the products yourself will take time. As orders increase, this can take up most of your day.
- It is costly as the business grows and can be very burdensome for a young business. You need the following:

  Warehouse space

  Warehouse equipment

  Additional staff

  Order fulfillment software requirements

2. Third-party fulfillment.

Handing off E-commerce fulfillment to a third-party often occurs when a merchant is spending too much time packing boxes and shipping orders, has run out of space to store their inventory, needs more time for strategic projects, and has no interest in managing their own distribution infrastructure.

When you outsource fulfillment to a 3PL company, they handle the entire fulfillment process for you — from receiving your inventory from your manufacturer to restocking returned products. Because 3PLs work with many merchants and typically operate a number of fulfillment centers, they have the logistical expertise and capacity and are able to negotiate substantial discounted bulk shipping rates from carriers due to the pure volume of shipments they are shipping out each day. The 3PL's staff will complete all tasks of the order fulfillment process within their fulfillment center:

- Receiving.
- Picking.
- Packing.
- Labeling.
- Returns processing.
- Quality control.
- Other specialized projects.

Each 3PL is unique and has their own services that will vary depending on your needs, including kitting, custom packaging, B2B orders, FBA (Fulfillment by Amazon) prep, temperature control or refrigeration, and more (see Figure 7-2).

The 3rd Party Fulfillment Model

Figure 7-2

Advantages:
- Inventory can be purchased in bulk in order to improve profit margins.
- No investment is required for warehouse space/real estate, WMS(Warehouse Management System) software, or a workforce to pick and pack orders.
- There is an added convenience of outsourcing the process to a trusted professional.
- Shipping discounts can be much better than if you were to negotiate on your own.

i. e.: Your business ships 5, 000 packages per month, but the third-party E-commerce fulfillment company may be handling 150, 000 orders per month. They're going to be able to get better shipping rates with FedEx/UPS than you can alone.

Disadvantages:

• Quality can be compromised.

You have to do your due diligence: a third-party E-commerce fulfillment company controls your E-commerce businesses' final handoff of value to your customers. In other words, they have the opportunity to make or break your customer satisfaction levels, which affects the lifetime value of these customers on your business.

3. Dropshipping.

Dropshipping means that the merchant never holds the products they sell in their online store; instead, the products are produced, stored, and shipped by the manufacturer. When a customer places an order on the merchant's online store, the order is forwarded either manually or automatically to the manufacturer. Then, the manufacturer dropships the product directly to the end customer. With dropshipping, the shipping process is completely in the hands of the manufacturer, who is often overseas. This means that your customers might have to wait for a product to be shipped from across the world. In addition, dropshipping does not necessarily allow you full control over inventory management and order fulfillment (see Figure 7-3).

Figure 7-3

Advantages:

• Easy to start: Dropshippers provide the products and the shipping, so all you need to do is focus on sales.

• Minimal business development: You're leveraging the network of your dropshipper, instead of personally building the relationships with every supplier. Essentially, every new partner allows you to grow by a significantly large number of new products.

• More products, faster: Growth in E-commerce begins with adding more products to your website. Integrating a dropshipper's products with your business is simple and straightforward because all you're doing is supporting the links and learning the prices — not lining up any other part of the logistics. This allows more people to discover you and increases the number of touchpoints by which interested shoppers can encounter your brand.

- Affordable: Low overhead makes dropshipping a great starting place for online retailers. All you do is pay for inventory when a sale is made, so you avoid operational expenses like warehousing. Profitability is not guaranteed, though, which we'll get to in the next section.

- Test before committing: Since you don't incur overhead, you can test out the viability of new markets for existing products anywhere you can establish a drop-shipper service.

- Focus on what you do well: The convenience of a hands-off product fulfillment experience thereby enables businesses to focus on other priorities, which is especially advantageous to new companies.

Disadvantages:

- No customization: Dropshipping usually means virtually no support for custom products. To achieve this type of support and customization, your dropshipper would have to function as a warehouse. Unfortunately, this is not likely unless their margins on custom products were worth the time and effort — in which case, the margins would likely not make sense for you.

- Lower quality control: Since the seller is removed from the fulfillment process, you're entrusting your brand's reputation to another party — while maintaining accountability. Buyers usually don't think about fulfillment models or dropshippers. If a defective product arrives or there is a miscommunication about the shipment, your customer doesn't want to hear that it was out of your control; all they care about is the overall experience.

- Reduced brand power: Your products are produced by others, so it's more difficult to establish a unique brand. The reduced quality control only increases the risk to your brand.

- Competitive disadvantage: Low barriers to entry mean it's hard to establish a competitive advantage over other businesses. You're competing on price, and that can easily become a losing game.

- Scale: Logistics can become challenging as a business scales up, especially when coordinating with multiple dropshippers.

(Adapted from https://www.bigcommerce.com/blog/ecommerce-fulfillment/
#deciding-which-ecommerce-order-fulfillment-model-to-use)

Words & Expressions

outsource	/aʊtˈsɔːs/	v.	obtain goods or services from an outside supplier; to contract work out 外包
sound	/saʊnd/	adj.	sensible and likely to produce the right results 明智的；合理的；正确的

infrastructure	/ˈɪnfrəˌstrʌktʃə/	*n.*	the basic systems and structures that a country or organization needs in order to work properly, for example roads, railways, banks etc 基础设施(建设)(如公路、铁路、银行等)
reside	/rɪˈzaɪd/	*v.*	to live in a particular place 居住
transit	/ˈtrænsɪt/	*n.*	the process of moving goods or people from one place to another(货物或人的)运输
distribute	/dɪˈstrɪbjuːt/	*v.*	to share things among a group of people, especially in a planned way(尤指有计划地)分发,分配,分送
proximity	/prɒkˈsɪmɪtɪ/	*n.*	nearness in distance or time (距离或时间的)接近,临近;邻近
seamlessly	/ˈsiː mləsli/	*adv.*	perfectly consistent and coherent 无缝地
duplicate	/ˈdjuːplɪkeɪt/	*v.*	to copy something exactly 复制
stockout	/ˈstɒkaut/	*n.*	an event that causes inventory to be exhausted 无存货,缺货
prevalent	/ˈprɛvələnt/	*adj.*	common at a particular time, in a particular place, or among a particular group of people 普遍的,盛行的,流行的
margin	/ˈmɑːdʒɪn/	*n.*	the difference between what it costs a business to buy or produce something and what they sell it for 利润,赚头
entail	/ɪnˈteɪl/	*v.*	to involve something as a necessary part or result 使必要;需要
forward	/ˈfɔːwəd/	*v.*	to send letters, goods etc to someone when they have moved to a different address 寄发;转寄;转交;转运
defective	/dɪˈfɛktɪv/	*adj.*	not made properly, or not working properly 有问题的,有毛病的,有缺陷的
coordinate	/kəʊˈɔː dɪˌneɪt/	*v.*	to organize an activity so that the people involved in it work well together and achieve a good result 协调(多人参加的活动)
apply to			适用于;应用于
aside from			除……以外
on the rise			在增加;在上涨
run out of			用完
in bulk			整批,散装;大批,大量
line up			排列起;整队
make sense			有意义;讲得通;言之有理

Notes & Terms

end consumer	a person who buys and uses a productor service 最终消费者,使用最终产品的人。一般制造厂商的促销活动和商业宣传皆针对此类消费者而设
a brick-and-mortar store	Brick and mortar (also **bricks and mortar** or **B&M**) refers to a physical presence of an organization or business in a building or other structure. The term brick-and-mortar business is often used to refer to a company that possesses or leases retail shops, factory production facilities, or warehouses for its operations. More specifically, in the jargon of E-commerce businesses in the 2000s, brick-and-mortar businesses are companies that have a physical presence (e.g., a retail shop in a building) and offer face-to-face customer experiences 实体店
FedEx	FedEx Corporation is an American multinational courier delivery services company headquartered in Memphis, Tennessee. The name "FedEx" is a syllabic abbreviation of the name of the company's original air division, Federal Express (now FedEx Express). The company is known for its overnight shipping service and pioneering a system that could track packages and provide real-time updates on package location (to help in finding lost packages), a feature that has now been implemented by most other carrier services. 联邦快递(FedEx)是一家国际性速递集团,提供隔夜快递、地面快递、重型货物运送、文件复印及物流服务,总部设于美国田纳西州,隶属于美国联邦快递集团(FedEx Corp)
UPS	United Parcel Service (UPS) is an American multinational package delivery and supply chain management company. Along with the central package delivery operation, the UPS brand name (in a fashion similar to that of competitor FedEx) is used to denote many of its divisions and subsidiaries, including its cargo airline (UPS Airlines), freight-based trucking operation (UPS Freight, formerly Overnite Transportation), and retail-based packing and shipping centers (The UPS Store). The global logistics company is headquartered in the U. S. city of Sandy Springs, Georgia, which is a part of the Greater Atlanta metropolitan area. UPS 快递(美国快递公司)
USPS	The United States Postal Service (USPS; also known as the Post Office, U.S. Mail, or Postal Service) is an independent agency of the executive branch of the United States federal government responsible for providing postal service in the United States, including its insular areas and

associated states. It is one of the few government agencies explicitly authorized by the United States Constitution. 美国邮政署,亦称美国邮局或美国邮政服务,是美国联邦政府的独立机构。美国邮政署是少数在美国宪法中提及设立的机构

WMS　　　A warehouse management system (WMS) is a software application, designed to support and optimize warehouse functionality and distribution center management. These systems facilitate management in their daily planning, organizing, staffing, directing, and controlling the utilization of available resources, to move and store materials into, within, and out of a warehouse, while supporting staff in the performance of material movement and storage in and around a warehouse. 仓库管理系统

Understanding the text

Ⅰ. Complete the following summary of the text.

As the _____ of storing inventory, picking and packing products, and shipping online orders to customers, order fulfillment can be completed in-house by an E-commerce company or outsourced to a third-party logistics (3PL) provider. E-commerce order fulfillment applies to both business-to-business (B2B) orders — where large quantities of product are shipped to big-box retailers — as well as business-to-consumer (B2C) orders that are shipped directly to a single shopper's home. In order to plan your order fulfillment strategy successfully, you need to take the infrastructure, systems, processes, and team into _____. You should attach importance to location, technology _____ and free 2-day shipping to attract customers. What's more, making the right choice for how you fulfill orders _____ on several factors, including your order volume, your products, what you're willing to manage yourself, and more. It is common to refer to three methods of order fulfillment and you can decide which _____ to use: In-house order fulfillment (also known as self-fulfillment), Third-party fulfillment and Dropshipping.

Ⅱ. Read the text and decide whether the following statements are true (T) or false (F).

(　　)1　Completed in-house by an E-commerce company or outsourced to a third-party logistics provider, order fulfillment is about storing inventory, picking and packing products, and shipping online orders to customers.

(　　)2　E-commerce order fulfillment promotes business-to-business (B2B) orders and business-to-consumer (B2C) orders. The former are shipped directly to a single shopper's home while in the latter large quantities of product are shipped to big-box retailers.

(　　)3　As affordable and fast shipping options are important to consumers, how to optimize your fulfillment operation depends on your customers' location.

(   ) 4   Offering free 2-day shipping helps attract more customers to your products in the first place.

(   ) 5   With the help of a third-party logistics provider, self-fulfillment means the merchant completes each step of the fulfillment process internally.

Ⅲ. Answer the following questions according to the text.

1. Why is an E-commerce order fulfillment important?

2. How to plan order fulfillment strategies successfully?

3. What are advantages of offering free 2-day shipping for E-commerce order fulfillment?

4. Which E-commerce order fulfillment model is common for merchants starting a new business? Why?

5. Why is Third-party fulfillment unique?

Language Work

Ⅰ. Choose the best choice to complete each of the following sentences.

1. _____ in 1999, *www.1688.com* is a leading wholesale marketplace that connects nearly 30 million enterprise bulk buyers and sellers worldwide and offers 250 million online goods.

A. Started   B. Begun   C. Launched   D. Opened

2. The 11.11 shopping festival began in 2009 with participation from just 27 _____ as an event for merchants and consumers to raise awareness of the value in online shopping.

A. customers   B. merchants   C. shoppers   D. buyers

3. David Roth, CEO of WPP Global Retail Business, noted that Chinese brands should go beyond product launching and make more efforts in building brand image with human touch and _____ identity.

A. own   B. only   C. special   D. unique

4. "While globalization _____ many benefits to multinational corporations, the Belt and Road Initiative aims to unlock the potential of small and medium-sized enterprises by enhancing connectivity, and E-commerce is a critical channel to attain that goal," said Zhao Lei, a professor at the Institute for International Strategic Studies, which is part of the Party School of the Central Committee of Communist Party of China.

A. offers   B. achieves   C. obtains   D. gets

5. The use of big data and intelligent and autonomous equipment has greatly improved the efficiency of the _____ business.

A. delivery   B. delivered   C. deliverable   D. deliver

Ⅱ. Match the English words in the left column with the English explanations in the right column.

_____   1. straightforward   A. to be important or to have an effect on what happens

_____　2. diligence　　　B. combine or work together in a way that makes something more effective

_____　3. matter　　　　C. simple and easy to understand

_____　4. integrate　　　D. the fact of being easy to see

_____　5. visibility　　　E. persevering determination to perform a task

Ⅲ. Translate the following sentences from the text into Chinese.

1. E-commerce order fulfillment applies to both business-to-business (B2B) orders — where large quantities of product are shipped to big-box retailers — as well as business-to-consumer (B2C) orders that are shipped directly to a single shopper's home.

_____

_____ .

2. Even if you don't operate a brick-and-mortar store, physical location still matters in E-commerce.

_____

_____ .

3. This means that as soon as an order is placed online, fulfillment staff can quickly be alerted to pick, pack, and ship the items to the customer.

_____

_____ .

4. This model ranges from small order volumes fulfilled from home to investments in a larger scale operation and more extensive facility.

_____

_____ .

5. When a customer places an order on the merchant's online store, the order is forwarded either manually or automatically to the manufacturer.

_____

_____ .

Ⅳ. Translate the following sentences into English using the proper forms of the words or expressions given in brackets.

1. 建议您提交投诉或问题时, 留下姓名、联系方式、投诉的涉嫌不道德或不合法可疑行为事件细节等详细信息。(submit)

_____

_____ .

2. 国内电商平台致力于为消费者提供选购品牌产品的优质购物体验。(cater to)

_____

_____ .

3. 据数据统计, 按 2017 年商品交易额(gross merchandise value)计算, 淘宝网是中国最大的

移动商业平台。(according to)

_____

_____ .

4. 这家物流公司致力于提供国内和国际的一站式物流服务。(aim to)

_____

_____ .

5. 哔哩哔哩弹幕网与淘宝在电商领域达成合作。(enter into an agreement)

_____

_____ .

Supplementary Reading: How Can Merchants Increase Transparency and Accuracy Around International Shipping Costs?

Making cross-border business transactions can be an expensive ordeal for both merchants and consumers. Add unexpected customs and tax charges after a purchase on top off that, and both parties are in for a rude awakening.

For many consumers, seeing additional charges tacked onto their bill can often be a good enough reason to walk away from their purchase altogether. An estimated 40 percent of E-commerce customers abandon their shopping carts if the checkout process is too frustrating, according to the most recent PYMNTS Checkout Conversion Index™. Adding the surprise of additional fees on goods can only exacerbate those frustrations.

For merchants focused on boosting their cart conversion, addressing these consumer vexations is a priority. But some companies, such as logistics provider Yakit, are offering ways to reduce the friction involved in international shipping by offering solutions that incorporate all shipping, taxes and customs costs into a final bill so that customers are not caught off-guard when they are ready to check out.

PYMNTS recently spoke with Rajiv Ayyangar, VP(Vice President) of product for Yakit, about how logistical shipping solutions are working to eliminate consumer surprises related to international E-commerce purchases.

Taking Surprises Out of International Shipping

Most merchants engaged in cross-border trade strive to deliver products to their customers as efficiently as possible. But one thing merchants don't want to deliver to their customers is the shock of being charged additional fees after the checkout process has been completed. Customers are likely to walk away from merchants after learning that the calculations of relevant taxes and customs were not included in the final bill.

However, merchants might not be aware of what a certain global region charges for the delivery of certain goods and hence be unable to offer customers an estimate of what additional fees they should expect to pay for their order. Without the ability to offer these estimates, international E-commerce merchants risk losing their customers because of a rocky delivery process.

Ayyangar said Yakit's services aim to help E-commerce merchants on Shopify by giving them access to a marketplace of cross-border services and tools. These tools allow merchants to pre-calculate duties and taxes into an order's final price tag to help consumers anticipate all charges involved. The company also allows Shopify's E-commerce merchants to compare various cross-border service providers, similar to how Kayak.com compares airline routes and prices, so they can choose a provider that meets their specific budget and timeline.

By offering more tools to merchants and consumers, the delivery process becomes more transparent for both parties, said Ayyangar. Keeping online shoppers informed about all of the charges involved in their purchase can help them avoid an unpleasant surprise during checkout. For merchants, customers who are not caught off guard by the cost of their order are less likely to abandon their shopping carts.

"Cart conversion for international customers is typically a lot lower because of the sticker shock of shipping, duties and taxes," Ayyangar said. "For a lot of shippers who are doing significant international direct to consumer business, this is the number one complaint."

Take this scenario as an example: a Canadian customer makes an international purchase valued at $100 and pays an additional $15 to $20 for shipping costs. But at their local post office, the customer is informed that an additional $20 must be paid in duties before the item can be released.

Ayyangar said discovering additional costs after a purchase is made which only adds another layer of exasperation to international shipping for everyone involved. "Consumers are likely to be annoyed by the surprise costs and, in some cases, might abandon their purchases at the post office rather than pay additional, unexpected fees", he said. "Meanwhile, merchants that shipped the goods risk losing return customers over an annoying experience".

"The biggest reason why people will switch off a platform when it comes to international B2C is a poor delivery experience, which includes being charged after the fact for duties and taxes which [they] didn't expect and couldn't predict," he said.

Ultimately, Ayyangar said merchants that can provide customers with a better delivery experience (one that avoids surprise charges) can go a long way toward improving retention rates.

Speed vs. Cost of Delivery

In the cross-border world, eliminating friction from checkout experience entails allowing E-commerce merchants to find a logistics provider with a rate that meets their budget and delivery needs. But when customers must choose between the cost and speed of their delivery, Ayyangar sees a familiar pattern.

Consumers are willing to wait longer for a delivery if it can save them money — a fact that has helped Yakit carve out business from competitors such as DHL and FedEx, which deliver a day or two faster but can cost 20 to 70 percent more, Ayyangar pointed out.

"We've found that's a sweet spot for E-commerce," he said. "We think there is always going to be an advantage to a slightly slower service with a significant cost advantage."

However, when needed, customers also expect faster deliveries, which have led Yakit to look for alternative options that can help boost the speed in the "last mile" of a delivery. To do that, the Sunnyvale, California-based company is considering partnering with Deliv and Uber to execute the last stretch of a delivery. "And as the demand for faster delivery grows, the company will also keep looking into the use of drone deliveries and autonomous vehicles to complete a delivery", Ayyangar said.

A Roadmap for Logistical Planning

Beyond offering customers pre-calculations on related taxes and fees and options for merchants to ship their products using a cheaper (but slower) delivery option, Ayyangar said Yakit's solutions also work to remove friction from cross-border logistics by gathering data on various deliveries. By collecting and analyzing this data, the company is able to anticipate challenges and avoid surprises when delivering goods to various global regions.

"Every country has its own challenges," Ayyangar said.

Deliveries can face "unusual" custom clearance challenges, logistical challenges like reaching certain parts of a country and technical challenges, such as whether a carrier's technical solutions are advanced enough to meet the delivery needs. Ayyangar said Yakit uses API integrations and FTP-type transfers to collect and analyze data and find ways to improve delivery systems.

"We get less and less surprised as we grow the network," he said.

As Yakit learns more from customer experiences with international shipping, Ayyangar hopes the company can work to reduce some of the barriers encountered when shipping worldwide. "Bringing down these barriers to cross-border trade will allow more innovative merchant products to reach the global market", he said.

"Our hope is to see an increasing richness of unique items being shared throughout the world," he said. "These types of innovations are connecting people in different parts of the world in a way that's more personal than making one mass-produced product and putting it in every store."

While Ayyangar anticipates demand for international E-commerce is poised for an "explosion," he worries that political climates in the U.S. and Europe could create barriers to international trade in the form of unexpected taxes and fees or logistical challenges. Nevertheless, he sees an opportunity for companies to step in and help merchants and consumers sort through whatever challenges may come.

(Adapted from https://www.pymnts.com/news/cross-border-commerce/
2017/removing-sticker-shock-from-cross-border-shipping-logistics/)

Words & Expressions

ordeal	/ɔːˈdiːl/	*n.* a terrible or painful experience that continues for a period of time 可怕的经历,痛苦的折磨
exacerbate	/ɪɡˈzæsəˌbeɪt/	*v.* to make a bad situation worse 使恶化;使加重
vexation	/vɛkˈseɪʃən/	*n.* a feeling of being annoyed, puzzled, and frustrated 恼火
friction	/ˈfrɪkʃən/	*n.* disagreement, angry feelings, or unfriendliness between people (人们之间的)不合,冲突,摩擦
eliminate	/ɪˈlɪmɪˌneɪt/	*v.* to completely get rid of something that is unnecessary or unwanted 消除,根除
scenario	/sɪˈnɑːrɪəʊ/	*n.* a situation that could possibly happen 可能发生的事,可能出现的情况
exasperation	/ɪɡˌzæspəˈreɪʃən/	*n.* actions that cause great irritation (or even anger) 恼怒,烦恼
check out		结账离开
strive to		努力
aware of		意识到,知道
rather than		而不是;宁可……也不愿
carve out		创业;开拓
sort through		分类,整理

Notes & Terms

Yakit	Yakit is a simple and powerful platform for international delivery with an experienced and agile team headquartered in the heart of Silicon Valley, California with presence in Bangalore, India and Berne, Switzerland. It is funded and supported by investors with deep roots in E-commerce. It provides customers with courier service at postal prices, and gives merchants the tools to unlock global markets (美国)一家国际物流公司
Shopify	Shopify is a Canadian E-commerce company headquartered in Ottawa, Ontario. It is also the name of its proprietary E-commerce platform for online stores and retail point-of-sale systems. Shopify offers online retailers a suite of services "including payments, marketing, shipping and customer engagement tools to simplify the process of running an online store for small merchants." The company reported that it had more than 800,000 businesses in approximately 175 countries using its platform as of December 31, 2018, with total gross merchandise volume exceeding $41.1 billion for calendar 2018 Shopify.是由托

比亚斯·卢克创办的加拿大电子商务软件开发商,总部位于加拿大首都渥太华,其提供的服务软件 Shopify 是一个 SaaS 领域的购物车系统,适合跨境电商建立独立站,用户支付一定费用即可在其上利用各种主题/模板建立自己的网上商店

Kayak.com   Kayak.com, sometimes styled as KAYAK, is a fare aggregator and travel metasearch engine operated by Booking Holdings. Its products are available in 18 languages. The company also runs travel search engines checkfelix and swoodoo. Formerly a separate company, the KAYAK Software Corporation was acquired by Booking Holdings on May 21, 2013. Kayak 是美国领先的旅游搜索引擎服务商,专注在线旅游,可以同时搜索上百家旅行网站,而将结果按多种方式排列出来,产品主要包括航班、酒店、汽车、旅行社等,另外还提供旅游管理工具服务

Deliv   Deliv is a Menlo Park-based crowdsourced, same-day delivery startup. Deliv bridges the last mile gap between multichannel retailers and their customers. Deliv offers same-day service to mall shoppers. Deliv was founded in 2012 by Daphne Carmeli, who also serves as CEO of the company. In 2017, the company announced an expansion of its service to 33 markets and 1,400 cities, up from 19 markets previously. (美国)一家快运公司

Uber   Uber Technologies Inc. is a transportation network company (TNC) headquartered in San Francisco, California. Uber offers services including peer-to-peer ridesharing, ride service hailing, food delivery, and a bicycle-sharing system. The company has operations in 785 metropolitan areas worldwide. Its platforms can be accessed via its websites and mobile apps. Uber is estimated to have 100 million worldwide users and a 67.3% market share in the United States. Uber has been so prominent in the sharing economy that the changes in industries as a result of it have been referred to as uberisation, and many startups have described their products as "Uber for X". The name "Uber" is a reference to the common (and somewhat colloquial) word uber, meaning "topmost" or "super", and having its origins in the German word über, cognate with over, meaning "above". 优步是一家美国硅谷的科技公司,由加利福尼亚大学洛杉矶分校辍学生特拉维斯·卡兰尼克和好友加勒特·坎普(Garrett Camp)于 2009 年创立。因旗下同名打车软件而名声大噪。Uber 目前已经进入中国的 60 余座城市,并在全球范围内覆盖了 70 多个国家的 400 余座城市

API   In computer programming, an application programming interface (API) is a set of subroutine definitions, communication protocols, and tools for building software. In general terms, it is a set of clearly defined methods of communication among various components. A good API makes it easier to develop a computer program by providing all the building blocks, which are then put together by the programmer. An API may be for a web-based system, operating system, database system, computer hardware, or software library. An API specification can take many forms, but often includes specifications for routines, data structures, object classes, variables, or remote calls. POSIX, Windows API and ASPI are examples of different forms of APIs. Documentation for the API usually is provided to facilitate usage and implementation. 应用程序编程接口是一些预先定义的函数，目的是提供应用程序与开发人员基于某软件或硬件得以访问一组例程的能力，而又无须访问源代码，或理解内部工作机制的细节

FTP　　　The File Transfer Protocol (FTP) is a standard network protocol used for the transfer of computer files between a client and server on a computer network. 文件传输协议是用于在网络上进行文件传输的一套标准协议，使用客户/服务器模式。它属于网络传输协议的应用层

Text Comprehension

Choose the best answer to each of the following questions according to the text.

1. According to the passage, which of the following is NOT the reason for E-commerce customers to abandon their shopping carts?

   A. Products delivered to customers as efficiently as possible.

   B. Unexpected customs and tax charges.

   C. Additional charges on the bill.

   D. Additional fees on goods.

2. Merchants strive to address consumer vexations by referring to the following solutions EXECPT _____.

   A. offering ways to reduce the friction involved in international shipping

   B. incorporating all shipping, taxes and customs costs into a final bill

   C. choosing a provider that meets specific budget and timeline

   D. helping consumers anticipate all charges involved

3. According to Ayyangar, how can the merchants improve retention rates?

   A. Merchants compare various cross-border service providers.

   B. Merchants provide customers with a better delivery experience that avoids unexpected charges.

   C. Merchants get access to a marketplace of cross-border services and tools.

   D. Merchants find a logistics provider that meets their budget and delivery needs.

4. What are solutions that work to remove friction from cross-border logistics?

   A. Merchants offer customers pre-calculations on related taxes and fees.

   B. Merchants ship their products using a cheaper (but slower) delivery option.

C. Merchants gather data on various deliveries.

D. All of the above.

5. How does Yakit anticipate challenges and avoid surprises when delivering goods to various global regions?

A. To reduce some of the barriers the company encountered when shipping worldwide.

B. To look for alternative options that can help boost the speed in the "last mile" of a delivery.

C. To collect and analyze data by using API integrations and FTP-type transfers.

D. To look into the use of drone deliveries and autonomous vehicles.

Language Work

Fill in the following blanks with the words or phrases given below. Change the forms where necessary.

investment	consecutive	logistics	boost	access
abandon	estimate	penalty	barrier	anticipate

1. _____ by booming E-commerce, the express delivery industry saw fast growth over the past few years, with the number of handled parcels increasing by 10 billion on average in each of the past three years.

2. In 2018, China has _____ the world's market for five consecutive years, surpassing the combined amount handled in developed economies.

3. China's _____ sector posted steady growth in 2018, with the value of goods carried by the sector up 6.4 percent year-on-year to 283.1 trillion yuan ($ 42.3 trillion).

4. The Chinese government's _____ in roads, water projects, logistics, and Internet facilities in rural areas has enabled the rise of E-commerce entrepreneurs seizing new opportunities throughout the country.

5. E-commerce provides _____ so that both the consumer and the producer can meet in a timely way.

Workshop

Presentation: Work in a group and share your experiences of buying things on cross-border E-commerce platforms, such as Alibaba.com, Tmall.com, Taobao.com etc. Discuss with your partners differences between traditional ways of shopping and shopping on E-commerce platforms nowadays. And make a presentation in the class to illustrate your ideas.

References

[1] https://smallbusiness.chron.com/definition-order-processing-systems-3197.html/, retrieved on 2019-04-02.

[2] https://www.bigcommerce.com/blog/ecommerce-fulfillment/#deciding-which-ecommerce-order-fulfillment-model-to-use/, retrieved on 2019-04-02.

[3] https://www.pymnts.com/news/cross-border-commerce/2017/removing-sticker-shock-from-cross-border-shipping-logistics/, retrieved on 2019-04-02.

[4] https://www.trackingmore.com/yakit-tracking.html/, retrieved on 2019-04-02.

[5] http://www.chinadaily.com.cn/business/.

[6] https://en.wikipedia.org/wiki/.

[7] http://www.youdao.com/.

[8] https://dictionary.cambridge.org/dictionary/english/end-consumer.

[9] https://en.wikipedia.org/wiki/Brick_and_mortar.

[10] https://en.wikipedia.org/wiki/FedEx.

[11] https://en.wikipedia.org/wiki/United_Parcel_Service.

[12] https://en.wikipedia.org/wiki/United_States_Postal_Service.

[13] https://en.wikipedia.org/wiki/Warehouse_management_system.

[14] https://en.wikipedia.org/wiki/Shopify.

[15] https://en.wikipedia.org/wiki/Kayak.com.

[16] https://en.wikipedia.org/wiki/Deliv.

[17] https://en.wikipedia.org/wiki/Uber.

[18] https://en.wikipedia.org/wiki/Application_programming_interface.

[19] https://en.wikipedia.org/wiki/File_Transfer_Protocol.

[20] https://m.hujiang.com/ciku/end-consumer/.

[21] https://baike.baidu.com/item/%E8%81%94%E9%82%A6%E5%BF%AB%E9%80%92/4759000.

[22] https://baike.baidu.com/item/USPS.

[23] https://baike.baidu.com/item/Shopify/17602573?fr=aladdin.

[24] https://baike.baidu.com/item/kayak/5143802#viewPageContent.

[25] https://baike.baidu.com/item/dhl%E5%9B%BD%E9%99%85%E5%BF%AB%E9%80%92.

[26] https://baike.baidu.com/item/Uber/14900884.

[27] https://baike.baidu.com/item/api/10154.

[28] https://baike.baidu.com/item/ftp/13839.

Unit 8

After-sale Services of Cross-border E-commerce

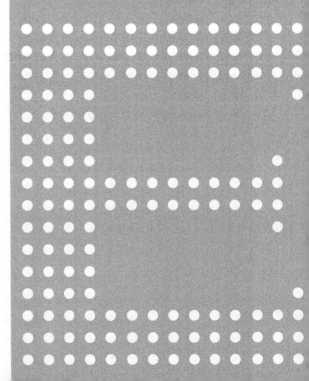

Learning Objectives

To learn how to contact customer service on Alibaba

To learn ways of settling disputes and complaints on cross-border E-commerce platforms

To get familiar with customer services on cross-border E-commerce platforms

Warming up

1. Work in a group and share your experience of buying products online that made you dissatisfied and your way to solve the problem.

2. Read the words or phrases and their explanations. Then complete the following paragraph(s) with the words or phrases. Change the form when necessary.

superlative	extremely good
operation	the work or activities done by a business or organization, or the process of doing this work
matter	to be important, especially to be important to you, or to have an effect on what happens
maximum	the largest number or amount that is possible or is allowed
investment	the use of money to get a profit or to make a business activity successful, or the money that is used

In the current scenario of intense global competition and Internet connectivity, the way we do business has undergone a sea change, and small businesses find it increasingly difficult to compete with the large players, who outdo them in terms of _____, manpower, quality of products or service, marketing and in fact in every possible field of _____. How then do small companies survive and make a name for themselves as successful enterprises? Also, the customer now has myriad options available at the click of a finger and it is definitely a buyer's market. How does one compete against large organizations and stay relevant? The answer to this question would be in using your small size to the _____ advantage. A small company would have to work that much harder to make the customer service so _____ that the customer keeps coming back for more. As is said, for the customer, it is not what he bought that _____, but how the whole purchase made him feel that is important. The service you received at the time of the business transaction stays in the customer's mind long after the purchase is made.

(Adapted from https://customercarecontacts.com/customer-
service-tips-to-help-your-brand-stand-out/)

Text: Alibaba Customer Service

Today, the name Alibaba is synonymous with wholesale trading, both buying and selling of products worldwide. With humble beginnings in the year 1999, the Chinese firm has grown to become one of the leading E-commerce companies in the world with over 45 million members. The wholesale model being one of the chief offerings, Alibaba today has hundreds of millions of products covering a wide range of categories. Catering to over 190 countries, Alibaba is free for registration and allows buyers and sellers to connect with each other, whether it is for product enquiry, price negotiation, shipping or others.

Some of the categories that have products listed include Agriculture, Apparel, Automobiles, Transportation, Shoes, Computer Hardware & Software, Home Appliances, Electrical Equipment, Sports, Toys, Beauty & Personal Care, Furniture, Tools, Hardware, among others. On the Alibaba website, one can narrow search results by type, source, and even location. Clicking on any of the results, a visitor is welcome with pictures relevant to the product, with details of product, warranty, payment terms, packaging, delivery and even sizes. If you are serious about the product listed, you can even reach the supplier directly on the page. For buyers, Alibaba offers specialized trade services such as Business Identity, Trade Assurance, Secure Payment, E-Credit Line and Inspection Service. Suppliers can choose from free membership and gold supplier membership. The latter provides privileges such as product showcases, verified icon, customized website, among others. One of the key offerings of Alibaba is its Inspection Service which allows you to find an inspector who will visit the manufacturing facility anywhere in China and make reports, including pictures, to ensure quality products are delivered.

If you are yet to try Alibaba, this is your time to explore wholesale trading. Visit the website and register for free. If you have concerns with regard to your payment, refund, cancellation, shipping, order quantity or the vendor itself, leave your complaints and feedback with the friendly customer service desk of Alibaba. Feel free to drop a mail or a support ticket to get faster responses. If you hail from Indonesia, Spain, Brazil, Germany, France, Turkey or Italy, Alibaba has an exclusive website catering the local populace.

The following suggestions shall be helpful for you to get familiar with customer services on Alibaba.

How to contact customer service team

If you have logged into your account, you may find our live chat entrance point at Account page, click on "get livechat" and select the category of your question and then you would directly enter our online chat. We have professional service team online 24 hours to provide help (see Figure 8-1).

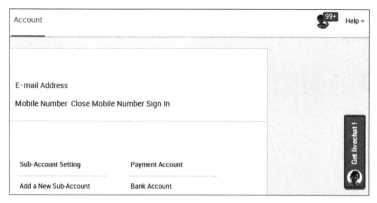

Figure 8-1

If you can't sign into your account somehow, you can still find us at our Help Center by clicking on "need help?" as below (see Figure 8-2).

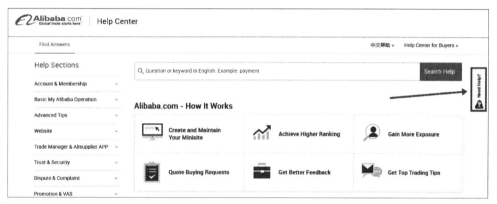

Figure 8-2

To contact live chat, please kindly select any question in the list page. And you shall see the page as below and then please click on the button "click here to contact live chat" (see Figure 8-3).

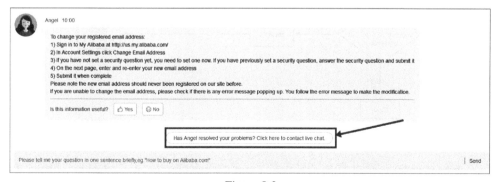

Figure 8-3

When it requires for login, you may directly click the button "click here for sign in issue" to contact online service as a tourist without the need of logging in (see Figure 8-4).

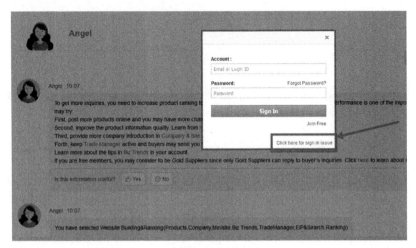

Figure 8-4

If you encounter any problem during the order process, you can submit a dispute. So what's the dispute process for offline order?

1. After the buyer submits a dispute, you two parties have 5 to 10 days to negotiate without the involvement of Alibaba. From the 6th day onward, the buyer can request Alibaba.com's assistance by clicking the "Escalate Dispute" button, or may continue to negotiate with the seller.

2. Alibaba.com will also act as a mediator for any disputes which remain unresolved after 10 days of initial opening.

Please find below dispute workflow:

1. Buyer makes a claim with the laptop.

2. Buyer and seller negotiate with each other. The process is as below (see Figure 8-5).

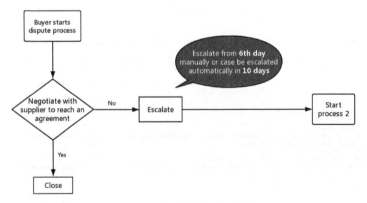

Figure 8-5

3. If no agreement is reached after negotiation and the case has been escalated, Alibaba dispute team will handle the case as follows:

If the defendant is China Gold Supplier or Global Gold Supplier on Alibaba.com (see Figure 8-6).

If the defendant is Free member on Alibaba.com (see Figure 8-7).

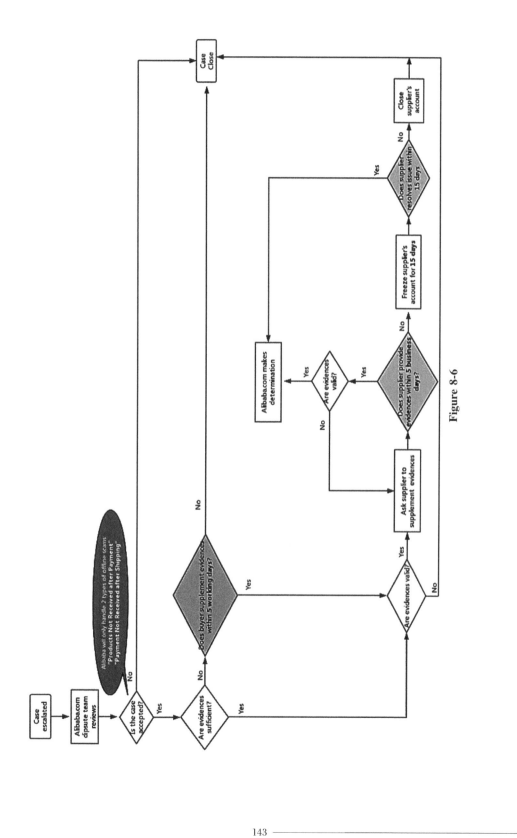

Figure 8-6

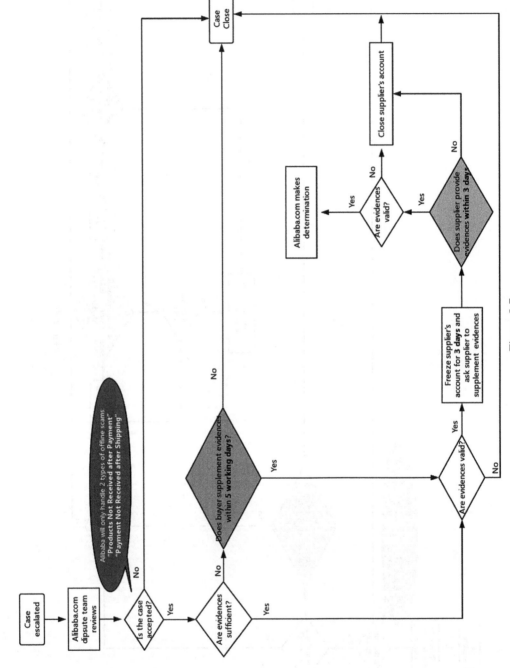

Figure 8-7

Case escalated

Alibaba.com dipsute team reviews

Alibaba will only handle 2 types of offline scams:
"Products Not Received after Payment"
"Payment Not Received after Shipping"

Is the case accepted?

Are evidences sufficient?

Does buyer supplement evidences within **5 working days**?

Are evidences valid?

Freeze supplier's account for **3 days** and ask supplier to supplement evidences

Does supplier provide evidences within **3 days**?

Are evidences valid?

Alibaba.com makes determination

Close supplier's account

Case Close

Important:

1. According to Alibaba dispute rules, Alibaba will only handle 2 types of offline scams: "**Products Not Received after Payment**" and "**Payment not Received after Shipping**". Other offline disputes will no longer be handled. Therefore, we strongly suggest that you make payments online via Alibaba.com and use Trade Assurance to protect your payments and products.

2. Please be advised that Alibaba.com is an information exchange platform only and the transaction is processed offline. We have no authority to impose compulsory sanction on any member. And if it is proved that the defendant should bear the responsibility for this trade dispute, then as punishment we will disable their Alibaba.com account. This is the utmost Alibaba.com can do for you.

Submit a Dispute for a Trade Assurance Order.

1. Go to the All Orders section in My Alibaba (see Figure 8-8).

Figure 8-8

2. If your order has not been paid for yet, you can cancel it online by clicking "Cancel Order" (see Figure 8-9).

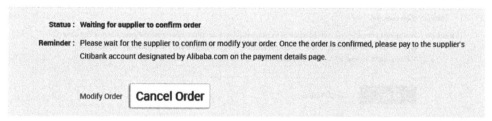

Figure 8-9

If you have paid for your order and the payment has been received, please click "Open a dispute" (see Figure 8-10).

If your order is complete, please click "Open a dispute" (see Figure 8-11).

3. Fill out the form and submit the dispute (see Figure 8-12).

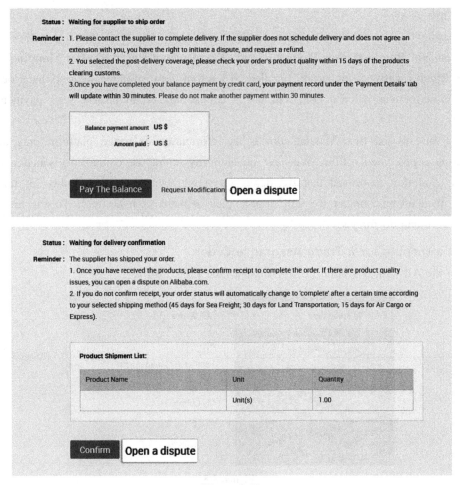

Figure 8-10

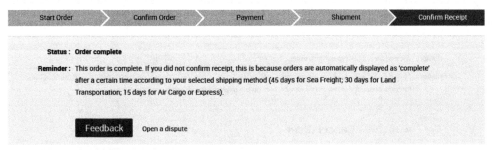

Figure 8-11

Submit a Dispute for a Secure Payment Order.

1. Go to the All Orders section in My Alibaba (see Figure 8-13).

2. If your supplier has not shipped the product, please click "Cancel Order Request" (see Figure 8-14).

* Reason for Dispute:	Please select a reason ▾
* Do you wish to continue with this order:	○ Yes, I want to continue with this order.　　○ No, I want to close this order.
* Desired Refund Amount:	Please enter a refund amount　　USD

Maximum refund amount available : 1143 USD ; Trade Assurance covered amount : 3333 USD

Please select which party shall be responsible for paying any refund process fees:

* Process fee⑦ :　● Buyer covers　○ Supplier covers　○ Buyer & supplier share

* Exchange rate difference⑦ :　○ Buyer covers　● Supplier covers

* Dispute Description:	

between 1-2000 characters

Upload Evidence:	[Upload]　Delete All

Max. file size: 5MB, Maximum of 6, format: jpg, pdf, doc, xls, png, docx, gif, xlsx, jpeg.

[Submit Dispute]　[Cancel]

Figure 8-12

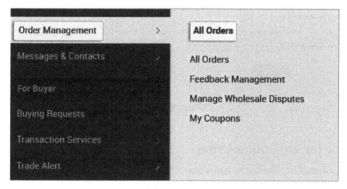

Figure 8-13

Figure 8-14

If your supplier has shipped the product, please click "Open Dispute" (see Figure 8-15).

3. Fill in the dispute form and click "Submit" (see Figure 8-16).

Please note that you can't open a dispute after your order is complete.

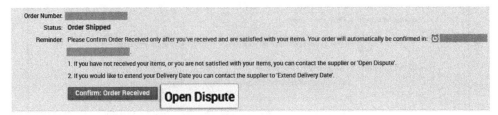

Figure 8-15

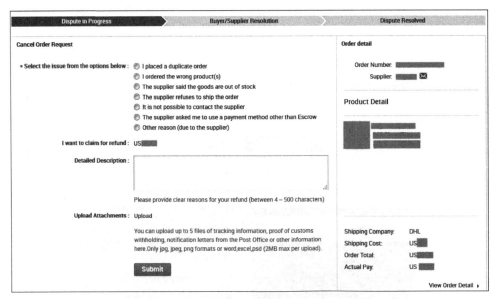

Figure 8-16

Submit a Dispute for an Offline Order.

1. Sign in to the Complaint Center with your Alibaba account (the one you used to contact the supplier).

2. Click "Offline Trade Dispute" (see Figure 8-17).

Figure 8-17

3. Fill out the complaint form and click "Submit".

Our team will review your case and contact you by phone or E-mail. Under normal circumstances, you will receive a reply from the team within 5 calendar days after submitting the dispute.

To check the status of your case.

1. Sign in to Alibaba Complaint Center.

2. Click on "Complaints I Submitted" under "Manage Complaints".

3. Select the case number for your complaint to view details (see Figure 8-18).

Figure 8-18

Note: Alibaba shall contact the complained party first after confirming your complaint. An agreement between you and the complained is what Alibaba encourages at the first period. Once solved with agreement, the complaint would be closed. However, if the complaint does not cooperate on this, Alibaba will give according punishment to the complained account. Meanwhile, to protect yourself from loss, you are advised to resort to embassy or overseas lawsuit for help.

(Adapted from https://customercarecontacts.com/contact-of-alibaba-customer-service/
https://service.alibaba.com/ensupplier/faq_detail/14455109.htm/
https://service.alibaba.com/ensupplier/faq_detail/1000091939.htm/
https://service.alibaba.com/helpcenter/47a9f417.html?spm=a273f.8140240.1992516.5795/
https://service.alibaba.com/ensupplier/faq_detail/1000126022.htm/)

Words & Expressions

synonymous	/sɪˈnɒnɪməs/	*adj.*	(~**with**) something that is synonymous with something else is considered to be very closely connected with it 相同的;近似的
warranty	/ˈwɒrəntɪ/	*n.*	a written agreement in which a company selling something promises to repair it if it breaks within a particular period of time 保修单
privilege	/ˈprɪvəlɪdʒ/	*n.*	a special advantage that is given only to one person or group of people 特权,特殊待遇
cancellation	/ˌkænsəˈleɪʃən/	*n.*	a decision to end an agreement or arrangement that you

			have with someone 取消,撤销
exclusive	/ɪkˈskluːsɪv/	*adj.*	available or belonging only to particular people, and not shared 独有的;独享的;专用的
populace	/ˈpɒpjʊləs/	*n.*	the people who live in a country 人民,百姓,大众
mediator	/ˈmiːdɪeɪtə/	*n.*	a person or organization that tries to end a quarrel between two people, groups, countries, etc. by discussion 调停者;斡旋者;解决纷争的人(机构)
initial	/ɪˈnɪʃəl/	*adj.*	happening at the beginning 开始的,最初的
escalate	/ˈɛskəˌleɪt/	*v.*	to become much worse (使)(战斗、暴力事件或不好的情况)升级;(使)恶化
defendant	/dɪˈfɛndənt/	*n.*	the person in a court of law who has been accused of doing something illegal 被告
scam	/skæm/	*n.*	a clever but dishonest way to get money 骗局,诡计,欺诈
process	/prəˈsɛs/	*v.*	to deal with information using a computer (计算机)处理(数据)
compulsory	/kəmˈpʌlsərɪ/	*adj.*	something that is compulsory must be done because it is the law or because someone in authority orders you to 规定的;强制的,强迫的;义务的
hail from			来自;出生于

Notes & Terms

Business Identity	商业身份
Trade Assurance	Trade Assurance is a free order protection service. It's designed to help create trust between buyers and suppliers and covers buyers in the event of payment, shipping and product quality-related disputes. 信保订单
Secure Payment	Secure payment 是阿里巴巴国际站针对国际贸易提供交易资金安全保障的服务,它联合第三方支付平台 Alipay 提供在线上交易资金支付的安全保障,同时保护买卖家从事在线交易,并解决交易中资金纠纷问题
Inspection Service	检验服务

Understanding the text

Ⅰ. Complete the following summary of the text.

Since established in 1999, Alibaba has now become one of the _____ E-commerce companies dealing with wholesale trading, both buying and selling of products with over 45 million members worldwide. The company has covered a wide range of categories for hundreds of millions of products, the wholesale being one of the chief models. For over 190 countries, Alibaba is free for registration and _____ buyers and sellers with each other. Its businesses include Agriculture, Apparel, Automobiles, Transportation, Shoes, Computer Hardware & Software, Home _____, Electrical Equipment, Sports, Toys, Beauty & Personal Care, Furniture, Tools, Hardware, among others. On the Alibaba website, one can get any information about products and even reach the supplier directly. Alibaba offers specialized trade services for buyers. Suppliers can choose from free membership and gold supplier membership. When you try wholesale trading on Alibaba, you may have concerns with _____ to your payment, refund, cancellation, shipping, order quantity or the vendor itself, leave your _____ and feedback with the friendly customer service desk of Alibaba. If you are from Indonesia, Spain, Brazil, Germany, France, Turkey or Italy, Alibaba has an exclusive website catering the local populace. You shall also be acquainted with contacting customer services on Alibaba and the process of submitting a dispute.

Ⅱ. Read the text and decide whether the following statements are true(T) or false(F).

(　)1　To log into your account and find live chat entrance point at Account page is the only way to contact service team on Alibaba.

(　)2　When the buyer submits dispute, both the buyer and the seller have 5 to 10 days to negotiate without the involvement of Alibaba.

(　)3　To avoid offline disputes and protect payments and products, the buyer is suggested to make payments online via Alibaba.com and use Trade Assurance.

(　)4　When submitting a dispute for a Trade Assurance Order on Alibaba, you can click "Open a dispute" if you have paid for your order.

(　)5　If a complaint is not solved, Alibaba will punish the complained account and suggest resorting to embassy or overseas lawsuit for help.

Ⅲ. Answer the following questions according to the text.

1. How to understand "the name Alibaba is synonymous with wholesale trading, both buying and selling of products worldwide"?

2. What businesses does Alibaba cover?

3. In what way can you guarantee your payment, refund, cancellation, shipping, order quantity or the vendor itself when you try wholesale trading on Alibaba?

4. Is it easy to get access to customer service on Alibaba? And how?

5. What does Alibaba function when solving a dispute between the buyer and the seller?

Language Work

Ⅰ. Choose the best choice to complete each of the following sentences.

1. _____ caused by online shopping and online loans were two major elements of Internet-

related cases heard by a court in Beijing's high-tech business hub over the past two years.

A. Facts   B. Questions   C. Phenomena   D. Disputes

2. The buyer _____ the bike he bought on the platform was different from the shopper's online description.

A. announced   B. claimed   C. acclaimed   D. protested

3. Several large online service platforms have realized their responsibility in keeping market order and protecting customers' rights, especially after the country's first E-commerce Law was put into _____ in January.

A. effect   B. efficiency   C. present   D. reality

4. Some Internet operators have made clearer and stricter rules on _____ products or services on their platforms to prevent unnecessary disputes.

A. selling   B. ordering   C. reviewing   D. promoting

5. In order to reduce tax burdens for all industries, the government _____ supporting measures, such as increased tax deductions for producer and consumer services.

A. adopted   B. adapted   C. accepted   D. invented

Ⅱ. Match the English words in the left column with the English explanations in the right column.

_____ 1. humble   A. an amount of money that is given back to you if you are not satisfied with the goods or services that you have paid for

_____ 2. apparel   B. buildings, pieces of equipment, or services that are provided for a particular purpose

_____ 3. icon   C. a small sign or picture on a computer screen that is used to start a particular operation

_____ 4. facility   D. of low birth or status

_____ 5. refund   E. clothes

Ⅲ. Translate the following sentences from the text into Chinese.

1. Catering to over 190 countries, Alibaba is free for registration and allows buyers and sellers to connect with each other, whether it is for product enquiry, price negotiation, shipping or others.

_____

_____.

2. Clicking on any of the results, a visitor is welcome with pictures relevant to the product, with details of product, warranty, payment terms, packaging, delivery and even sizes.

_____

_____.

3. Alibaba.com will also act as a mediator for any disputes which remain unresolved after 10 days of initial opening.

_____

4. And if it is proved that the defendant should bear the responsibility for this trade dispute, then as punishment we will disable their Alibaba.com account.

_____

5. Meanwhile, to protect yourself from loss, you are advised to resort to embassy or overseas lawsuit for help.

_____

Ⅳ. Translate the following sentences into English using the proper forms of the words or expressions given in brackets.

1. "互联网 + 护理服务"（Internet Plus Nursing Service）是供康复期患者或失能老人（discharged patients and elderly or disabled people）联系注册护士上门提供护理服务的一个在线平台。（register）

_____

2. 电商经营者和平台应自律守信。（take responsibility for）

_____

3. 美国智能手机巨头苹果公司下调了部分 iPhone 产品的在华售价,试图以此推高销量。（boost）

_____

4. 中国跨境电商行业发展迅速对海关的监管提出了严峻的挑战。（pose）

_____

5. 国内主要电商平台"淘宝"近日发布的报告显示,2018 年中国人花了 160 亿元在线购买商品和服务。（issue）

_____

Supplementary Reading: Developing a Customer Service Policy

With more ways to contact businesses than ever before — phone, websites, E-mail, social media, in person — customers expect more and more responsive companies. Quality of service has gone from a competitive advantage to a necessity. Research shows that over two-thirds of customers who stop using businesses do so because they find the service staff unhelpful, while

55% would pay more to guarantee good service. In order to improve the service of your company, or to establish that your new venture is customer oriented, you will need to evaluate your current service, investigate your customer's needs, and develop a flexible customer service policy that addresses those needs.

Learning More about Your Customers' Needs

1. Set up a system to document customer complaints and comments. Your customer service policy should be tailored to the needs of your customers, and if you listen, your customers will tell you what those needs are. If you don't have a systematic way to compile this information, develop one. The information recorded should include:

- The customer's name, address, and phone number
- The name of the employee receiving the complaint
- The date and time of the complaint and of its resolution
- The nature of the complaint
- The agreed-upon solution, whether it was implemented on the spot, and if not when it was promised
- What steps are currently being taken
- The date and time of follow-up to ensure the customer is satisfied
- Any compensation given to the customer
- Suggestions on how the problem can be avoided in the future

2. Create surveys and run focus groups. In both cases, your goal should be to gather useful information rather than positive feedback. To do so:

- Ask open-ended questions that lend themselves towards specific feedback, rather than focusing on rankings, which tell you little about how to address them. Ratings are less important than why you are getting those ratings.
- Use professional firms or online survey sites to help develop questions that are truly objective and don't stack the deck to get you favorable results. What you need is useful feedback, not praise.
- Use online surveys to gather information in real time. You need to know what your customers need today, not two months ago. The best way to do this is to use a self-serve or full-service online system to gather customer feedback.

3. Consult your employees and operational data. Organize focus groups to talk to your employees about frequent customer issues they deal with. Also look at stats like the number of returns and return rate to determine how happy customers are with your products. Other stats to consult include:

- The status of backlogs and stockouts — If your products are unavailable, you can bet your customers are less than satisfied.
- Internal reject rate — If the rate is high, then there is a good chance some bad products are

reaching customers. Bad products mean dissatisfied customers, and the typical dissatisfied customer tell 9-15 people about their experience.

4. Talk to your vendors and service providers. If you outsource various aspects of your business like shipping or website management, these service providers may have valuable information about your customers.

- Ask your website administrator to categorize types of feedback and transmit it to you.
- Ask your shipping unit how frequently it must re-do orders that are rejected the first time they ship due to defects or other problems.
- Ask your customer service call-center to categorize complaints and other feedback and transmit it to you. Also ask about typical customer wait time and how many customers call and hang up before reaching a service agent.

5. Identify your top three significant customer service issues. Combine internal and vendor input and compare it to information from your customers in order to create a list of problems. Focus on the ones that come up frequently, affect your bottom line, and are actionable (i.e. "my order was defective" rather than "I was dissatisfied").

Creating your Customer Service Policy

1. Develop a vision statement. This is the guiding principle that informs how your company seeks to interact with its customers. It is both a daily reminder and a goal to be aspired to. It should be simple vision for McDonald's: "Quality, Service, Cleanliness, Value." To come up with your vision statement:

- Looking 3 to 5 years into the future, imagine your company's success and list five reasons for it.
- Now list the reasons for your success from the customer's viewpoint.
- From the vantage point of this future success, list the steps you have taken to upgrade customer service.
- Based on these lists, summarize the key elements of your vision.
- List the verbs from you summary and use them to build a concise vision statement.

2. Set customer service goals in line with your vision and based on your research into customer needs. These goals should provide quantifiable targets to address the customer service areas you identified as most important. For example:

- A time limit by which all calls to the service center will be answered
- A target for the percentage of products returned
- A target for the percentage of customers who report that they are satisfied with how their complaint was handled
- A target for the percentage of customers who complain but go on to purchase your service or products again

3. Make your customer policies straightforward and customer-friendly. Review your customer

feedback to see which policies have proven most troublesome. If possible, get rid of them. Be sure to consult your employees to get their feedback on any proposed policies. They will often have a better feel for how the customer interacts with the customer service policy.

- You can find examples of straightforward, succinct customer service plans at *www. thethrivingsmallbusiness.com* and *www.aa.com* (American Airlines).

4. Use your goals as a guide in creating your customer service policy. Once you have hashed out a policy, take time to consider it from the customers' point of view. Policy areas to touch on include:

- Product or service overview — Do you have policies in place to make it as easy as possible for customers to learn about what you sell?

- Speed — Can your customers order quickly and painlessly? Are knowledgeable customer service representatives readily available? Consider setting a maximum wait time for in store and phone service, and then consider what it will take to achieve those service standards.

- Communication — Do you do a good job of informing customers of everything they need to know to do business with you? Return and shipping policies should be easy to locate. Accepted forms of payment should be clearly displayed. Add-on services and warranties should be explained without pressure to buy.

- Follow up — Your customers should be given the name, phone number, and E-mail of a person to contact if they need help after a purchase. Show them a timeline for service or product delivery. Give information on how to seek technical support or other help. Make it easy for them to complain if they need to do so.

- Complaints — Are complaints handled promptly? Are employees given the freedom to solve problems to reach the best solution? Is higher level management involved quickly? How are customers compensated for various problems? Is there follow-up to ensure customer satisfaction?

- Retention — Are you building long-term relationships with your customers? Contact them a month after the transaction to be sure they are satisfied. Consider sending out a newsletter or coupons to customers. Create customer forums on your website.

- Employee monitoring — Are you encouraging your employees to provide good customer service? Do you share customer feedback with them and confront them when they are not meeting service standards? Do you recognize and reward them when they provide good service?

5. Give your employees discretion to deal with customer problems. What you don't want are policies that are used as weapons against the customer — e.g. "I'm sorry I can't do more, but it's company policy" — or problems that drag on and frustrate customers. Instead of strict rules, give your employees broad guidelines to help them solve the problem:

- Understand the problem — Let the customer speak without interrupting, note the important facts, and repeat them to be sure you got it right. "Just to confirm, you want to receive a new unit and get a refund, right?"

- Identify the cause — Find out what the customer did, review what should have happened, and isolate the problem. Identifying the cause often means accepting that the company, not the customer, is responsible for the problem. "You ordered a unit that our website says works with your system. You should have been able to plug it in and use it, but the literature on the website must be mistaken, because the unit is not compatible with your system."

- Propose solutions — First ask the customer for ideas. If he or she has a clear idea of how they want the situation resolved, either agree or work with them to finalize a plan that works for the customer and the company.

- Solve the problem — Take corrective action and ask the customer if they are pleased with the way the problem was resolved. Apologize for the trouble and ideally, offer the customer something as compensation for their trouble.

6. Train your employees in the new policy. Hold a mandatory meeting to introduce the plan and to explain its purpose. Afterwards, work training into regular meetings, as well as holding training workshops to teach your personnel particular skills such as problem solving for complaints.

(Adapted from https://www.wikihow.com/Develop-a-Customer-Service-Policy)

Words & Expressions

responsive	/rɪˈspɒnsɪv/	adj.	reacting quickly, in a positive way 反应快的;灵敏的;积极的
venture	/ˈventʃə/	n.	a new business activity that involves taking risks 风险项目,风险投资;冒险事业
implement	/ˈɪmplɪm(ə)nt/	v.	to take action or make changes that you have officially decided should happen 执行;贯彻;实施
stats	/stæts/	n.	statistics 统计数字
backlog	/ˈbæklɒg/	n.	a large amount of work that you need to complete, especially work that should already have been completed 积压未办之事,积压的工作
reject	/rɪˈdʒekt/	v.	to refuse to accept, believe in, or agree with something 拒绝接受
succinct	/səkˈsɪŋkt/	adj.	clearly expressed in a few words — use this to show approval 言简意赅的,简明扼要的,简练的
mandatory	/ˈmændətərɪ/	adj.	if something is mandatory, the law says it must be done 依法必须做的,强制性的,义务的
on the spot			立刻,当场
stack the deck			暗中布局(使情况对某人有利或不利),预先做手脚,暗中策划

hang up	搁置,拖延
hash out	消除,经过长时间讨论解决一个问题

Notes & Terms

service agent	服务代理
The Thriving Small Business.com	The Thriving Small Business（TSB）is a business performance consulting company that was created out of a passion to help small business owners see their vision come to life by creating infrastructures that support business development and growth through strategic customer focus 蓬勃发展的小企业平台
American Airlines	美国航空公司

Text Comprehension

Choose the best answer to each of the following questions according to the text.

1. In order to improve the service of your company, you need to do the following EXCEPT _____.

   A. to establish a new venture

   B. to assess your current service

   C. to research on what your customers need

   D. to set up a flexible customer service policy

2. What's the goal of creating surveys and running focus groups?

   A. To get positive feedback.

   B. To use a self-serve or full-service online system.

   C. To praise.

   D. To gather useful information.

3. Which is the guiding principle that informs how your company seeks to interact with its customers?

   A. Talk to your vendors and service providers.

   B. Give your employees discretion to deal with customer problems.

   C. Identify your top three significant customer service issues.

   D. Develop a vision statement.

4. When creating your customer service policy, use your goals as a guide. Policy areas to touch on include the following EXCEPT _____.

   A. product or service overview, speed.   B. communication, follow up.

   C. employer monitoring.   D. complaints, retention.

5. How to give your employees guidelines to deal with customer problems?

A. To understand the problem.
B. To identify the cause.
C. To propose solutions.
D. All of the above.

Language Work

Fill in the following blanks with the words or phrases given below. Change the forms where necessary.

cash	launch	scan	compete	clarify
frustrate	interrupt	identify	compatible	contact

1. The E-commerce law, which _____ E-commerce operators into E-commerce platform operators, merchants on E-commerce platforms, and those doing business on their own websites or via other web services, covers not only famous platforms such as Alibaba's Taobao but also those selling goods via social networks including the popular chatting app WeChat.

2. The International Olympic Committee (IOC) and its Worldwide Top Partner Alibaba Group announced that the first-ever Olympic official online store had been _____ on Tmall, China's largest E-commerce platform.

3. Chinese E-commerce giant Alibaba Group Holding Ltd _____ a record 213.5 billion yuan in sales during its 24-hour online retail frenzy Singles' Day in 2018.

4. As high as 60.3% of payments made via Alibaba's T-mall and Taobao during the Singles' Day shopping frenzy were verified by users _____ their fingerprints or faces instead of entering passwords, according to the E-commerce giant. Bio-payments are gradually replacing passwords to become the primary means of payment in future.

5. The British Museum opened an online store on China's E-commerce platform Tmall, _____ with the Palace Museum on the platform, which has successfully been selling souvenirs.

Workshop

Presentation: Work in a group and discuss which factor plays the most important role in customer service. And make a presentation in the class to illustrate your ideas.

References

[1] https://customercarecontacts.com/customer-service-tips-to-help-your-brand-stand-out/, retrieved on 2019-04-03.

[2] https://customercarecontacts.com/contact-of-alibaba-customer-service/, retrieved on 2019-04-03.

[3] https://service.alibaba.com/ensupplier/faq_detail/14455109.htm/, retrieved on 2019-04-03.

[4] https://service.alibaba.com/ensupplier/faq_detail/1000091939.htm/, retrieved on 2019-04-03.

[5] https://service.alibaba.com/helpcenter/47a9f417.html?spm=a273f.8140240.1992516.5795/, retrieved on 2019-04-03.

[6] https://service.alibaba.com/ensupplier/faq_detail/1000126022.htm/, retrieved on 2019-04-03.

[7] https://waimaoquan.alibaba.com/bbs/read-htm-tid-2259649-fid-215.html.

[8] https://baike.1688.com/doc/view-d43868730.html.

[9] https://www.wikihow.com/Develop-a-Customer-Service-Policy/, retrieved on 2019-04-02.

[10] https://newssearch.chinadaily.com.cn/.

[11] http://www.chinadaily.com.cn/business/.

[12] https://en.wikipedia.org/wiki/.

[13] http://www.youdao.com/.

[14] https://tradeassurance.alibaba.com/.

[15] https://activities.alibaba.com/alibaba/secure-payment-supplier.php/.

[16] https://thethrivingsmallbusiness.com/about/.

Unit 9

Business
Communication

Learning Objectives

To learn how to establish business relations and exchange business information

To study business letters for different purposes

To master main contents and useful expressions of business letters

Warming up

1. Work in a group and discuss the questions: 1) What does a business letter look like? 2) What is the purpose of a business letter? 3) In what situation is a business letter used?

2. Read the words or phrases and their explanations. Then complete the following paragraph with the words or phrases. Change the form when necessary.

client   a person who uses the services or advice of a professional person or organization

recipient   a person who receives sth

relationship the way in which two people, groups or countries behave towards each other or deal with each other

format   the general arrangement, plan, design, etc. of sth

permanent   lasting for a long time or for all time in the future; existing all the time

Business letters are usually letters from one company to another, or between such organizations and their customers, _____ and other external parties. As important marketing tools, business letters exchange information in a written _____ for the process of business activities. The overall style of letters depends on the _____ between the parties concerned. They can take place between organizations, within organizations or between the customers and the organization. Business letters can have many types of contents, for example, to request direct information or action from another party, to order supplies from a supplier, to point out a mistake by the letter's _____, to reply directly to a request, to apologize for a mistake, or to convey goodwill. They are sometimes useful because they produce a _____ written record, and may be taken more seriously by the recipient than other forms of communication.

(Adapted from https://en.wikipedia.org/wiki/Business_letters/)

Text: Business Letters

Business letters are different from other types of writing because they need to be purposeful, economical and reader-oriented. It is important for business writers to focus on expressing their ideas rather than impressing the intended audience. The goal is to get the message across in a clear and simple manner. As the Internet has changed a lot of things within the business world, quick business E-mails now rule the day. E-mails are so accessible and the following situations engage business E-mails for different purposes.

1. Establishing Business Relations

Businesses relations can be defined as a commercially oriented connection between a small business and other two organizations. Based on mutual interests and benefits, businesses relations are essential for success in trade. The most known types are alliances and networks, forming relationships within different organizations together into one. An example of forming such a relationship based on networking is engaged in a foreign organization, to increase financial gain and market share within the industry. This emphasizes the importance of forming external relationships, as this can push the business into having a more effective and higher position in the market, ahead of its competitors with greater brand awareness and recognition. Small businesses have a difficult time building good business relations as business relations is connected with such marketing performances and the need of having a good starting profit, time, planning and marketing expertise, therefore establishing strong social ties from different organizations can strengthen the overall performance.

【Sample 1】

Dear Sir or Madam,

On the recommendation of your Chamber of Commerce, we have learned with pleasure the name and address of your firm. We wish to inform you that we are a textile supply based in London, UK, with more than 30 retail stores located in Southern Britain. We shall be glad to enter into business relations with you on the basis of equality and mutual benefit.

We are very interested in learning more about your products of impressive silk and cotton for possible import and sale in our chain stores and would greatly appreciate a copy of your full product catalogue, along with pricing lists.

We look forward to your early reply.

Yours faithfully,

John Marx, Director of Purchasing Department

Dear Mr. Marx,

Thank you for your interest in our products. Dongwu Exports has been in the business of producing a variety of textiles for over 10 years. I am sure you will be very satisfied with our quality and service. To give you a general idea of our products, we are sending you a file containing a catalogue together with a range of pamphlets for your reference.

Please contact us with any questions if you are interested in receiving samples of any of the items listed in the catalogue. We shall make offers promptly.

Sincerely,

Victor Wu, Export Manager

---

2. Inquiries

A business inquiry letter is a letter written for communication between two organizations or persons belonging to two different organizations inquiring some business they are doing together or hoping to do in future. In some cases, the sender may not have ever met the receiver. One has to be precise and to the point and does not drag the letter. It can be of many types. It can be about certain products or services of the receiving company. It can refer to the status of the ongoing work being done by the company receiving the letter. Such a letter also serves as a proof for the business being done between two organizations and as a history for future references. This type of letter is brief and to the point. To keep the letter brief and concise, the sender should stick to the point and ask for what he/she wants straightforwardly.

【Sample 2】

Dear Sir or Madam,

With regard to your advertisement in the Business Journal of 2nd March, we are very interested in importing silk dresses from Hangzhou. We would be obliged if you will let us have detailed information about sizes, colors and prices.

We have been importers of textiles for many years and there is a steady demand in our market for textiles of good quality.

We should appreciate the catalogs and quotations of your products. Please indicate any new items not yet introduced into U.S.A and send some samples if possible.

We look forward to hearing from you soon.

Yours sincerely,

Lina Smith, Sales Manager

Dear Ms. Smith,

Thank you for your inquiry dated 5 March for silk dresses. We have pleasure in enclosing a quotation for silk dresses as follows:

"SOFT" silk dresses sizes 36-44 in white, purple, blue, yellow, black

per 100 $ 1,800.00

We will allow you a discount of 20% if the order exceeds 100 items (100 inclusive).

As requested, we have sent out 5 sets of samples via UPS express, tracking No. is 9638572X.

We require payment by irrevocable sight Letter of Credit, and we can guarantee delivery within 15 days after we receive the L/C.

Please let us know your comments on the samples and questions for any further information. Any orders you place with us will be processed promptly.

Yours sincerely,

Lili，Product Manager

---

3. Orders

An order letter is the one that conveys the message for a supply of goods. It is written by a company or an individual who wants to place an order or place a purchase request to another company. Before planning to write an order letter, it is important to carry out some research work related to desired products or services. Having detailed information can provide the company or the person concerned with the clear picture of placing on order. There are lots of commitments involved with this type of letter so it is important to draft it carefully. There are several things, which can be included in an order letter like order details, quantity, quality, delivery time, after sales services etc. Before drafting an order letter, it is necessary to write down the terms and conditions related to purchases that can be beneficial to both the parties. When it comes to adding the information about the items, few things should be added as names of the product, required quantity, catalogue number, weight of the product, model number of the product, price, size and color details, etc.

【Sample 3】

Dear Ms. Li,

We have received your letter of March 5 with illustrated catalogue and price list. Thank you for the samples you sent us and we are satisfied with the quality. The prices are also up to our requirement. Please find enclosed here with our Order No. 9875 for 1,500 units of "SOFT" silk dresses with a total value of USD 21,600.

Quantity	Size	Color
50	36, 44	white
100	38, 40, 42	white
50	36, 44	purple
100	38, 40, 42	purple
100	38, 40, 42	blue
100	38, 40, 42, 44	black

As summer is coming and the goods are in great need, we hope the shipment can be made before May 10. We shall open our confirmed irrevocable L/C in your favor as soon as we receive your confirmation on the order.

We are pleased to have transacted this initial business with you and look forward to further expansion of trade to our mutual benefit.

Very truly yours,

Lina Smith

Dear Ms. Smith,

Thank you very much for the Order No. 9875 dated on 10th March 2018. We now have pleasure in confirming you that all the items you required are in stock. The goods can be shipped by the end of March and are due to arrive in London on May 6.

We can also confirm you that your banker, Bank of England, have accepted our draft for USD 21,600, payable within 30 days at sight.

It is a pleasure doing business with you and we look forward to the opportunity to serve you in the future.

Yours faithfully,

Lili

---

4. Payment

Payment is the trade of value from one party (such as a person or company) to another for goods, or services, or to fulfill a legal obligation. The most common means of payment involve use of money, cheque, or debit, credit or bank transfers. Payments may also take complicated forms, such as stock issues or the transfer of anything of value or benefit to the parties. As an important and complicated issue in international trade, payments are frequently preceded by an invoice or bill and mainly include Letter of Credit (L/C), Remittance and Collection.

【Sample 4】

Dear Ms. Smith,

With reference to the 1500 "SOFT" silk dresses concerning our Sales Confirmation No. TEL158, we wish to remind you that the date of delivery is approaching. However, up to present we have not received the covering L/C. This caused us some inconvenience and made it difficult for us to process the order as agreed.

In order to complete shipment before the scheduled date, please see to it and open the relevant L/C immediately in conformity with the terms of the contract.

Yours sincerely,

Lili

Dear Ms. Li,

I regret having to ask you for extending the deadline for payment on our order No. 9875. Due to the unexpected computer attacks, it is nearly impossible for us to make payment on time. Under such circumstances, we can not get access to our computer systems. This may cause a delay of about one week before everything recovers. In light of this situation, we respectfully request an extension of 30 days on our account.

Yours faithfully,

Lina Smith

---

5. Shipment

Shipping originally referred to transport by sea, but in American English, it has been extended to refer to transport by land or air (International English: "carriage") as well. Freight transport is the physical process of transporting commodities and merchandise goods and cargo. "Logistics", a term borrowed from the military environment, is also fashionably used in the same sense. Modes of shipment include land or "ground" shipping, ships, air freight and intermodal freight transport. Intermodal freight transport refers to shipments that involve more than one mode. More specifically it usually refers to the use of intermodal shipping containers that are easily transferred between ship, rail, plane and truck.

Common trading terms used in shipping goods internationally include free on board (FOB), carriage and freight (now known in the US as "cost and freight") (C&F, CFR, CNF), carriage, insurance and freight (now known in the US as "cost, insurance and freight") (CIF). The shipper chooses the carrier who offers the lowest rate (to the shipper) for the shipment. In some cases, however, other factors, such as better insurance or faster transit time will cause the shipper to choose an option other than the lowest bidder.

【Sample 5】

Dear Ms. Smith,

We are pleased to inform you that we have received your L/C No. 5565 under our Sales Confirmation No. TEL158. We have had the 1500 "SOFT" silk dresses loaded on board M.V. "Shunfeng", which is scheduled to leave for London on April 4, and is due on the end of this month.

Enclosed are shipping documents including Bill of Lading, Invoice, Packing List and Insurance Policy.

All items have been examined carefully before being packed and we are sure that they will reach you in good order.

We hope that this initial order will lead to further business.

Yours sincerely,

Lili

Dear Ms. Li,

Our order No. 9875   1500 "SOFT" silk dresses

As it is now more than two months since we opened a letter of credit in your favor, we should like to know exactly when you could arrange shipment of the goods. Your prompt response will be highly appreciated.

Sincerely,

Lina Smith

(Adapted from https://en.wikipedia.org/wiki/Business_relations/,

https://www.letters.org/category/order-letter/)

Words & Expressions

orient	/ˈɔːrɪent/	v.	~ **sb/sth** (**to/towards sb/sth**) to direct sb/sth towards sth; to make or adapt sb/sth for a particular purpose 朝向;面对;确定方向;使适应
accessible	/əkˈsesəbl/	adj.	that can be reached, entered, used, seen, etc.可到达的;可接近的;可进入的;可使用的;可见到的; easy to understand 容易理解的;易懂的
alliance	/əˈlaɪəns/	n.	~ (**with sb/sth**) / ~ (**between A and B**) an agreement between countries, political parties, etc. to work together in order to achieve sth that they all want (国家、政党等的)结盟,联盟,同盟
expertise	/ˌekspɜːˈtiːz/	n.	~ (**in sth/in doing sth**) expert knowledge or skill in a particular subject, activity or job 专门知识;专门技能;专长
retail	/ˈriːteɪl/	n.	the selling of goods to the public, usually through shops/stores 零售
pamphlet	/ˈpæmflət/	n.	a very thin book with a paper cover, containing information about a particular subject 小册子;手册
concise	/kənˈsaɪs/	adj.	giving only the information that is necessary and important, using few words 简明的;简练的;简洁的
straightforward	/ˌstreɪtˈfɔːwəd/	adj.	honest and open; not trying to trick sb or hide sth 坦诚的;坦率的;率直的
oblige	/əˈblaɪdʒ/	v.	to force sb to do sth, by law, because it is a duty, etc.(以法律、义务等)强迫,迫使
quotation	/kwəʊˈteɪʃən/	n.	a statement of how much money a particular piece of work will cost 报价;估价
enclose	/ɪnˈkləʊz/	v.	~ **sth** (**with sth**) to put sth in the same envelope, package, etc. as sth else 附入;随函(或包裹等)附上
discount	/ˈdɪskaʊnt/	n.	~ **on/off sth** an amount of money that is taken off

			the usual cost of sth 折扣
exceed	/ɪkˈsiːd/	*v.*	to be greater than a particular number or amount 超过(数量)
irrevocable	/ɪˈrevəkəbl/	*adj.*	that cannot be changed 无法改变的;不可更改的
confirm	/kənˈfɜːm/	*v.*	to state or show that sth is definitely true or correct, especially by providing evidence(尤指提供证据来)证实,证明,确认
initial	/ɪˈnɪʃl/	*adj.*	happening at the beginning; first 最初的;开始的;第一的
due	/djuː/	*adj.*	~ (**to do sth**) / ~ (**for sth**) arranged or expected 预定;预期;预计
extend	/ɪkˈstend/	*v.*	to make sth last longer 延长;使延期
get across			使通过;解释清楚;使被理解;清楚
on the basis of			根据;在……的基础上;按照
to the point			中肯,扼要;切题
with regard to			关于;至于
in need			急需
in stock			有存货,现有
see to			负责;注意;照料;注意做到
in conformity with			遵循(规则);与……相符合(或一致)
in light of			根据;鉴于;从……观点

Notes & Terms

Chamber of Commerce	It is a form of business network, for example, a local organization of businesses whose goal is to further the interests of businesses. Business owners in towns and cities form these local societies to advocate on behalf of the business community. Local businesses are members, and they elect a board of directors or executive council to set policy for the chamber. The board or council then hires a President, CEO or Executive Director, plus staffing appropriate to size, to run the organization. A chamber of commerce is a voluntary association of business firms belonging to different trades and industries. They serve as spokesmen and representatives of business community. They differ from country to country. The first chamber of commerce was founded in 1599 in Marseille, France. 商会
Letter of Credit	It is also known as a documentary credit or banker's commercial credit, provides an economic guarantee from a bank to an exporter

of goods. Being safe and reliable, it is most frequently adopted in the international trade and goods delivery. It is particularly useful where the buyer and seller may not know each other personally and are separated by distance, differing laws in each country, and different trading customs. It is a primary method in international trade to mitigate the risk a seller of goods takes when providing those goods to a buyer. It does this by ensuring that the seller is paid for presenting the documents which are specified in the contract for sale between the buyer and the seller. That is to say, L/C is a payment method used to discharge the legal obligations for payment from the buyer to the seller, by having a bank pay the seller directly. Thus, the seller relies on the credit risk of the bank, rather than the buyer, to receive payment. 信用证

Remittance

It is a transfer of money by which the buyer sends the payment to the seller through a bank or other ways according to the terms and time stipulated in the contract. It is commonly used for payment in advance, cash with order and open account business. It falls into three forms: mail transfer (M/T 票汇), telegraphic transfer (T/T 电汇) and demand draft (D/D 信汇). 汇付

Collection

It means that the creditor (exporter) draws a bill of exchange and entrusts the bank to collect the payment of the shipment from the debtor (importer). It has two forms: Documents against Payment (D/P 付款交单) and Documents against Acceptance (D/A 承兑交单). D/P means the shipping documents are to be delivered against payment only. There are D/P at sight and D/P after sight. D/P at sight(即期付款交单) means to pay against documentary draft at sight. D/P after sight (远期付款交单) is to duly accept the documentary draft drawn at X X days' sight upon first presentation and make payment on its maturity. D/A calls for delivery of documents against acceptance of the draft drawn by the exporter/seller. D/A is always after sight. 托收

bill of lading

A bill of lading (sometimes abbreviated as B/L or BoL) is a document issued by a carrier (or their agent) to acknowledge receipt of cargo for shipment. Bills of lading are one of three crucial documents used in international trade to ensure that exporters receive payment and importers receive the merchandise. 提单;提货单

invoice

a commercial document issued by a seller to a buyer, relating to a sale transaction and indicating the products, quantities, and agreed

	prices for products or services the seller had provided the buyer. Payment terms are usually stated on the invoice. These may specify that the buyer has a maximum number of days in which to pay and is sometimes offered a discount if paid before the due date. The buyer could have already paid for the products or services listed on the invoice. 发票;(发货或服务)费用清单
FOB	The exporter delivers the goods at the specified location (and on board the vessel). Costs paid by the exporter include load, lash, secure and stow the cargo, including securing cargo not to move in the ships hold, protecting the cargo from contact with the double bottom to prevent slipping, and protection against damage from condensation. For example, "FOB JNPT" means that the exporter delivers the goods to the Jawahar lal Nehru Port, India, and pays for the cargo to be loaded and secured on the ship. This term also declares where the responsibility of shipper ends and that of buyer starts. The exporter is bound to deliver the goods at his cost and expense. In this case, the freight and other expenses for outbound traffic are borne by the importer. 离岸价
C&F, CFR, CNF	Insurance is payable by the importer, and the exporter pays all expenses incurred in transporting the cargo from its place of origin to the port/airport and ocean freight/air freight to the port/airport of destination. For example, C&F Los Angeles (the exporter pays the ocean shipping/air freight costs to Los Angeles). most of the governments ask their exporters to trade on these terms to promote their exports worldwide such as India and China. Many of the shipping carriers (such as UPS, DHL, FedEx) offer guarantees on their delivery times. These are known as GSR guarantees or "guaranteed service refunds"; if the parcels are not delivered on time, the customer is entitled to a refund. 成本加运费
CIF	Insurance and freight are all paid by the exporter to the specified location. For example, at CIF Los Angeles, the exporter pays the ocean shipping/air freight costs to Los Angeles including the insurance of cargo. This also states that responsibility of the shipper ends at the Los Angeles port. 成本、保险费加运费
M.V.	motor vessel 货轮

Understanding the text

Read the text and answer the following questions.

1. What's the importance of establishing business relations?
2. What are the features of a business inquiry letter?
3. What is an order letter? What is necessary information included in an order letter?
4. Which payment is most liked by the buyer? Why?
5. How many modes of shipment do you know in international trade? If shipment is delayed, what will happen to the buyer?

Exercise

Exercise 1

Ⅰ. Translate the following sentences into Chinese.

1. We shall be glad to enter into business relations with you on the basis of equality and mutual benefit.

2. We are writing to express our desire to build direct business relations with you.

3. We have come to know your address from the Commercial Counselor of your embassy in Beijing who has informed us that you are in the market for office equipment.

4. ABC is a China based company engaged in the manufacture and export of industrial machinery to more than 50 countries.

5. We have obtained from the Web that your business scope coincides with us, so we are writing to you in the hope of establishing business relations with you.

Ⅱ. Translate the following sentences into English.

1. 我们愿意在贵已双方都接受的条件下建立贸易关系。

2. 我们从广告上得悉贵公司,特此致函希望与贵方建立贸易关系。

3. 随函附上一份最新的商品目录参考,若贵方对其中任何一款感兴趣,请告知我方。

4. 这些年来,我们率先开发和生产适用于家饰用途的系列产品,并建立了自己的加工厂。

5. 我们对贵公司的丝织品感兴趣。如贵方能寄来最新的商品目录、价格表和样品,我们将不胜感激。

Ⅲ. Task Assignment

You obtain from The Journal of Commerce the name and address of a clothes company, which is one of the leading manufacturers and exporters of Children's Garments in China. Please write to establish business relations with it.

****

Exercise 2

Ⅰ.Translate the following sentences into Chinese.

1. We will allow you a discount of 20% if the order exceeds 100 items (100 inclusive).

2. If you decide to take advantage of our offer, please kindly fax us acceptance.

3. We should be obliged if you could quote your best price for the product and state your best terms and discount allowable.

4. We feel sorry to say that the price we quoted is our bottom price so we are unable to make a further reduction.

5. Thank you for your inquiry. Would you tell us the quantity you require so that we can work out the offers?

_____

_____.

II. Translate the following sentences into English.

1. 如果您能为我方提供这些电子产品的报价, 我方将不胜感激。

_____

_____.

2. 你方的报价已经超出了我方能接受的范围。

_____

_____.

3. 感谢您有兴趣了解我们的优质电子产品, 我们很高兴就您感兴趣的产品为您报价。

_____

_____.

4. 我们请贵方提供样品、最低报价和其他条款及情况。

_____

_____.

5. 为使你方对我公司产品有全面了解, 现随附有关我公司经营的小册子和价目表, 内有详细规格和包装情况。

_____

_____.

III. Task Assignment

You have seen the advertisement in the Business Journal and want to ask for a quotation for the motorcycles described.

****

Exercise 3

I. Translate the following sentences into Chinese.

1. We now have pleasure in confirming you that all the items you required are in stock.

_____

_____.

2. We suggest a reduction of 5% on orders of 500 pieces for each.

_____

_____.

3. As some items under your order are beyond our business scope, we can only accept your order partially.

．

4. I have received your order and would like to confirm with you the terms of transaction.

．

5. What's your policy for canceling an order?

．

II. Translate the following sentences into English.

1. 兹回复贵方 4 月 20 日牛肉罐头报价函,现寄去 500 箱牛肉罐头订单,作为试购。

．

2. 感谢您订购我们手工制作的首饰。

．

3. 我们已经收到您订购 100 辆自行车(型号 A580-1)的订单。

．

4. 由于该产品在库房没有库存,所以您的订单被延误。

．

5. 如果我们对这些产品满意的话,我们会续订的。

．

III. Task Assignment

Write a letter to your customer that you regret your company can not accept the order at the price quoted 3 months ago, since wages and prices of materials have risen considerably.

****

Exercise 4

I. Translate the following sentences into Chinese

1. In light of this situation, we respectfully request an extension of 30 days on our account.

2. Payment is to be made by D/P at sight and we hope that it will be acceptable to you.

3. Upon receipt of your payment, we will ship the goods by air.

4. We thank you very much for your check for RMB 26, 000 yuan in full settlement of our invoice No. 4521 of July 15th.

5. As detailed in the signed contract between our two firms, if an account is not paid in full within 60 days of receipt of product, we have the legal right to pursue payment.

II. Translate the following sentences into English

1. 一旦收到贵方关于此次订货的确认书,我方即要求银行开出以贵方为受益人的信用证。

2. 你们如果提前支付货款,可以给你们打八五折。

3. 感谢您及时付款。

4. 我们很高兴地通知贵方,以贵方为受益人的不可撤销信用证已经开出,金额为 15 000 美元。

5. 我们愿承兑你方根据信用证金额开具的汇票。

III. Task Assignment

Until April 30th, you haven't received your customer's payment of $ 3000, originally due March 31st. Write a letter to remind it of the overdue and state that you may pursue legal means if the payment is not received by May 31st.

****

Exercise 5

Ⅰ. Translate the following sentences into Chinese

1. Enclosed are shipping documents including Bill of Lading, Invoice, Packing List and Policy of Insurance.

 .

2. Please make shipment of the contracted goods without further delay.

 .

3. The order is so urgently required that we have to ask you to speed up shipment.

 .

4. We'll do our utmost to deliver the goods at an earliest possible date. But the shipment date depends on the L/C opening date reaching us.

 .

5. We will take delivery of the goods as soon as they are released from the Customs.

 .

Ⅱ. Translate the following sentences into English

1. 如果我们能及时收到信用证,我方保证在六月底完成装运。

 .

2. 希望尽早收到贵方发货的通知。

 .

3. 这种新式包装适合长途海运。

 .

4. 我们会尽最大努力帮助你们提前装船。

 .

5. 你方货号为 4578 的货物下周一会备好,请问你们走海运还是空运?

 .

III. Task Assignment

As the season is approaching, your company is in great need of the goods. Please write a letter to urge an early shipment.

****

Supplementary Reading: How's Your E-mail Etiquette?

In a fast-moving global economy, E-mail offers you the convenience of being able to quickly get your message across to your colleagues or clients at any hour of the day or night. The Internet revolution has had the unintended effect of decreasing the use of oral communication and increasing the importance of text — particularly E-mails — as the primary means of business communication. Employees are no longer writing memos to each other; they are sending E-mails. But are we taking E-mails as seriously as our other business correspondence? Remember, your correspondence says a lot about you, and E-mail etiquette (also called netiquette) not only makes for effective professional communication, but also helps you build a good professional image within your organization and with clients.

Mind Your Manners

Be conversant with the fact that there are some people who are very sensitive to being addressed by their first names. When in doubt, use Mr., Ms., Sir, Madam or Dr. (if appropriate). When you are replying to an E-mail and the sender of the original message has used his or her first name only, then you could safely assume it's all right to use that person's first name as well. Next, there are three words in the dictionary that are very important to netiquette. People may not notice these words when they're there, but if you forget to use them, you'll come across looking disrespectful and ungrateful. These very powerful words are "Please" and "Thank You".

Don't Use That Tone with Me

Tone is a difficult thing to explain. Remember when your parents would say "Don't use that tone of voice with me, young lady (or young man)?" Your feelings come across by the way you say something. It is easy to change your tone when you're speaking. When you're writing, it's very hard to do so. Whenever you write an E-mail, you should read your message over several times before you hit "Send". Make sure that you come across as respectful, friendly, and approachable. And don't sound curt or demanding. Sometimes just rearranging your paragraphs will help. If you're writing to someone you've communicated with before, you might want to begin by saying "I hope you are well." E-mail writers often use emoticons to convey a certain tone. For those of you who don't know what these are, emoticons are little faces made up by arranging parentheses, colons, and semi-colons. Use good judgement here. If you are writing to someone frequently and share an informal relationship, then emoticons are okay. If you're writing to a prospective client or your boss, stick to words only. Avoid writing your message using all uppercase letters. It looks like you're shouting.

And Your Point Would Be...?

When possible, don't ramble. Be concise and get to your point as quickly as you can. However, don't leave out necessary details. If providing a lot of background information will help the recipient answer your query, by all means, include it. You may even want to apologize for being so verbose at the beginning of the message.

Plz Don't Abbrvt.

Never ever use U instead of you, 2 instead of to or too, plz instead of please, and thanx instead of thanks. It's fine for personal E-mails. Business E-mails should be more formal. Of course, frequently used abbreviations such as Mr. and Ms., FYI (for your information), Inc., and etc. are fine.

Spelling Counts... Grammar Too

Use your spell checker. That's what it's for. Don't rely entirely on the spell checker though. If you're using the wrong spelling for a particular use of a word, i.e. two vs. to vs. too, the spell checker won't pick it up. A minor typographical error in a lengthy E-mail will generally go unnoticed, but a series of typographical, spelling, and grammatical errors will indicate a lack of professionalism and has the potential to cost your business or maybe even your job.

Use a Descriptive Subject Line

Always use a subject line in your E-mails. Make sure the subject line is brief, but descriptive. Make an effort to keep your subject line to six or fewer words. The subject line is supposed to be brief and summarize the message, and not become the whole E-mail content. You can summarize the action item of E-mail in the subject line, e.g., "Tues. meeting canceled."

Keep Check on Numbers

Be conservative about who you send your E-mails to. Only send it to those who are directly affected by the issue in question. Ask yourself, is this information useful to this person? Is this level of detail appropriate for this person, or should I send them a summary when everyone's input is gathered and we have come to a conclusion? Send the E-mail "To" the person or people that you are asking for an answer or action, and be specific about what you are asking of whom. Send a courtesy copy (cc) to those who need to be aware of the request but are not asked to act upon it or respond to it. Double check that you have properly attached documents to avoid sending a second message. Check messages frequently — at least three times a day. Immediately respond, delete, forward, or save to a folder as appropriate. The more you leave messages sitting in your Inbox, the bigger the chore to gain control again. It is also easy to lose track of an important action item, or message, if you do not keep it organized. Just like any other type of written message, be aware that it could be forwarded to others or saved indefinitely. Be prudent in what you decide to write in an E-mail.

Include a signature of no more than four lines. Your signature should provide the recipient with a means to contact you other than E-mail, and should mention your designation, company name, etc. For internal communication, it is not necessary to always produce highly organized and precisely worded E-mails. However, etiquette is not totally abandoned in internal communication, particularly when it comes to professional courtesy.

Make A Good First Impression

Though E-mails are less intrusive than a phone call and faster than a letter, first impressions are as important here as any other business communication tool. An E-mail may be your introduction to someone you never met before like a prospective client or new boss or colleague or even a prospective employer. Take your time putting together a well-written message. Once you hit the "Send" button you won't have another chance.

(Adapted from http://www.en8848.com.cn/article/ecommerce/E-mail/12656.html/)

Words & Expressions

conversant	/kən'vɜːsənt/	*adj.*	~ **with sth** knowing about sth; familiar with sth 通晓的;熟悉的
curt	/kɜːt/	*adj.*	(of a person's manner or behavior) appearing rude because very few words are used, or because sth is done in a very quick way 简短而失礼的;唐突无礼的
uppercase	/'ʌpəˌkeɪs/	*adj.*	capital 大写的(字母)
ramble	/'ræmbəl/	*v.*	~ (**on**) (**about sb/sth**) to talk about sb/sth in a confused way, especially for a long time 漫谈;闲聊;瞎扯
query	/'kwɪəri/	*n.*	a question, especially one asking for information or expressing a doubt about sth 疑问;询问
verbose	/vɜː'bəʊs/	*adj.*	using or containing more words than are needed 冗长的;啰唆的;唠叨的
typographical	/ˌtaɪpə'græfɪkəl/	*adj.*	relates to the way in which printed material is presented.印刷上的
in question			讨论中的;成问题的;考虑中的

Text Comprehension

Choose the best answer to each of the following questions according to the text.

1. Which of the following is nowadays the primary means of business communication?

   A. Memos.

   B. E-mails.

   C. Phone calls.

   D. Business letters.

2. Which of the following is NOT an appropriate tone in business E-mails?

   A. Friendly and approachable.

   B. Respectful and grateful.

   C. Formal and serious.

   D. Curt and demanding.

3. What does the author suggest about business E-mail etiquette?

   A. Emoticons should be often used to make the E-mail lively.

   B. All capital letters should be used to show that you are serious.

   C. The point should be stated clearly at the beginning of the E-mail.

   D. No abbreviation should be used in E-mail writing.

4. What does the author suggest about the subject line of a business E-mail?

   A. A business E-mail can be sent without a subject line.

   B. The subject line should include as many details as possible.

   C. The subject line should be concise and contain the key points.

   D. Action words must be used in the subject line.

5. Which of the following should be checked for the business E-mails?

   A. The spelling and grammar of the message.

   B. The recipient of the message.

   C. The attachments.

   D. All of the above.

Language Work

Fill in the following blanks with the words or phrases given below. Change the forms where necessary.

confident	conservative	designation	antique	get across
etiquette	prospective	organization	prudent	come across

1. Whether we are buying, selling, consulting, or simply trying to obtain information, we will

need to _____ ideas to the audience we are not used to dealing with.

2. Office _____ and rules might also imperil new employees who haven't yet made the switch from campus mind to office mind.

3. Social networks have reduced friction in the labor market by allowing employers and _____ employees to connect more easily than ever before.

4. After the approval of the Board of Directors, her new official _____ is Financial Controller.

5. It might be more _____ to get a second opinion before going ahead in business operations.

Workshop

Presentation: Work in a group and share your experiences of writing an E-mail. Discuss with your partners advantages and disadvantages of handwritten letters and E-mails. And present your ideas to the class.

References

［1］董晓波. 实用商务英语写作教程［M］.2 版. 北京：北京交通大学出版社,2014.

［2］肯·欧奎恩. 商务信函写作一本通［M］.高勤,译. 北京：人民邮电出版社,2013.

［3］李蕾. 商务英语函电［M］. 北京：对外经济贸易大学出版社,2015.

［4］杨荔,刘彩勤. 商务英语函电阅读与写作［M］. 北京：对外经济贸易大学出版社,2014.

［5］叶晓英. 商务谈判英语即学即用［M］. 北京：对外经济贸易大学出版社,2011.

［6］周邦友. 商务英语写作教程［M］. 上海：东华大学出版社,2016.

［7］https：//en.wikipedia.org/wiki/Business_relations/on receid 2019-3-16.

［8］https：//www.letters.org/category/order-letter/on receid 2019-3-16.

［9］http：//www.doc88.com/p-9189488447560.html/on receid 2019-3-12.

［10］https：//en.wikipedia.org/wiki/Payment/on receid 2019-3-11.

［11］https：//en.wikipedia.org/wiki/Business_letter/on receid 2019-1-10.

［12］http：//www.tingroom.com/lesson/ttswky/394811.html2019-3-16.

［13］https：//www.letters.org/inquiry-letter/business-inquiry-letter.html/on receid 2019-1-10.

［14］http：//www.en8848.com.cn/article/ecommerce/E-mail/12656.html/on receid 2019-3-16.

［15］http：//www.en8848.com.cn/bec/waimao/wm-jiaoji/312073.html/on receid 2019-3-16.

［16］http：//www.en8848.com.cn/BEC/waimao/E-mail/104717.html/on receid 2019-3-16.

Unit 10

Business Contract

Learning Objectives

To know the types and components of a business contract

To get acquainted with the different conditions in a business contract

To master main terms and useful expressions in writing a business contract

Warming up

1. Work in a group and discuss the basic elements of a business contract.

2. Read the words or phrases and their explanations. Then complete the following paragraph(s) with the words or phrases. Change the form when necessary.

deliver   to take goods, letters, etc. to the person or people they have been sent to

grocery   food and other goods that are sold by a grocer or a supermarket

breach   a failure to do sth that must be done by law

unaware   not noticing or realizing what is happening

valid   legally or officially acceptable

We all make contracts almost every day. As a consumer we probably enter a number of contracts every day online or in a store — even if we do not realize it. Whenever we buy a coffee, hire a car, join a gym, do the _____ shopping, fill the car up with petrol, sign up for a mobile phone plan or purchase a ticket for public transport, we are entering into a contract. We are often _____ we are contracting (or at least don't turn our minds to that fact) and in most cases it is unnecessary to do so; most contracts are made and performed instantly (or almost instantly) without any problems arising. However, should something go wrong (e.g., one party fails to perform, or goods _____ or services performed are defective in some way), it may become important to assess when and whether a _____ contract was entered into, the nature of its terms and obligations and what, if any, remedies may be available in the event of a _____.

(Adapted from

https: //comcom.govt.nz/consumers/your-rights-as-a-consumer/unfair-contract-terms/

http: //www.australiancontractlaw.com/)

Text: Contracts

A contract is a legally-binding agreement which recognizes and governs the rights and duties of the parties to the agreement. A contract is legally enforceable because it meets the requirements and approval of the law. An agreement typically involves the exchange of goods, services, money, or promises of any of those. In the event of breach of contract, the law awards the injured party access to legal remedies such as damages and cancellation.

Contracts may be bilateral or unilateral. A bilateral contract is an agreement in which each of the parties to the contract makes a promise or set of promises to each other. For example, in a contract for the sale of a house, the buyer promises to pay the seller \$ 200,000 in exchange for the seller's promise to deliver title to the property. These common contracts take place in the daily flow of commerce transactions, and in cases with sophisticated or expensive precedent requirements, which are requirements that must be met for the contract to be fulfilled. A contract is often evidenced in writing or by deed; the general rule is that a person who signs a contractual document will be bound by the terms in that document.

Typically, contracts are oral or written, but written contracts have typically been preferred in common law legal systems. An oral contract may also be called a parol contract or a verbal contract, with "verbal" meaning "spoken" rather than "in words", an established usage in British English with regards to contracts and agreements, and common although somewhat deprecated as "loose" in American English. If a contract is in a written form, and somebody signs it, then the signer is typically bound by its terms regardless of whether they have actually read it provided the document is contractual in nature. However, affirmative defenses such as duress or unconscionability may enable the signer to avoid the obligation. Further, reasonable notice of a contract's terms must be given to the other party prior to their entry into the contract. Contracts are widely used in commercial law, and form the legal foundation for transactions across the world. Common examples include contracts for the sale of services and goods (both wholesale and retail), construction contracts, contracts of carriage, software licenses, employment contracts, insurance policies, sale or lease of land, and various other uses.

A business contract is a formal written agreement, which sets forth rights and obligations of the parties concerned. He/She will send a Sales Contract or a Purchase Contract to the other side to ask for counter-signature. When the contract is made by the buyer, it is called the Purchase Contract and when made by the seller, the Sales Contract. In sending out the contracts or confirmation, special attention should be paid to the price, terms of payment, specifications, quality, quantity, time of delivery, port of destination, etc. According to the degree and simplicity, a business contract can fall into different types, such as Contract, Agreement, Confirmation, Memorandum, Order, etc. Its contents include:

1. Title (合同名称)

2. Preamble (前文)

2.1 Date and place of signing (订约日期和地点)

2.2 Signing parties and their nationalities, principal place of business or residence addresses (合同当事人及其国籍、主营业场所或住所)

2.3 Each party's authority (当事人合法依据)

2.4 Recitals or WHEREAS clause (订约缘由/说明条款)

3. Body (正文)

3.1 Definition clause (定义条款)

3.2 Basic conditions (基本条款)

3.3 General terms and conditions (一般条款)

3.3.1 Duration (合同有效期)

3.3.2 Termination (合同的终止)

3.3.3 Force Majeure (不可抗力)

3.3.4 Assignment (合同的让与)

3.3.5 Arbitration (仲裁)

3.3.6 Governing law (适用的法律)

3.3.7 Jurisdiction (诉讼管辖)

3.3.8 Notice (通知手续)

3.3.9 Amendment (合同修改)

3.3.10 Others (其他)

4. Witness clause (结尾条款)

5. Concluding sentence (结尾语)

6. Signature (签名)

7. Seal (盖印)

(Adapted from

http://www.lawtime.cn/info/hetong/yingwen/2010031036234.html/

https://wenku.baidu.com/view/cd4e4d8b84254b35eefd349f.html?rec_flag=

default&sxts=1553678623540/)

【Sample 1】

出 口 合 同
SALES CONTRACT

合同号 / S/C No.:

日　期 / DATE:

卖方：

SELLER:

ADD:

FAX: TEL:

买方：

BUYER:

ADD:

FAX: TEL:

兹经双方同意,按下列条款达成如下交易：

The Seller and the Buyer have agreed to close the following transactions according to the following conditions stipulated below:

1. 商品：

Commodity:

商品名称、规格 Commodity, Specification	数　量 Quantity	单　位 Unit	单　价 Unit Price	金　额 Amount
总计 / TOTAL:				

（允许卖方在装货时溢装或短装_____%,价格按照本合同所列的单价计算。）

(The Sellers are allowed to load the quantity with _____% more or less, the price shall be calculated according to the unit price stipulated in this contract.)

2. 包装：

Packing:

3. 唛头：

Shipping mark:

由卖方决定,除非在装运前得到买方的及时通知。

To be designated by the sellers, unless otherwise advised by the Buyer in time before shipment.

4. 装运：

Shipment:

从_____口岸到_____,分批_____, 转船_____

From _____ to _____, Partial shipment _____, Transshipment _____ .

5. 检验：

Inspection:

6. 保险：

Insurance:

按发票金额的110%投保。

To be covered for 110% of invoice value.

7. 付款：

Payment:

开立100%不可撤销的_____天信用证。提交装运单据到中国任一银行议付。信用证必须于_____到达卖方,并保证于装运后15天内在中国有效。

By 100% irrevocable L/C payable at _____ sight and negotiable against presentation of shipping documents to any bank in China. The L/C must reach the Sellers on _____ and is to remain valid in China for 15 days after the date of shipment.

8. 不可抗力：

Force Majeure:

如由于战争、地震、水灾、火灾、暴风雨、雪灾或其他不可抗力的原因,致使卖方不能全部或部分装运或延期装运合同货物,卖方对这种不能装运或延期装运本合同货物不负有责任。卖方须于 15 天内用传真通知买方。

The sellers shall not be held responsible for late delivery or non-delivery for all or part of the contracted goods owing to such Force Majeure causes as war, earthquake, flood, conflagration, rainstorm and snowstorm. However, in such a case, the sellers shall inform the buyers by fax within 15 days.

9. 异议与索赔：

Discrepancy and Claim:

货物到达目的地后,买方若对货物的质量/数量/重量有异议,应在货物到达目的地后 15 天内凭卖方承认的公众鉴定人出具的检验证明向卖方提出,否则卖方将不承担责任。对由不可抗力造成的损失,或属于承运人或保险人责任范围内的,卖方不予赔偿。任何一方未按上述规定的期限履约,无论是卖方没有发运还是买方没有开证,或者信用证不符合合同条款而买方又没有及时修改,对方都有权解除合同,并向另一方索赔补偿直接损失。遭受不可抗力除外。

In case any discrepancy on quality/quantity/weight of the goods is found by the Buyers after the goods arrive at the port of destination, claim which should be loaded with the Sellers within 15 days after the goods arrive at the port of destination; otherwise the sellers will not undertake the responsibility. However, the Sellers shall not be held responsible either for compensation of loss(es) due to natural cause(s) or for that (those) within the responsibility of the Ship owners or Underwriters. In the event either the Sellers fail to effect the shipment or the Buyers fail to establish the relevant L/C within the respective time limits as set forth in the above, or the L/C does not correspond with the Contract terms and the Buyers fail to amend it in time, the Complaining Party shall have the right to cancel this contract and to claim on the Party at fault for compensation of direct losses if any, sustained there from, unless in cases where Force Majeure is applicable.

10. 仲裁：

Arbitration:

凡因执行本合同所发生的或与本合同有关的一切争议,双方应通过协商解决;如果协商不能解决,应提交北京中国国际经济贸易仲裁委员会,根据该会的仲裁规则进行仲裁。仲裁裁决是最终的,对双方都有约束力。仲裁费用除仲裁机构另有规定外,均由败诉方承担。

Any dispute arising from the execution of, or in connection with, this Contract shall be settled through Arbitration Commission of China, for settlement by arbitration in accordance with the Commission's Provisional Rules of Procedures. The award and decision made by the Commission shall be final and binding on both parties. The arbitration charges, unless otherwise stipulated by the arbitration unit, shall all be born by the party losing the lawsuit.

11. 本合同以中文和英文两种文字书就,两种文字的条款具有同等效力。

This contract is issued in both Chinese and English, the clauses in which have the same effects.

12. 其他条款/Other Terms:

请签署后退回一份,供我方存档。/Please sign and return one copy for our file.

卖方:　　　　　　　　　　买方:

Seller:　　　　　　　　　Buyer:

【Sample 2】

CONTRACT

Contract No.:

Date:

The Buyer:

Add:

Tel:　　　　　　　　Fax:

Contact person:

E-mail:

The Seller: HANGZHOU SOFT SILK DRESSES IMP. & EXP. CO., LTD.

Add: 5TH FLOOR, JINGHUA BUILDING, NO.9, HIGHWAY G156, HANGZHOU CITY, ZHEJIANG PROVINCE, CHINA

Tel and Fax: 0086-0571-1234567

Contact person:

E-mail:

This contract is made by and between the buyer and the seller, whereby the buyer agrees to buy and the seller agrees to sell the commodity according to the terms and conditions stipulated hereunder:

1. DESCRIPTION OF COMMODITY AND PRICE:

Item	Description	Q'ty	CIF XX Port, (Country/Area) in USD	
			Unit Price	Amount
1	XXX			
2	XXX			
	SAY IN TOTAL XXXXX (IN CAPITAL) US DOLLARS AND XX CENTS ONLY.			

2. SPECIFICATIONS

The seller guarantees that the commodity will be tested strictly before the delivery, the commodity is brand new, and the quality, specifications and technical requirement of the commodity are in accordance with the factory standard.

3. PAYMENT

ⅰ. The payment is made out to be XX% deposit within 10 calendar days from the date of signing this contract by T/T, (100-XX)% by T/T before delivery.

ⅱ. irrevocable L/C at sight.

ⅲ. irrevocable usance L/C 90/180/360 days with/without confirmation.

ⅳ. O/A 90/180/270/360 days after shipment date.

Bank details of the seller:

ⅰ. BANK OF CHINA LTD HANGZHOU BRANCH

ADD.: B.O.C. TOWER, 58 QINHE ROAD, HANGZHOU, ZHEJIANG, P.R. CHINA

POSTCODE: 310000

SWIFT CODE: BKCHCNBJ100

ACCOUNT: HANGZHOU SOFT SILK DRESSES IMP & EXP CO., LTD

ACCOUNT NO. (USD): 1234567890

ACCOUNT NO. (EURO): 8765432101

ACCOUNT NO. (RMB): 1357901113

ⅱ. AGRICULTURAL BANK OF CHINA JINING BRANCH

SWIFT CODE: ABOCCNBJ200

ACCOUNT: HANGZHOU SOFT SILK DRESSES IMP & EXPCO., LTD

ACCOUNT NO. (USD): 191817654321

4. TIME OF SHIPMENT

Under CIF XX Port, (Country/Area) terms, the commodity should be prepared for transport to the loading port within XX calendar days after receiving the deposit payment.

5. PORT OF SHIPMENT

Main port (Shanghai/Tianjin/Qingdao) of China

6. PORT OF DESTINATION

XX port, XX

7. SHIPMENT

By sea, in container/in bulk vessel

Under CIF XX port, XX Terms.

The transshipment is accepted/not accepted. The partial shipment is allowed/not allowed.

8. PACKING

The packing of the commodity shall be in accordance with the export standard packing of the manufacturer, be suitable for long distance transportation of ocean and inland.

9. SHIPPING MARK

10. INSURANCE

Covering All Risks for 110% of CIF Invoice Value to be effected by the Seller.

11. DOCUMENTS

The following documents will be submitted to the Buyer:

1) Bill of Lading: Three (3) originals bills of lading clean on board and three non-negotiable copies,

2) Commercial Invoice,

3) Packing list,

4) Quality Certificate: (optional, depending on the market)

5) Origin Certificate: (optional, depending on the market)

6) Inspection Certificate: (optional, depending on the market)

12. WARRANTY

12 months from B/L date or 2000 working hours, whichever comes first.

13. LICENSE, DUTIES AND TAXES

Except as otherwise provided herein, all import permits and licenses and the import duties, customs fees and all taxes levied by any government authority other than the Seller's country shall be the sole responsibility of the Buyer.

14. ARBITRATION

All disputes in connection with this contract or the execution thereof shall be settled through friendly negotiation. In case no settlement can be reached, the disputes shall be submitted for arbitration to China International Economic and Trade Arbitration Commission which shall be trialed in Beijing and conducted in accordance with the Commission's arbitration rules in effect at the time of applying for arbitration. The arbitral award should be final and binding upon both parties. Arbitration fee shall be borne by the losing party.

15. LATE PAYMENT

If the payment is not made to the seller according to the payment terms under this contract, the Buyer shall pay compensation fees to the Seller; such compensation fees are 0.5% of amount payable for each full month considering of 30-60 days deferred payment. If the time doesn't reach one full month but more than fifteen days, it will be treated as one full month.

16. FORCE MAJEURE

The Seller will not be held responsible for failure or delay to perform all or any part of this contract due to Acts of God, Restraint of the Government, Strikes, Lockouts, Industrial Disturbances, War, Blockades, Insurrections, Riots, Epidemics, Civil Disturbances,

Explosions, Fires, Floods, Earthquakes, Storms, Lightnings or any other events which could not be predicted, controlled, avoided or overcome by the Seller. However, the Seller affected by the event of Force Majeure shall inform the Buyer of its occurrence in writing as soon as possible and thereafter sends a certificate of the event issued by the relevant authorities to the Buyer within 15 days after its occurrence.

17. GOVERNING LAW

This contract and its revisions, amendments are made, signed and executed in accordance with the laws of the People's Republic of China.

18. ASSIGNMENT

Neither party shall have the right to directly or indirectly assign, transfer or designate rights and/or obligations hereunder, in whole or in part, to any third party without prior written consent of the other party.

19. MISCELLANEOUS

No oral agreement, promise, statement or mutual understanding, which may affect this contract, shall be recognized or enforceable.

Any notice, requirement, amendments, acknowledgment, waiver or request brought forward based on this contract shall be made in writing through negotiations by both parties. A notice shall be deemed duly received by its addressee if it is sent by courier service.

20. CONTRACT SIGNING

This contract is made in English in two originals, with each party keeping one. Both parties agree to honor the confidentiality of this contract.

21. EFFECTIVENESS

This contract is coming into force dating from the stamp and the signature of authorized representatives from the Seller and the Buyer.

The Buyer: XXXXXXXXXX	The Seller: Hangzhou SOFT Silk Dresses Import & Export Co., Ltd.
_____ (Name) (Title)	_____ (Name) (Title)

Words & Expressions

| party | /ˈpɑːtɪ/ | n. | one of the people or groups who are involved in a legal argument or agreement(法律争议或协议 |

的)一方

breach	/briːtʃ/	*n.*	(~ **of**) an action that breaks a law, rule, or agreement 违背,违反
sophisticated	/səˈfɪstɪˌkeɪtɪd/	*adj.*	clever and complicated in the way that it works or is presented 复杂巧妙的;先进的;精密的
precedent	/ˈprɛsɪdənt/	*n.*	an action or official decision that can be used to give support to later actions or decisions 可援引的先例
parol	/pəˈrəʊl/	*adj.*	expressed or given by word of mouth 口头的
deprecate	/ˈdɛprɪkeɪt/	*v.*	to strongly disapprove of or criticize something 坚决反对;强烈批评
duress	/djʊˈrɛs/	*n.*	illegal or unfair threats 胁迫,威逼
lease	/liːs/	*n.*	a legal agreement which allows you to use a building, car etc for a period of time, in return for rent (房子、汽车等的)租约,租契
countersignature	/ˌkaʊntəˈsɪgnətʃə/	*n.*	a second confirming signature endorsing a document already signed 副署,连署;会签
memorandum	/ˌmɛməˈrændəm/	*n.*	a short legal document that contains the important details of an agreement 协议;备忘录
preamble	/priːˈæmbəl/	*n.*	a statement at the beginning of a book, document, or talk, explaining what it is about (书、文件、讲话的)前言,序言;开场白
duration	/djʊˈreɪʃən/	*n.*	the length of time that something continues 持续时间
termination	/ˌtɜːmɪˈneɪʃən/	*n.*	the act of ending something, or the end of something 结束,终止,停止
arbitration	/ˌɑːbɪˈtreɪʃən/	*n.*	the process of judging officially how an argument should be settled 仲裁;公断
jurisdiction	/ˌdʒʊərɪsˈdɪkʃən/	*n.*	the right to use an official power to make legal decisions, or the area where this right exists 司法权;审判权;管辖权;管辖区域
stipulate	/ˈstɪpjʊˌleɪt/	*v.*	if an agreement, law, or rule stipulates something, it must be done (协议、法律、规则等)规定,约定
conflagration	/ˌkɒnfləˈgreɪʃən/	*n.*	a very large fire that destroys a lot of buildings, forests, etc. 大火
hereunder	/ˌhɪərˈʌndə/	*adv.*	(in documents, etc.) below this; subsequently; hereafter (文件等中)在下文中

usance	/ˈjuːzəns/	*n.*	the period of time permitted by commercial usage for the redemption of foreign bills of exchange (商业用国外支票的支付)期限
defer	/dɪˈfɜː/	*v.*	to delay something until a later date 延期，推迟
miscellaneous	/ˌmɪsəˈleɪnɪəs/	*adj.*	a miscellaneous set of things or people includes many different things or people that do not seem to be connected with each other (物或人)各种各样混在一起的，混杂的；多种多样的
in the event of			如果，万一
in nature			本质上，事实上
prior to			先于，在前，在之前，在……之前
set forth			阐明；陈述
correspond with			符合，一致
in accordance with			依照；与……一致
in effect			实际上；生效
come into force			生效；开始实施

Notes & Terms

Unconscionability	A defense against the enforcement of a contract or portion of a contract. If a contract is unfair or oppressive to one party in a way that suggests abuses during its formation, a court may find it unconscionable and refuse to enforce it. A contract is most likely to be found unconscionable if both unfair bargaining and unfair substantive terms are shown. An absence of meaningful choice by the disadvantaged party is often used to prove unfair bargaining. 显失公平
Force Majeure	Force majeure refers to a clause that is included in contracts to remove liability for natural and unavoidable catastrophes that interrupt the expected course of events and restrict participants from fulfilling obligations. 不可抗力
Recitals	statements of fact as they pertain to an agreement. They lay out the context and purpose of the agreement, providing courts with an indication of each party's intent should disputes arise and the agreement be challenged. Well-crafted recitals are an essential part of any contract.(契约等中)陈述事实的部分
Transshipment	the shipment of goods or containers to an intermediate destination, then to another destination. Transshipment usually takes place in

transport hubs. Much international transshipment also takes place in designated customs areas, thus avoiding the need for customs checks or duties, otherwise a major hindrance for efficient transport. Transshipment is normally fully legal and an everyday part of world trade. However, it can also be a method used to disguise intent, as is the case with illegal logging, smuggling, or grey-market goods. 转运

China International Economic and Trade Arbitration Commission

The China International Economic and Trade Arbitration Commission (CIETAC) is permanent arbitration institutions. CIETAC independently and impartially resolves economic and trade disputes by means of arbitration. With its headquarters in Beijing, CIETAC also has sub-commissions in Shenzhen, Shanghai, Tianjin and Chongqing, respectively known as the CIETAC South China Sub-Commission, Shanghai Sub-Commission, Tianjin International Economic Financial Arbitration Center (Tianjin Sub-Commission) and Southwest Sub-Commission. The aim of the CIETAC South China Sub-Commission office is "to conciliate foreign-related economic and trade disputes in the special zone and to take cognizance of arbitration application for the Foreign Economic and Trade Arbitration Commission. With the approval of the Arbitration Commission the arbitral tribunal could conduct proceedings in Shenzhen, and provide arbitration and legal consultancy services". The office is under the direct leadership of CCPIT in respect of its arbitration business and it is under the leadership of the Shenzhen Municipal Government in terms of personnel and administrative affairs. 中国国际经济贸易仲裁委员会

Understanding the text

I. Complete the following summary of the text.

Meeting the requirements and _____ of the law, contracts govern the rights and duties of the parties and are usually about the exchange of goods, services, money, or promises of any of those. On one hand, contracts may be _____ or unilateral; on the other hand, oral or written. Widely used in commercial law, contracts form the legal foundation for transactions across the world. A business contract is a _____ written agreement and regulates rights and obligations of the parties concerned. The party will send a Sales Contract or a _____ Contract to the other to ask for counter-signature. In sending out the contracts or confirmation,

special attention should be paid to the price, terms of payment, specifications, _____,
quantity, time of delivery, port of destination, etc. A business contract can be in different
forms, such as Contract, Agreement, Confirmation, Memorandum, Order, etc.

Ⅱ. Read the text and decide whether the following statements are true (T) or false (F).

(   ) 1   A contract is bound by law and governs the rights of the parties to the agreement.

(   ) 2   If one party breaches the contract, the injured party can get access to legal remedies
by law.

(   ) 3   In a unilateral contract, two parties make a promise or set of promises to each other.

(   ) 4   Before signing the contract, terms must be given to the other party as a reasonable
notice.

(   ) 5   The Sales Contract is made by the seller in business.

Ⅲ. Answer the following questions according to the text.

1. What are the common forms of a contract?

2. What does a business contract mean?

3. What elements are included in a business contract?

4. What's the difference between Sales Contract and Purchase Contract?

5. What factors should be considered before sending out the contracts or confirmation?

Language Work

Ⅰ. Choose the best choice to complete each of the following sentences.

1. If one party wants to _____ the contract before the terms are up, he/she should notify the
other party.

    A. end   B. finish   C. terminate   D. eliminate

2. A business agreement needs to properly name the _____ and use clear and concise
language to accurately describe the deal and the proper execution of the agreement.

    A. companies   B. parties   C. sides   D. opponents

3. The contract is made out in English and Chinese languages in quadruplicate, both texts being
equally _____, and each Party shall hold two copies of each text.

    A. genuine   B. real   C. approved   D. authentic

4. The contract shall be governed by and construed _____ the laws of the People's Republic
of China.

    A. in accordance with   B. conformed to

    C. consistent with   D. identical to

5. If the Buyer will not make payment according to the article _____ in this contract, the
Seller will not make delivery.

    A. stipulated   B. prescribed   C. regulated   D. enforced

II. Match the English words in the left column with the English explanations in the right column.

_____ 1. amendment   A. a moral or legal duty to do something

_____ 2. execute   B. to promise to do something or to promise that something will happen

_____ 3. obligation   C. a small change, improvement, or addition that is made to a law or document, or the process of doing this

_____ 4. guarantee   D. a product that is bought and sold

_____ 5. commodity   E. to do something that has been carefully planned

III. Translate the following sentences from the text into Chinese.

1. This contract is made by and between the buyer and the seller, whereby the buyer agrees to buy and the seller agrees to sell the commodity according to the terms and conditions stipulated hereunder.

_____
_____.

2. In case no settlement can be reached, the disputes shall be submitted for arbitration to China International Economic and Trade Arbitration Commission which shall be trialed in Beijing and conducted in accordance with the Commission's arbitration rules in effect at the time of applying for arbitration.

_____
_____.

3. However, the Seller affected by the event of Force Majeure shall inform the Buyer of its occurrence in writing as soon as possible and thereafter sends a certificate of the event issued by the relevant authorities to the Buyer within 15 days after its occurrence.

_____
_____.

4. No oral agreement, promise, statement or mutual understanding, which may affect this contract, shall be recognized or enforceable.

_____
_____.

5. This contract is made in English in two originals, with each party keeping one.

_____
_____.

IV. Translate the following sentences into English using the proper forms of the words or expressions given in brackets.

1. 为避免违反合同或发生争议,双方都应该意识到签订合同的重要性。(be aware of)

_____

2. 保险可以由买方或卖方投保。(cover)

3. 本合同自双方签字盖章之日起生效。(come into force)

4. 卖方保证所供货物在发货前经过严格测试,保证货物是全新的。(guarantee)

5. 卖方要确保本合同规定下的所有货物安全按时完好地交付买方指定的承运人。(nominated)

Supplementary Reading: How to Write a Business Contract

Business contracts are crucial to the relationships between companies and business partners. Contracts specify the terms of agreements, services or products to be exchanged and any deadlines associated with the partnership. Business contracts prevent disputes and misunderstandings, providing for legal remedies if one party does not uphold his end of the contract. Use these tips to write a business contract for your company. Knowing how to write a business contract can protect you and your business.

Determine if all parties are legally able to participate.

The contract will not be valid unless everyone entering into the contract is fully able to understand what they are signing.

Evaluate the contract's consideration.

In a legal contract, something of value must be exchanged for something else of value. This is known as "consideration", and a contract cannot exist without it. Two types of goods or services can be exchanged, though most contracts involve the exchange of a product or service for money.

Oftentimes businesses that are involved in selling goods must buy these goods from a manufacturer. To guarantee quantity, quality, and date of delivery, they will often enter into a contract setting out the terms of the sale. Here the manufacturer is giving the business something of value (goods) in exchange for something else of value (money).

Determine the legal purpose of the contract.

The purpose of the contract (the exchange of consideration) should be established clearly. In creating a legal contract, the purpose of the contract may not be illegal. A contract for an illegal exchange is not valid.

Set the terms of the agreement.

For a contract to be legal and binding, an offer must be clearly made and accepted. Before you write up a final contract, both parties should have the same idea about what the contract will stipulate. A contract that does not suit the needs of both parties will have to be altered.

A basic contract may already be on the table before final terms are agreed to. Before the contract is finalized, both the offering party and the accepting party should agree to all terms in the contract. When an offer is made, and the other party — while responding favorably — includes additional or alternate terms in his response, that is considered to be a counteroffer, not an agreement.

Come to an agreement in good faith. Good faith — an understanding that both sides will fulfill the requirements of the agreement — is presumed to be the basis of all contracts. The exact definition of good faith may vary, but it generally refers to the duty to act honestly toward the other parties to the contract. When a party does not act in good faith, the contract may have been breached. There are a few activities that courts consider a violation of the good-faith agreement. Lying about the condition of a property, bribing the agent who signed the contract, or outright violations of the agreement all serve to demonstrate a breach of good faith.

In some cases, verbal agreements are considered legal contracts. Generally speaking, verbal agreements are legally binding, as long as they can be proven. For example, if your business is considering hiring a specific wholesaler to provide a certain product, the wholesaler should quote you a price for it. If you call the wholesaler and verbally accept the terms of the agreement, you have entered into a contract. Generally, it is better to get a contract in writing. Written contracts do a better job of preventing confusion about terms and assist all parties in understanding their obligations. To avoid accidentally accepting a verbal contract, ask for a written statement declaring the price and other terms before accepting anything verbally.

Writing the Contract

1. Begin with the basic information.

Write the date at the top of the page, then write the names or company names of both parties in this format: " This contract is between _____ and _____." If there is identifying information you want to include, such as a title or business designation, include it here. If you are contracting on behalf of a business, include both the business name and the names of the people who are authorized to contract on behalf of the business. This could include names of the

CEO, president or director.

2. Detail the exchange of items.

Clearly describe what services or goods are being exchanged. For example, "Business A agrees to provide 100 sweaters per month to Business B. Business A will charge $ 20 per sweater for a total of $ 2,000 to be paid in full by business B within 30 days of delivery."

Use plain language, rather than legalese. If you end up going to court, the judge will adjudicate the case based on how the contract would be interpreted by the average person.

Use concise language. It should explain what one business is offering and promising to deliver and what the other business agrees to pay or do in exchange. State exactly what is being sold. If payments are to be made, include acceptable means of making payments (cash, check, or credit card, for example) as well as the amounts that will be due and the due dates.

If your business is selling property, provide a legal description of the property and its exact location. The description may pinpoint the location of the subject property within its particular Township, Range and Section. To find the legal description of a property, go to the records office nearest the property. The clerk there can look up the legal description based on the address. Additionally, some property deeds include the legal description.

When selling goods or services, describe them in detail. Describe the color, size, make, model, delivery date and any other identifying details. If services are in consideration, indicate what services will be performed. Specify who will perform the services, for whom, where, when, for how long and for how much money or other consideration.

3. Consider adding a confidentiality clause.

If you don't want the other party to share the information in the contract with others, you can add a confidentiality clause. All businesses have some important, confidential information, be it a sales plan, a recipe, or the company's marketing strategy. Companies often insert a confidentiality clause into an employment contract if the employee will deal with sensitive information. This type of clause is not necessary when the other party to the contract will not be exposed to any secret information.

The basic principles of a confidentiality clause are similar to those of non-disclosure agreements. You may also want to include a non-compete clause, which would prohibit someone from engaging in a similar service for a competitor for a given period of time (such as one year) after termination of employment with you. A confidentiality clause can be worded like this: "The parties acknowledge that each may receive or have access to confidential information. For the purposes of this agreement, the party that receives the confidential information will not reveal this information to anyone for any reason."

4. Add dispute resolution terms to the contract.

The contract should specify how the issue will be handled if a breach occurs. Note who will pay attorney's fees and court costs, and what the remedy for breach is. Also note the district in which disputes will be settled, particularly if the parties to the contract reside or are licensed in different localities.

If a party to the contract breaches, and lawyers get involved, it is usually customary for each party to pay their own legal fees. However, parties can require the losing side in a legal dispute to pay the winner's attorney's fees. To include a provision for payment of attorney fees, include language such as: "The winning party has the right to collect from the other party its reasonable costs and attorney's fees incurred in enforcing this Agreement."

5. Include a clause describing the termination of the contract.

Specify how long the contract will last. If it's for a one-time exchange of services, state that it will be terminated upon completion of the transaction. If it's a contract for ongoing services, you may want to state terms for either party to terminate the contract.

The contract should contain language allowing for termination if one party is in violation of the agreement, including a provision for how much termination notice should be given (such as two weeks). For example, you could include language stating what constitutes a breach and what the other party will do if there is a breach: "If Company X does not deliver [the product] within three weeks of signing this Agreement, X has breached the contract. Company Y is entitled to buy [the product] from another vendor and recover any difference in price from Company X." If neither party breaches the contract, it will terminate whenever the performance is completed. This does not need to be explicitly spelled out in the contract. Whenever both parties have done everything the contract stipulates, the contract will automatically terminate.

6. Make sure the contract is in accordance with applicable law.

Research which laws pertain to the contract so you can ensure that it is legally enforceable. For example, certain contracts must be in writing to be enforceable. Additionally, different places have different rules regarding the way contracts are interpreted if there is a breach.

7. Reserve the last page for the parties to sign and date the contract.

Provide spaces for each name and accompanying dates.

8. Hire a lawyer to review your contract.

A lawyer can ensure that your contract is written in accordance with applicable law. She/He can also help with the termination clause, suggesting appropriate cover (recovery of losses) in the case of a breach of contract.

(Adapted from https://www.wikihow.com/Write-a-Business-Contract/)

Words & Expressions

| uphold | /ʌpˈhəʊld/ | v. | to defend or support a law, system, or principle so that it continues to exist 支持,维护(法规、制度或原则) |

facilitate	/fəˈsɪlɪteɪt/	v.	to make it easier or more likely to happen 促进
counteroffer	/ˈkaʊntərɔːfə/	n.	an offer that someone makes, for example, for a house or business, in response to an offer by another person or group 还价
violation	/ˌvaɪəˈleɪʃn/	n.	an action that breaks a law, agreement, principle, etc. (对法律、协议、原则等的)违背,违反
bribe	/braɪb/	v.	to illegally give someone, especially a public official, money or a gift in order to persuade them to do something for you 贿赂,收买
outright	/ˌaʊtˈraɪt/	adj.	complete and total 完全的,彻底的
designation	/dezɪɡˈneɪʃən/	n.	a name or title 名称,称号
authorize	/ˈɔːθəraɪz/	v.	to give official permission for something 授权,批准,许可
legalese	/liːɡəˈliːz/	n.	language used by lawyers that is difficult for most people to understand 法律术语,法律用语
adjudicate	/əˈdʒuːdɪkeɪt/	v.	to make an official decision about who is right in a disagreement between two groups or organizations 判决,裁决
pinpoint	/ˈpɪnpɒɪnt/	v.	to discover or explain exactly the real facts about something or the cause of a problem 查明,准确地说出,描述(事实真相)
confidentiality	/ˌkɒnfɪˌdenʃɪˈælɪtɪ/	n.	a situation in which you trust someone not to tell secret or private information to anyone else 机密,秘密;保密
acknowledge	/əkˈnɒlɪdʒ/	v.	to admit or accept that something is true or that a situation exists 承认(某事属实或某情况存在)
localities	/ləʊˈkælɪtɪs/	n.	a small area of a country, city, etc. 地区
provision	/prəˈvɪʒən/	n.	a condition in an agreement or law (协议或法律中的)规定,条款,条件
enter into			进入;讨论;成为……的一部分
in exchange for			作为……的交换
on the table			公开地
on behalf of			代表;为了
be exposed to			接触;遭受;暴露;面对
be entitled to			有权;有……的资格
spell out			讲清楚
pertain to			关于;从属于;适合

Notes & Terms

CEO　　The chief executive officer (CEO) or just chief executive (CE), is the most senior corporate, executive, or administrative officer in charge of managing an organization — especially an independent legal entity such as a company or nonprofit institution. CEOs lead a range of organizations, including public and private corporations, non-profit organizations and even some government organizations (e. g., Crown corporations). The CEO of a corporation or company typically reports to the board of directors and is charged with maximizing the value of the entity, which may include maximizing the share price, market share, revenues or another element. In the non-profit and government sector, CEOs typically aim at achieving outcomes related to the organization's mission, such as reducing poverty, increasing literacy, etc. 首席执行官,一种高级职务名称。在经济组织机构中,首席执行官是在一个企业中负责日常事务的最高行政官员,主司企业行政事务,又称作司政、行政总裁、总经理或最高执行长。在政治组织机构中,首席执行官为政府首脑,相当于部长会议主席、总理、首相、行政院院长、政府主席等级别的行政事务最高负责高官。

Text Comprehension

Choose the best answer to each of the following questions according to the text.

1. For companies and business partners, there are many factors to consider before signing a contract EXECPT _____.

　　A. to confirm all parties' legal participation

　　B. to consider the contract's evaluation

　　C. to determine the legal purpose of the contract

　　D. to establish the terms of the agreement

2. How to make the exchange of items clearly in a contract?

　　A. Using plain language instead of legalese.

　　B. Stating the products sold exactly.

　　C. Describing goods or services in detail.

　　D. All of the above.

3. What situation is NOT necessary for adding a confidentiality clause in the contract?

　　A. One party shares the information in the contract with others.

　　B. One party has some important, confidential information of the company.

　　C. One party has sensitive information of the company.

　　D. One party has no secret information of the company.

4. According to the passage, which of the following is TRUE?

A. In the contract, there is no need to specify which party will pay attorney's fees and court costs.

B. Once a contract is signed, there is no time limit upon completion of the transaction.

C. The winning party has the right to require the other party to pay for attorney fees.

D. The contract will not terminate even if both parties have done everything the contract stipulates.

5. Why is it important for a company to hire a lawyer to review the contract?

A. A lawyer can check if the contract meets the law and helps to recover the losses.

B. Lawyer can suggest the breach of the contract.

C. Lawyer can help to research which laws pertain to the contract.

D. A lawyer can handle all issues in a breach of the contract.

Language Work

Fill in the following blanks with the words or phrases given below. Change the forms where necessary.

set up	dispute	right	apply to	indication
set in	concern	contribute	apply for	commerce

1. Shanghai plans to expand its e-stamp service for enterprises engaging in trade and investment, E-commerce and contracts, and individuals will be able to _____ an e-stamp for their community affairs such as medical and health insurance.

2. According to the law, The State protects the investment, income and other legitimate _____ and interests of foreign investors in China.

3. The Foreign Investment Law has corrected many deficiencies of the previous laws and it has _____ lots of rules at the institutional level to protect foreign investment.

4. The law protects the intellectual property rights and encourages technology cooperation based on voluntary principles and _____ rules.

5. According to the research, cases accepted by the court were _____ involving securities, financial borrowing contracts, corporate bond trading, financial lease contracts and business trust.

Workshop

Presentation: Work in a group and discuss how to write a business contract legally. Write either Purchase Contract or Sales Contract based on the samples given and make a presentation in the class.

References

[1] 李蕾. 商务英语函电[M]. 北京：对外经济贸易大学出版社,2015.

[2] 杨荔,刘彩勤. 商务英语函电阅读与写作[M]. 北京：对外经济贸易大学出版社,2014.

[3] 叶晓英. 商务谈判英语即学即用[M]. 北京：对外经济贸易大学出版社,2011.

[4] https://wenku.baidu.com/view/cd4e4d8b84254b35eefd349f.html?rec_flag=default&sxts=1553678623540/, retrieved on 2019-03-25.

[5] http://www.lawtime.cn/info/hetong/yingwen/2010031036234.html/, retrieved on 2019-03-27.

[6] https://comcom.govt.nz/consumers/your-rights-as-a-consumer/unfair-contract-terms/, retrieved on 2019-03-25.

[7] http://www.australiancontractlaw.com/, retrieved on 2019-03-24.

[8] https://wenku.baidu.com/view/cd4e4d8b84254b35eefd349f.html?rec_flag=default&sxts=1553678623540/, retrieved on 2019-03-25.

[9] http://www.lawtime.cn/info/hetong/yingwen/2010031036234.html/, retrieved on 2019-03-27.

[10] http://www.europeanchamber.com.cn/en/past-events-archive/4426/Government_meeting_China_International_Economic_and_Trade_Arbitration_Commission_and_Members_of_European_Chamber/, retrieved on 2019-03-28.

[11] https://www.wikihow.com/Write-a-Business-Contract/, retrieved on 2019-03-27.

[12] https://en.wikipedia.org/wiki/Contract/, retrieved on 2019-03-27.

[13] https://language.chinadaily.com.cn/, retrieved on 2019-04-02.

[14] http://www.chinadaily.com.cn/business/.

[15] http://www.youdao.com/.

[16] https://baike.baidu.com/.

[17] https://www.law.cornell.edu/wex/unconscionability/.

[18] https://www.investopedia.com/terms/f/forcemajeure.asp/.

[19] https://baike.baidu.com/item/%E9%A6%96%E5%B8%AD%E6%89%A7%E8%A1%8C%E5%AE%98/26567?fr=aladdin/.

[20] https://en.wikipedia.org/wiki/Recital_(law)/.

[21] https://en.wikipedia.org/wiki/Transshipment/.

[22] http://www.chinalawwiki.com/index.php?title=The_China_International_Economic_and_Trade_Arbitration_Commission_(CIETAC)/.

[23] https://en.wikipedia.org/wiki/Chief_executive_officer/.

Appendix

Supplementary
Glossary

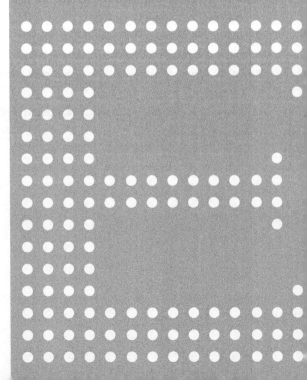

A

abandon *v.*	废弃
abandonment *n.*	撤销
abate *v.*	废止
abatement *n.*	冲销,扣减
ABC(Agent-Business-Consumer) *abbr.*	代理商-商家-消费者
abeyance *n.*	暂缓
abide *v.*	坚持,遵守
abolish *v.*	废除
abortive *adj.*	失败的(计划等)
abroad *adj.*	国外的
abrogate *v.*	废除,取消
absorb *v.*	分配
absorb the price difference *v.*	分担差价
absorption *n.*	分摊(费用等),合并,吸收
abstract *n.*	文摘,摘要
accede *v.*	继承,同意(勉强地)
accept *v.*	接受
accept the bid *v.*	接受投标
acceptance *n.*	承兑,承付,接受,验收
accepted letter of credit *n.*	已承兑信用证
acceptor *n.*	承兑人,承付人
access *n.*	通道,通过
accessory *n.*	附件
accident *n.*	事故
Accommodate *v.*	(房间、建筑物等)容纳
accordance *n.*	按照
account *n.*	账目,账户
accountant *n.*	会计师
accumulate *v.*	累计
accuracy *n.*	准确性
accusation *n.*	诉讼
achieve *v.*	达到,完成
achievement *n.*	成就
acknowledge *v.*	承认,收到通知
act *n.*	行为,行动

addition *n.*	补充
additions *n.*	增加,增添
address *n.*	地址
addressee *n.*	收电人,收件人,收信人
addresser *n.*	发电人,发件人,发信人
adjudication *n.*	裁决
adjust *v.*	调整
adjustment *n.*	调整
administer *n.*	管理
admission *n.*	准允
admonition *n.*	警告
adopt *v.*	采纳
adoption *n.*	采纳
adulterate *v.*	掺假,掺杂
advance *adj.*	垫付,提前的,预付,预付款,预支
advancing *adj.*	价格上涨
advantage *n.*	利益,优势
advertise *v.*	广告
advertisement *n.*	通告
Advertorial *n.*	付费文章(软文广告)
advice *n.*	建议,通知
affect *v.*	影响
affidavit *n.*	宣誓书
affiliate *n.*	分机构,联营
after-sale service *n.*	售后服务
agency *n.*	代理
agenda *n.*	备忘录,记录
agent *n.*	代理人
agent's staff *n.*	代理人的工作人员
aggregate *v.*	综合,总和,总计
aggregation *n.*	集团(公司的),集中(货物的)
air-condition *n.*	空气调节
air-freight *n.*	空运
airmail *n.*	航寄
airport *n.*	机场
alarm *n.*	警报,警告
allocate *v.*	拨(款),分配资金
allocation *n.*	分配,分摊

allotment *n.*	拨款,分配(预算的)
allowance *n.*	补助,津贴
alter *v.*	改动
alternative *adj.*	备选的,可替换的,选择性的
altitude *n.*	高度
aluminum window *n.*	铝窗
ambiguity *n.*	含糊
amend *v.*	修改
amendment *n.*	修改
amortization *n.*	摊还,摊销
amount *n.*	金额,总数
amusement *n.*	娱乐设施
analysis *n.*	分析
angle steel *n.*	角钢
annex *n.*	附件,附录
announce *v.*	宣布
announcement *n.*	通告
annuity *n.*	年金
annul *adj.*	取消,无效
answer *n.*	答复,回答
antedate *n.*	早填日期
anticipate *v.*	预见,预计
anticipation *n.*	预期
antique *n.*	古董,古物
APC (annual production capacity) *abbr.*	年生产能力
apparatus *n.*	仪器,装置
appeal *v.*	上诉
appeal to arbitration *v.*	诉诸仲裁
appear *v.*	刊登
appearance in court *n.*	出庭
appendix *n.*	附录
appendix to contract *n.*	合同附件
applicant *n.*	申请人
application *n.*	申请书,要保书
appoint *v.*	委派,约定
appraisal *n.*	鉴别,评价书
appraise *v.*	评价
appraiser *n.*	估价人

appreciation *n.*	增值,涨价
appropriate *adj.*	拨款,拨用
approval *n.*	批准
approve *v.*	批准
approved *adj.*	已批准的
approximate *adj.*	近似,约数
arbitral *adj.*	仲裁的
arbitrate a dispute *v.*	仲裁争端
arbitration *n.*	仲裁
arbitrator *n.*	仲裁员
architect *n.*	建筑师
architectural design *n.*	建筑设计
architectural engineer *n.*	建筑工程师
architecture *n.*	建筑设计,建筑学
area *n.*	地区,面积
argument *n.*	争论
arithmetical error *n.*	算术错误
arrange *v.*	安排
arrangement *n.*	安排
arrears *n.*	拖欠
arrestment *n.*	财产扣押
arrive *v.*	到达
arrow network *n.*	箭形网络图
article *n.*	条款,章程
article No. *n.*	货号
as well as	也;和……一样;不但……
Asian Development Bank *n.*	亚洲开发银行
ask *v.*	讨价,询问
ask for loan *v.*	告贷,借债
asked price *n.*	要价
assay *v.*	化验
assembly *n.*	装配
assess *v.*	估定,征收
assessor *n.*	估税员
assets *n.*	资产
assign *v.*	分派,指派
assignee *n.*	受让人
assigner *n.*	转让人

assignment	*n.*	转让
assignor	*n.*	转让人
assistance	*n.*	协助
assistant	*n.*	助理
assistant engineer	*n.*	助理工程师
assistant superintendent	*n.*	助理监督
associate	*v.*	联合
association	*n.*	协会
assortment	*n.*	花色(搭配)
assurer	*n.*	保险人
at sight	*adv.*	见票时
A-to-Z (Amazon A-to-Z Guarantee claim)	*n.*	亚马逊 A-to-Z 担保索赔
attach	*v.*	随附
attachment	*n.*	附件
attendance	*n.*	出席
attention	*n.*	注意
attestation	*n.*	证明,作证
attorney	*n.*	代理人,律师
auction	*n.*	拍卖
audit	*v.*	审计
authentication	*n.*	证明;鉴定;证实
authority	*n.*	当局,权力
authorization	*n.*	授权
authorize	*v.*	授权
autograph	*n.*	签署
available	*adj.*	可用的,有效的
avoid	*v.*	避免
avoidance	*n.*	避免
award	*n.*	判标,判给,授标,授予

B

B/L Bill of Lading	*n.*	海运提单
B/R Bill Rate	*n.*	买价
B2B	*abbr.*	经济组织对经济组织
B2B2C	*abbr.*	企业对企业对消费者
B2C	*abbr.*	经济组织对消费者
B2F	*abbr.*	企业对家庭

B2G *abbr.*	政府采购
B2M *abbr.*	面向市场营销的电子商务企业
B2S *abbr.*	分享式商务,或体验式商务
BAB *abbr.*	企业-联盟-企业
BAF Bunker Adjustment Factor *abbr.*	燃油附加费
balance *n.*	平衡,余额
balance sheet *n.*	收支平衡表,资产负债表,资产负债平衡表
ballast age *n.*	压仓费
bank *n.*	银行
bank account *n.*	银行账户
bankrupt *adj.*	破产的
bankruptcy *n.*	破产
banner *n.*	横幅广告
Banner Ad *n.*	横幅广告(网页顶部、底部或者侧边的广告展示位置)
barrel *n.*	桶(石油计量)
barrister *n.*	律师
barter *n.*	易货交易
basis *n.*	基准
BCR(benefits-costs ratio) *abbr.*	效益成本比率
be subject to	受支配,从属于;有……倾向的
bear *n.*	空头
bearer *n.*	持票人,持有人
bearer B/L *n.*	不记名提单
belated *adj.*	误期的
belated claim *n.*	迟索的赔款
beneficiary *n.*	受益人
benefit *n.*	利润,利益,效益
biased *adj.*	偏差,有偏见的
bid *v.*	投标
bidder *n.*	投标人
bidding *n.*	投标
bill *n.*	票据,期票,清单
bind *v.*	使确定不变,使受法律约束
binder *n.*	保险单,保证金
bond *n.*	保证金,债券
bonus *n.*	红利,奖金
book *n.*	订货

book-keeper *n.*	簿记员
BOQ (bill of quantity) *abbr.*	工程量表,工程量清单
borehole *n.*	钻孔
borrow *v.*	借用
borrower *n.*	借款人,借款者
boundary *n.*	界限
bouquet *n.*	一揽子
branch *n.*	分公司,分支
breach *v.*	违反
breakage *n.*	破坏
break-down *n.*	明细表
bribes *n.*	贿赂
brief *n.*	大纲,提要
broker *n.*	经纪人
brokerage *n.*	经纪人佣金,经纪业
broking *n.*	经纪业
browse *v.*	浏览(信息)
bubble *n.*	商业骗局
budget *n.*	预算
bulk *n.*	散装
bull *v.*	买空
bulletin *n.*	公报,公告
burden *n.*	间接费用
bureau *n.*	局
business *n.*	商务,生意
BUYBOX *n.*	黄金购物车
buyer *n.*	采购员,购买人,买主
by rail	由铁路,乘火车
by-law *n.*	细则,章程
by-product *n.*	副产品

C

C&F (cost and freight) *abbr.*	成本加运费
C(check) *abbr.*	检查
C(control) *abbr.*	控制
C.I.F.(cost insurance and freight) *abbr.*	成本,保险费加运费,到岸价
C.Q.D.(customary quick dispatch) *abbr.*	港口习惯快速装卸

C2B(T) *abbr.*	消费者集合竞价-团购
C2C *abbr.*	消费者对消费者
cancel *v.*	撤销,注销
cancellation *n.*	取消,撤销
capacity *n.*	容积
capital *n.*	资本
cargo *n.*	货物
cartage *n.*	搬运费,运货费
Cartel *n.*	卡特尔
case *n.*	案件
cash *n.*	现金
cashier *n.*	出纳员
casting *adj.*	浇筑,现浇的
casual *adj.*	非正式的,临时的
casualty *n.*	伤亡人员,意外
catalogue *n.*	商品目录
cater to	迎合;为……服务
CBA(cost-benefit analysis) *abbr.*	成本效益分析
centigrade *n.*	摄氏度
central bank *n.*	中央银行
ceramic tile *n.*	瓷砖,陶瓷面砖
ceremony *n.*	典礼,仪式
certificate *n.*	证明,证书
cessation *n.*	终止
CFR (Cost and Freight) *abbr.*	成本加运费价
chairman *n.*	董事长,主席
change *v.*	变更,改动
characteristics *n.*	性能
charge *v./n.*	费用,收费,索价
charter *n.*	公司执照
chattels *n.*	动产
check *v./n.*	检查
cheque *n.*	支票
choice *n.*	选择
CIF (Cost Insurance and Freight) *abbr.*	到岸价
CIP (Carriage and Insurance...) *abbr.*	运费保险费付至……
CIP (freight or carriage & insurance paid to) *abbr.*	运费,保险费付至

claim　*n.*	索偿,索赔,索赔金额,要求权
claimant　*n.*	索赔的债权人,索赔人
claimee　*n.*	索赔的债务人
claimer　*n.*	索赔人
clause　*n.*	(合同)条款
clear　*v.*	清除
clearance　*n.*	海关清税,清关
clerk　*n.*	办事人员
Click (Click through)　*n.*	点击量/点击次数 (用户点击广告的次数,评估广告效果的指标之一)
Click Rate (Click-through Rate)　*n.*	点击率/点进率 (网络广告被点击的次数与访问次数的比例), 即 clicks/impressions. 如果这个页面被访问了 100 次,而页面上的广告也被点击了 20 次,那么 CTR 为 20%,CTR 是评估广告效果的指标之一
client　*n.*	当事人,顾客,客户,业主
COD (cash on delivery)　*abbr.*	到货付款
code　*n.*	代码,法规
code of practice　*n.*	施工规范
coefficient　*n.*	系数
co-guarantor　*n.*	共同担保人
coincide　*v.*	符合,重合
co-insurance　*n.*	共同保险
collaborate　*v.*	合作
collateral　*n.*	抵押品
color sample　*n.*	色彩样品
combination　*n.*	合并,联合
commence　*v.*	开工
commitment　*n.*	承诺
committee　*n.*	委员会
commodity　*n.*	货物,商品
community　*n.*	公众,团体
compact　*n.*	契约
company　*n.*	公司
comparability　*n.*	可比性
compelling　*adj.*	极为有趣的;令人激动的;引人入胜的
compensation　*n.*	报酬,补偿,补贴
competency　*n.*	权限

competition	*n.*	竞争
competitive	*adj.*	竞争性的
competitiveness	*n.*	竞争力
competitor	*n.*	对手,竞争者
complain	*v.*	申诉,控诉
complainant	*n.*	起诉人,申诉人
complaint	*n.*	申诉,控诉
complement	*n.*	补充
complementary	*adj.*	补充的
complete	*v.*	完成
complexity	*n.*	复杂性;难懂
compliance	*n.*	屈从,依从
comprehensive	*adj.*	综合的
compromise	*v.*	和解,妥协
compute	*v.*	计算
concern	*n.*	担心,忧虑
concerned	*adj.*	有关的
concession	*n.*	让步,特许
conciliation	*n.*	调解,和解
concise	*adj.*	简洁的,简练的,简明的
conclude	*v.*	结束
conclusive	*adj.*	确定性的,最后的
concurrent	*adj.*	共同的,同时发生的
condemnation	*n.*	征用
condition	*n.*	条件
conference	*n.*	会议,会谈
confident	*adj.*	信任
confidential	*adj.*	机密的
confinancing	*n.*	联合贷款
confine	*v.*	限制
confirm	*v.*	保兑
confirmation	*n.*	确认,确认书
confiscate	*v.*	没收,征用
conflict	*n.*	冲突,抵触
conform	*v.*	依从,遵守
conformity	*n.*	符合,一致
confute	*v.*	驳斥
conjunction	*n.*	连接,连带

conjuncture　*n.*	行情
connect　*v.*	连接,联系
consent　*n.*	同意
consequence　*n.*	后果
consider　*v.*	考虑
consideration　*n.*	补偿,体谅
considering　*n.*	鉴于
consign　*v.*	托运,委托
consignee　*n.*	收货人,受托人
consignment　*n.*	代售
consistency　*n.*	一贯性,一致性
constrain　*v.*	强制
constraint　*adj.*	强制
construct　*v.*	建设
construction　*n.*	建设,建筑,施工
constructive　*adj.*	建设性的
construe　*v.*	解释
consulate　*n.*	领事馆
consult　*v.*	咨询
consultant　*n.*	顾问
consultation　*n.*	协商,咨询
consume　*v.*	消费
consumption　*n.*	消耗量
contact　*v.*	接触,联系
contain　*v.*	包含
container　*n.*	集装箱
content　*n.*	内容
contention　*n.*	争论
contestant　*n.*	争执方
context　*n.*	上下文
contingencies　*n.*	偶发事件
contingency　*n.*	意外事件
contraband　*n.*	禁运品,走私货
contract　*n.*	承包,合同
contrast　*n./v.*	对比,对立
contravene　*v.*	违反
contribute　*v.*	贡献
control　*v.*	控制

controller *n.*	检验员
controversy *n.*	争论
convene *v.*	召集
convenience *n.*	方便
convention *n.*	惯例
conventional *adj.*	常规的
conventions *n.*	风俗习惯
conversation *n.*	会话,会谈
conversion *n.*	转变;改造;转换;(金融)兑换,换算
convince *v.*	使确信,信服
convoke *v.*	召集
cook *n.*	厨师
cooperate *v.*	合作,协作
coordinate *v.*	协调
coordination *n.*	协调
copy *n.*	副本,复印件
copy-right *n.*	版权
copywriting *n.*	文案策划;文案写作
core *n.*	核心
corporate *adj.*	共同的
corporation *n.*	公司,股份有限公司,有限公司
corpus *n.*	本金
correspondence *n.*	符合,通信
correspondent *n.*	客户
correspondent bank *n.*	代理银行
corrigendum *n.*	勘误
corrosion *n.*	腐蚀,锈蚀
cost(s) *n.*	成本
costing *n.*	成本计算
costly *adj.*	昂贵的
council *n.*	会议,委员会
councilor *n.*	参赞,顾问
counsellor *n.*	参赞,顾问
count *v.*	计算
counter *n.*	反对,柜台
counter sample *n.*	对等样品
counterbalance *v.*	抵消
counterclaim *n.*	反索赔

counterfeit *n.*		假冒,伪造
counterpart *n.*		对方
course *n.*		科目
court *n.*		法庭
courtesy *n.*		礼节性会见
covenant *n.*		缔约,契约
cover *v.*		包括,保额,抵偿
coverage *n.*		保额
CPA (Cost Per Action) *abbr.*		每次动作成本
CPC (Cost Per Click; Cost Per Thousand Click-Through) *abbr.*		每点击成本
CPC (Cost-Per-Click) *abbr.*		点击付费站内广告(根据点击数付费)
CPM (Cost Per Mille, or Cost Per Thousand) *abbr.*		每千人成本
CPP (Cost Per Purchase) *abbr.*		每购买成本
CPR (Cost Per Response) *abbr.*		每回应成本
CPS (Cost Per Sales) *abbr.*		销售分成
CPT (Carriage Paid To…) *abbr.*		运费付至目的地
CR (Conversion Rate) *abbr.*		转化率(指访问某一网站访客中转化的访客占全部访客的比例)
crack *n.*		裂缝
craft *n.*		手艺
craft men *n.*		技工
credit *n.*		信贷,信任
credit card *n.*		信用卡
credit guarantee *n.*		贷款信用担保
creditor *n.*		借方
criterion *n.*		标准
critical *adj.*		关键的,重要的
CRM (Customer Relationship Management) *abbr.*		客户关系管理
currency *n.*		货币
current *adj.*		流动的
custody *n.*		保管
customer *n.*		顾客,买主
customs *n.*		关税,海关

D

D/A (documents against acceptance)	*abbr.*	承兑交单
D/D (demand draft)	*abbr.*	汇票
DAF (delivered at frontier)	*abbr.*	边境交货
damage	*n.*	赔偿,损害
danger	*n.*	危险
database	*n.*	数据库
date	*n.*	日期
DCF method (discounted cash flow method)	*abbr.*	资金流动折现评估法
DDP (delivered…duty paid)	*abbr.*	完税后交货
deal	*n.*	交易
dear	*adj.*	昂贵的
debasement	*n.*	贬值
debate	*n.*	辩论
debenture	*n.*	公司债券,无担保债券
debit	*n.*	借方
debt	*n.*	欠债,债务
debtor	*n.*	债务人
decade	*n.*	十个一组的数,旬
deceit	*n.*	诈骗
decide	*v.*	决定,判决
decision	*n.*	决定
declarant	*n.*	报关人,申请人
declaration	*n.*	报关单
declaration inwards	*n.*	进口报关单,入境报关单
declaration outwards	*n.*	出口报关单
declare	*v.*	申报
decrease	*v.*	减少
decrease in cost	*n.*	费用的减少
decree	*n./v.*	判决
deduct	*v.*	扣除
deed	*n.*	契约
default	*n.*	拖欠
defect	*n.*	缺陷
defendant	*n.*	被告

defer	*v.*	推迟
deficit	*n.*	赤字,亏空
definite	*adj.*	肯定的,明确的
definiteness	*n.*	肯定性
definition	*n.*	定义
deform	*v.*	变形
defraud	*v.*	诈骗
defray	*v.*	支付
delay	*v.*	拖延,延缓
delegate	*n.*	代表,委派
delete	*v.*	取消
deliver	*v.*	递交,制服
delivery	*n.*	交货
delve into		深入研究;钻研
demand	*v.*	需要,要求
demonstrate	*v.*	示范;演示
demurrage	*n.*	装运滞期费
denim	*n.*	粗斜棉布,劳动布
denomination	*n.*	单位,名称
denote	*v.*	指示
denounce	*v.*	通告废除
density	*n.*	密度
depart	*v.*	出发,违背
department	*n.*	部门
departure	*n.*	离开
depend	*v.*	依靠
depletion	*n.*	损耗,折损
deposit	*n.*	折扣
depreciation	*n.*	贬值,折旧
depression	*n.*	萧条
depth	*n.*	深度
depute	*v.*	委托
deputy	*n.*	代表,副手
describe	*v.*	描述
description	*n.*	描述,摘要,说明书
design	*n.*	设计
designate	*v.*	任命,指派
destination	*n.*	目的地

destination port *n.*	目的港
destroy *v.*	破坏
detail *n.*	细节
determine *v.*	决定
devaluation *n.*	贬值
devastate *v.*	毁坏
develop *v.*	发展,开发
diagram *n.*	图表
dimension *n.*	尺寸,度量
diminish *v.*	减少,减低
diplomatic *adj.*	外交的
director *n.*	董事,主任
disburse *v.*	拨款,支付
disbursement *n.*	支付
discharge *v.*	清偿
discontinue *v.*	停止,中断
discount *n.*	打折扣,贴现,折扣
discretion *n.*	处置权,自行处理
discrimination *n.*	歧视
discussion *n.*	讨论
dispatch *v.*	派遣
disproof *v.*	驳斥
dispute *n.*	争端,争议
disqualification *n.*	不合格,取消资格
district *n.*	地区
dividend *n.*	股息,红利
division *n.*	分部
document *n.*	文件
dollar *n.*	美元
domestic *adj.*	国内的
draw *v.*	提款
draw back *v.*	退税
drawee *n.*	付款人
drawing *n.*	冷拉
drone *n.*	无人驾驶飞机
DSP (Demand-Side Platform) *abbr.*	展示广告(即需求方平台)
due *adj.*	到期的,应付的
dues *n.*	会费,捐款

duly *adv.*   及时地,适当地

duplicate *adj.*   复制的,加倍的

duplicate sample *n.*   复样

duration *n.*   持续时间

duties *n.*   税金,职务

duty *n.*   关税

duty-free *adj.*   免税

E

EAN (European Article Number) *abbr.*   欧洲商品编码（13 位数的 GTIN 码,有时为 8 位数）

earnest *n.*   定金

ECC (estimate contract coverage) *abbr.*   预计合同范围

economy *n.*   经济,节约

EDI (Economic Development Institution) *abbr.*   经济发展学院

EDM *abbr.*   (Electronic Direct Marketing 的缩写) 电子邮件营销

EEC (European Economic Community) *abbr.*   欧洲经济共同体

effectiveness *n.*   有效性

efficiency *n.*   效率

efficient *adj.*   有效的

elevator *n.*   电梯

eligible *adj.*   合格的;有资格的

eliminate *v.*   消除,根除

embassy *n.*   大使馆

emergency *n.*   紧急情况

emigration *n.*   移民

employ *v.*   雇用

employee *n.*   雇员

end-user *n.*   用户

energy *n.*   能量,能源

enforce *v.*   强制,实施

engineer *n.*   工程师

engineering *n.*   工程

entertaining *adj.*   有趣的;娱乐的;使人愉快的

entrance *n.*   入境,入口

entrust	*v.*	委托
entry	*n.*	报关单,报关手续,登记,入境
enumeration	*n.*	细目
envelope	*n.*	包封,信封
equipment	*n.*	设备
equitable	*adj.*	公正的
equivalent	*adj.*	等量的,等值的
ERP (Enterprise Resource Planning)	*abbr.*	企业资源计划
escalator	*n.*	自动扶梯
escrow	*n.*	(协议未达成期间)暂由第三方保管的资金(地产,合约等)
essential	*adj.*	基本的,实质的
establish	*v.*	建立
estimate	*v.*	估算,预算
estimating	*n.*	估算
evaluate	*v.*	评价
evaluation	*n.*	评估
event	*n.*	事件
evidence	*n.*	凭证,证据
evoke	*v.*	引起,唤起
exact	*adj.*	正确的
except	*v.*	除外
exchange	*v.*	换汇,交换
exclude	*v.*	除外
exclusion	*n.*	除外责任
exclusive	*adj.*	独占的,专一的
exculpatory	*adj.*	开脱罪责的,无责任的
executive	*adj.*	执行者
exercise	*v.*	行使
ex-factory price	*n.*	工厂交货价
exhibition	*n.*	展览
exit-visa	*n.*	出境签证
expand	*v.*	扩展
expect	*v.*	预期
expedite	*v.*	加快速度
expend	*v.*	耗费
expenditures	*n.*	费用
expense	*n.*	开支

experience *n.*	经验
experiment *n.*	实验
expert *n.*	专家
expertise *n.*	鉴别
expiration *n.*	到期,期满
expire *v.*	期满
explanation *n.*	解释
export *n./v.*	出口,输出
exportation *n.*	出口
EXQ (ex-quay) *abbr.*	码头交货,码头交货价
EXS (ex-ship) *abbr.*	输入港船上交货价
ex-showroom *n.*	展室交货价
extension *n.*	延长
extreme *adj.*	极端的
EXW (ex-works) *abbr.*	工厂交货
ex-warehouse *n.*	仓库交货价
ex-works price *n.*	工厂交货价,出厂价

F

F.O.B. air port *abbr.*	启运地机场交货
F.P.A.(free from particular average) *abbr.*	平安险
fail *v.*	失败
failure *n.*	破产,违约
fair *adj./n.*	公正的,展销会
fair average quality (F.A.Q) *abbr.*	良好平均品质
FAS (free along side ship) *abbr.*	船边交货
favor *v.*	有助于
fax *n.*	传真
FBA (Fulfillment by Amazon) *abbr.*	亚马逊物流
FC (foreign currency) *abbr.*	外币
feasibility *n.*	可行性
fee *n.*	费
feedback *n.*	反馈
festival *n.*	节日
file *n.*	档案
filling *n./v.*	填充,填上,归档
filter *n./v.*	过滤,过滤器

finance *n.*	财政,筹资,金融,资金
financing *n.*	筹资,融资
finder *n.*	中间人
fine *v.*	罚款
finish *v.*	完工
float *v.*	浮动
flood *n./v.*	洪水
fluctuate *v.*	波动,升降
FOB（free on board） *abbr.*	离岸价
foot-notes *n.*	附注
forecast *n.*	预测
foreclosure *n.*	取消赎取权
foresee *v.*	预见
foreseeability *n.*	预见性
formatting *n.*	格式化
formula *n.*	公式
forward *n.*	期货
foundation *n.*	基础,基金
franchise *n.*	经营特许权
freight *n.*	运费
from … perspective	从……的角度来看
fruitful *adj.*	富有成果的
ft（foot） *abbr.*	英尺
fuel *n.*	燃料
fulfill *v.*	履行,完成
function *n.*	职能
fund *n.*	基金,资金

G

G2B（Government to Business）*abbr.*	（企业与政府机构间电子商务的）政府抛售
gage *n.*	抵押品
gain *v.*	获得,收益,盈余
gain and loss *n.*	损益
gal（gallon） *abbr.*	加仑
gasoline *n.*	汽油
GCID（Global Catalog Identifier） *abbr.*	全球目录编码
generic *adj.*	一般的;普通的;通用的

gift	*n.*	礼品,赠品
glass	*n.*	玻璃
GNP (gross national product)	*abbr.*	国民生产总值
goal	*n.*	目标
goodwill	*n.*	好信誉
government	*n.*	政府
grade	*n.*	等级
grant	*v.*	补贴,授予
graph	*n.*	图表
gratuitous	*adj.*	免费的
gross	*n.*	毛值,总值
gross for net	*n.*	毛作净
gross weight	*n.*	毛重
group	*n.*	集团
growth	*n.*	增长
growth rate	*n.*	增长率
GSP (generalized system of preferences)	*abbr.*	普遍优惠率
guarantee	*n./v.*	保证,保证书
guideline	*n.*	指南

H

hand-book	*n.*	手册
handle	*v.*	操作,管理
hand-over	*v.*	移交
harbor	*n.*	海港
harm	*v.*	伤害,损害
harmless	*adj.*	无害的
here-after	*adv.*	此后,下文
here-by	*adv.*	特此
here-in	*adv.*	此中,于此
highlight	*v.*	突出;强调
hire	*v.*	租用
hold	*v.*	持有
holiday	*n.*	假期,节日
hospital	*n.*	医院
host	*n.*	主人
hotel	*n.*	旅馆

I

I/S (international shopping)	*abbr.*	国际询价采购
IaaS	*abbr.*	基础服务
ICB (international competitive bidding)	*abbr.*	国际竞争性招标
identification	*n.*	鉴别,认定
identify	*v.*	验明
identity	*n.*	身份
IFC (International Finance Corporation)	*abbr.*	国际金融公司
IMF (International Monetary Fund)	*abbr.*	国际货币基金组织
immunity	*n.*	豁免
imperfect	*adj.*	不完善的
implement	*v.*	落实,执行
import	*v.*	进口
important	*adj.*	重要的
imposition	*n.*	课税
impost	*n.*	进口税
impound	*v.*	扣押
imprint	*v.*	盖印
improper	*adj.*	不合格的
improvement	*n.*	改进
in(inch)	*abbr.*	英寸
inalienable	*adj.*	不可剥夺的权利
inauguration	*n.*	典礼
include	*v.*	包括
inclusive	*adj.*	包括的
income	*n.*	收入
income accounts	*n.*	收益账户
incorporate	*v.*	将……包括在内;包含;吸收;使并入
Incoterms (International Rules for the interpretation of Trade Terms)	*abbr.*	国际贸易术语解释通则
increase	*v.*	增加
increment	*n.*	增值
incumbent	*adj.*	负有义务的
indemnify	*v.*	保护,补偿
indent	*n.*	订货单
indenture	*n.*	契约

indicate *v.*	象征;暗示
indicator *n.*	指标
ineffective *adj.*	无效的
inefficient *adj.*	低效的,无能的
inequality *n.*	不平等
inevitable *adj.*	不可避免的
inexpensive *adj.*	廉价的
inexperience *n.*	缺乏经验
inferior goods *n.*	低档货
inflation *n.*	通货膨胀
inflow *v.*	流入
inform *v.*	报告,通知
inheritor *n.*	继承人
initial *adj.*	最初的,最开始的,草签
initial a contract *v.*	草签合同
initial cost *n.*	最初成本
initial data *n.*	原始资料
initial payment *n.*	定金,最初付款
initial price *n.*	初步价格
initial ranking *n.*	初步排列顺序
injustice *n.*	不公平
innovation *n.*	革新
input *n.*	输入,投入
inquiry *n.*	查询,询价
insight *n.*	洞悉;了解
insolvent *n.*	破产者,无力偿还者
inspect *v.*	检查
inspection *n.*	检查
inspector *n.*	检查员
installation *n.*	安装
installment *n.*	分期付款
instant *adj.*	立即
instill *v.*	逐渐灌输,逐步培养
institute *n.*	协会,学会,学院
instruction *n.*	指令,指示
instrument *n.*	仪表,仪器
insulation *n.*	绝缘材料
insulator *n.*	绝缘体

insurable liabilities *n.*	保险责任
insurance *n.*	保险
insurant *n.*	被保险人
insure *v.*	投保
Insured *n.*	被保险人
insurer *n.*	保险人
intent *v.*	意向
intention *n.*	意图
interest *n.*	兴趣
interest rate *n.*	利率
interests *n.*	利息
internal rate of return (IRR) *abbr.*	内部收回率,内部收益率
International Chamber of Commerce (ICC) *abbr.*	国际商会
interpretation *n.*	解释,口译
interpreter *n.*	口译员
interview *n.*	会见
introduce *v.*	介绍
introduction *n.*	简介,简述
invalid *adj.*	无效的,作废的
invariable *adj.*	不变的
inventory *n.*	财产目录,存货,提单
invite *v.*	邀请
invoice *n.*	发票
involve *v.*	包含,卷入
inward *adj./adv.*	向内的
inward charge *n.*	入港费
IOU (I owe you) *abbr.*	借据
irreconcilable *adj.*	不可调和的
ISBM(International Standard Book Number) *abbr.*	国际标准书号
issue *v.*	颁布,公布
item *n.*	条款,项,项目

J

jargon *n.*	行话;黑话;行业术语
jerry *adj.*	偷工减料

job *n.*	工作、职业
jobber *n.*	批发商
JS(JavaScript) *abbr.*	前端开发
judge *v.*	法官,审理
judgement *n.*	判决
judicial *adj.*	公正的,司法的
jurisdiction *n.*	管辖权,司法权
justice *n.*	公正,审判
justification *n.*	证明,证实

K

Kg *abbr.*	公斤,千克
kickback *n.*	回扣;佣金
kite *n.*	空头支票
kiting *n.*	挪用
know-how *n.*	技术,诀窍,专有技术
knowledge *n.*	理解,知道

L

L/C (letter of credit) *abbr.*	(银行发行的)信用证
L/G (letter of guarantee) *abbr.*	(贸易)信用保证书
label *n.*	标记,标签
labor *n.*	劳力
lack *v.*	缺少
lading *n.*	船货
lapse *n.*	失效
larceny *n.*	盗窃
law *n.*	法律,法规
lawsuit *v.*	诉讼
lawyer *n.*	律师
lay *v.*	放置
lb *n.*	磅
LC (local currency) *abbr.*	当地货币
LCB (local competitive bidding) *abbr.*	国内竞争性报价
lease *v.*	租赁,租约
legality *n.*	合法

legislation *n.*	法规
legitimacy *n.*	合法;合理;正统
lend *v.*	贷款,借出
lender *n.*	出借人
length *n.*	长度
letter *n.*	信函
liability *n.*	义务,责任,债务
licence *n.*	许可证,执照
licensee *n.*	接受方,引进方
licensor *n.*	出让方,许可方
lien *n.*	扣押权,留置权
limitation *n.*	限制
Limited (Ltd.) *n.*	有限公司
liquidate *v.*	清偿,清算
list *n.*	列表,清单
litigant *n.*	诉讼当事人
loan *v.*	贷款
log into *v.*	登录计算机
lose *v.*	丢失,丧失,损失
loss *n.*	损失

M

M.O. (money order) *abbr.*	汇款单
M/T (mail transfer) *abbr.*	信汇
M/T advice *n.*	信汇委托书
M2C (Manufacturers to Consumer) *abbr.*	生产厂商对消费者的商业模式
machinery *n.*	机器,机械
mail *v.*	邮寄
maintenance *n.*	维修
make a difference	有影响;有关系
management *n.*	管理
manager *n.*	管理人员
mandate *v.*	委托,指定
mandator *n.*	委托人
mandatory *n.*	受托人
manual *adj.*	手工的
mark *n.*	标记

market *n.*	市场
material *n.*	材料,资料
maturity *n.*	到期
max *adj.*	最大,最多
M-B *abbr.*	移动电子商务
MD (managing director) *abbr.*	执行董事,总经理
mean *n.*	平均数
means *n.*	收入
measure *n.*	措施
media *n.*	宣传媒介
mediation *n.*	调解,仲裁
mediator *n.*	调解人
meeting *n.*	会议
merchant *n.*	商人
adj.	商业的
message *n.*	消息
metric *n.*	度量标准
adj.	公制的
middleman *n.*	中间人,经纪人
milestone *n.*	里程碑
million *n.*	百万
min *adj.*	最小,最少
mineral *n.*	矿物
minimum *adj.*	最小的,最少的;最低限度的
minister *n.*	部长
ministry *n.*	部
minutes *n.*	会谈纪要,纪要
mission *n.*	代表团,任务
misstatement *n.*	错报
mistake *n.*	错误
misunderstanding *n.*	误解
mitigation *n.*	减轻
mode *n.*	模式
model *n.*	模型
modification *n.*	修改
money *n.*	货币,金钱
mortgage *v.*	抵押
mortgagee *n.*	受押人

motion clarity index	运动清晰度指数
MT (metric ton) *abbr.*	吨
multiple *adj.*	多重的

N

N/M (no mark) *abbr.*	无唛头
nationality *n.*	国籍
native *adj.*	本地的,本地人,本国的
necessary *n.*	必需品
negative *adj.*	否定,负的
neglect *v.*	疏忽,玩忽
negligence *n.*	粗心大意,过失,玩忽
negligible *adj.*	可以忽略的
negotiate *v.*	会谈,协商
negotiation *n.*	谈判,协商
net *adj.*	净的
net asset *n.*	净资产
net present value (NPV) *abbr.*	净现值
net present value method (NPV method) *abbr.*	净现值法
net weight *n.*	净重
nil *n.*	零,无
NNP (net national product) *abbr.*	国民生产净值
no mark (N/M) *n.*	无标记
noise *n.*	噪音
nominate *v.*	提名,推荐
nominee *n.*	被指定人,被提名者
non performance of contract *n.*	合同的不履行
non-acceptance *n.*	拒绝承兑
noncompetitive bid *n.*	非竞争性投标
non-contractual document *n.*	非契约性文件
non-excusable delays *n.*	不可原谅的拖期
non-implementation of contract *n.*	合同的不履行
non-operating revenue *n.*	营业外收入
non-refundable payment *n.*	不退的付款
non-responsive bid *n.*	没有作出反应的投标
non-tariff barriers (NTBs) *abbr.*	非关税壁垒

norm *n.*	定额
notarization *n.*	公证
notary *n.*	公证人,公证行
notary public *n.*	公证人
note *n.*	附注,票据,期票
notice *n.*	通告,通知
notification *n.*	通知书
notification of approval *n.*	批准通知
novelty *n.*	新颖性
NPV (net present value) *abbr.*	净现值
NPV method (net present value method) *n.*	现净值法
NTBs (non-tariff barriers) *abbr.*	非关税壁垒
null *n.*	无效
number *n.*	数量,数目
numerous *adj.*	大批量的

O

o/d (on demand) *abbr.*	即付
O/D (overdraft) *abbr.*	透支
O2O *abbr.*	网上与网下相结合
obey *v.*	服从
object *v.*	对象,反对
objection *n.*	反对,拒绝
objective *n.*	经营目标
objectivity *n.*	客观性
obligation *n.*	义务,责任
oblige *n.*	债权人
obligor *n.*	债务人
oblong *n.*	长方形
observance *n.*	观察,遵守
observation *n.*	观察,评论
observatory *n.*	气象台
observe *v.*	遵守(法律、法规)
obsolete *adj.*	过时的
obstacle *n.*	障碍,障碍物
obstruct *v.*	妨碍
obtain *v.*	获得

obviate *v.*	排除
occasion *n.*	机会,时机
occupant *n.*	占有人
occupation *n.*	居住,占用,职业
occupy *v.*	从事,占用,占有
occur *v.*	发生
occurrence *n.*	发生,事件
odd *adj.*	零散的,临时的
odds *n.*	差别,优势,胜算
ODR (Order Defect Rate) *abbr.*	订单缺陷率
Off-day *n.*	休息日
offend *v.*	违反
offer *v.*	报价,发盘,卖价
offeree *n.*	接受报价者,买主
offerer *n.*	(贸易)发价人,报价人
office *n.*	办公室
officer *n.*	公务员,官员
officiate *v.*	行使职务,主持会议
offset *v.*	冲销,抵消
omit *v.*	省略,遗漏
OMS (Order Management System) *abbr.*	订单管理系统
open *v.*	开放
operating *n.*	操作,营业,运营
Operation Manager *n.*	运营经理
operator *n.*	操作者,经纪人
opinion *n.*	意见书
opponent *n.*	对手
optimization *n.*	最优化
order *n.*	订单,命令
order B/L *n.*	指示提单
ordinance *n.*	法令
organic *adj.*	有机的;组织的
organization *n.*	机构,组织
Organization of Petroleum Exporting *n.*	石油输出国组织
orientation *n.*	定位
origin *n.*	原产地
original *n.*	原件
original sample *n.*	原样

original *adj.*	独创的;新颖的
outdoors *n.*	户外
outgo *n.*	支出
outlay *n.*	开支
outlet *n.*	排水口
outline *n.*	轮廓,外形,要点
over *prep.*	超过
overdraft（O/D） *v.*	透支
overdue *v.*	过期未付,逾期
overhaul *v.*	检修
overhead *n.*	管理费,间接费用
overland *adj.*	陆上的
overload *v.*	超负荷
overproduction *n.*	生产过剩
oversight *v.*	失察
overstep *v.*	越权
overtime *v.*	加班
overweight *v.*	超重
owe *v.*	欠债
owing *adj.*	未付的
owner *n.*	业主
ownership *n.*	所有权
oxidized *adj.*	生锈的,氧化的

P

P（plan） *abbr.*	计划
P2C（production to consumer）*abbr.*	生活服务平台(产品从生产企业直接送到消费者手中,中间没有任何的交易环节的商业模式)
P2P（peer to peer） *abbr.*	点对点、渠道对渠道
PaaS（Platform as a Service） *abbr.*	平台服务
pack *v.*	包装,打包
package *n.*	包,包装,一揽子
packing *n.*	包装
pact *n.*	公约
paid *adj.*	已支付的
paint *n.*	油漆

pamphlet *n.*	宣传小册
panel *n.*	仪表板
paper *n.*	票据,纸币
par *n.*	票面额
paragraph *n.*	段落
parallel *adj.*	平行的
parameter *n.*	参数
parapet *n.*	短墙,女儿墙
parcel *n.*	包裹,部分,一块
park *n.*	公园,停车场
parliament *n.*	国会,议会
part *n.*	部分
participate *v.*	参加
particular *adj.*	特别的,细节
partition *n.*	隔墙,间墙
partner *n.*	合伙人
partnership *n.*	合伙
party *n.*	一方(合同中的一方)
party A *n.*	甲方
party B *n.*	乙方
pass *v.*	通行
passport *n.*	护照
patent *n.*	专利
path *n.*	路径
pattern sample *n.*	款式样品
patterns *n.*	图样
pawn *n.*	抵押,典当
pay *v.*	支付
pay as you earn (PAYE) *v.*	预扣所得税
payable *adj.*	应付的,应付款
pay-back *v.*	收回
PAYE (pay as you earn) *abbr.*	预扣所得税
payee *n.*	收款人,受款人
payer *n.*	付款人
payment *n.*	付款,支付
PDM (Product Data Management) *abbr.*	产品数据管理
penalty *n.*	罚金,罚款
pension *n.*	退休金

per diem *adj.*	按日计
percent *n.*	百分比
percentage *n.*	百分数
perfect *adj.*	完美的
perform *v.*	履行,履约,执行
performance *n.*	履约,实施
period *n.*	周期
permission *n.*	准许
permit *n.*	通行证,许可证
permits *n.*	许可证费用
person *n.*	人
personnel *n.*	人员
petition *n.*	申请
picture *n.*	图片,照片
plaintiff *n.*	原告
plan *n.*	计划
plant *n.*	工程设备
play a role in	在……中起作用;在……扮演一个角色
pledge *v.*	抵押,抵押品
plenipotentiary *adj.*	有全权的
PLS (please) *abbr.*	请
PLSCONFM (please confirm) *abbr.*	请确认
plus or minus *n.*	正负号;增减
policy *n.*	保单,政策
pollution *n.*	环境污染
POP(Point Of Purchase) *abbr.*	卖点广告(又名:店头陈设)
populace *n.*	人民,百姓,大众
population *n.*	人口
populous *adj.*	人口稠密的
port *n.*	港口
porter age *n.*	搬运费
position *n.*	位置,职位,状况
positive *adj.*	正的
possession *n.*	占有
possibility *n.*	可能性
possible *adj.*	可能的
postpone *v.*	推迟,延期
potential *adj.*	潜在的,可能的

power *n.*	权利
powerless *adj.*	无权的,无效的
PR *abbr.*	软文推广
practical *adj.*	实际的
precede *v.*	领先,优先
precedence *n.*	先决的,优先权
precedent *n.*	先例
precise *adj.*	精确的
precision *n.*	精确度
prejudice *n.*	偏见,损害
premise *n.*	前提
prepare *v.*	编制,准备
prepayment *n.*	预付款
present *v.*	出席
present contract *n.*	本合同
presentation *n.*	交单,提交
preservation *n.*	保护,防腐
preserve *v.*	保持
president *n.*	总裁,总统
pressure *n.*	电压,压力
price *n.*	价格
principal *n.*	本金,委托人(代理人的)
prioritize *v.*	优先处理
priority *n.*	优先权
private *adj.*	私营的
private enterprise *n.*	私营企业
privilege *n.*	特许
probability *n.*	概率,可能性
probable *adj.*	可能的
probation *n.*	试用,试用期
probation period *n.*	试用期
problem *n.*	问题
procedural law for arbitration *n.*	仲裁使用的程序法
procedure *n.*	程序
procedure for claims *n.*	索赔程序
procedure of approval *n.*	批准程序
proceed *v.*	继续进行,开始,起诉
proceeding *n.*	会议录,诉讼

proceeds	*n.*	收入,收益
process	*v.*	加工
process cost	*n.*	加工成本
process data	*n.*	处理数据,整理资料
proclamation	*n.*	公布,公告
procurement	*n.*	采购
produce	*v.*	生产
product page	*n.*	产品说明页
production	*n.*	产量,生产
production volume	*n.*	产量
productivity	*n.*	生产率
profession	*n.*	技能,职业
professional	*adj.*	职业的,专业的
proficiency	*n.*	精通,熟练
profile	*n.*	外形,轮廓
profit	*n.*	利润
profiteer	*n.*	投机商
Prohibit	*v.*	禁止
project	*n.*	工程,计划,项目
projection	*n.*	估算,预测
prominently	*adv.*	显著地;突出地
promise	*n.*	受约人
promise	*v.*	承诺
promisor	*n.*	立约人
promissory note	*n.*	期票
promoters	*n.*	业主
promotion	*n.*	促销,推销
proof	*n.*	证明
property	*n.*	财产
proprietary	*adj.*	所有人的,专卖的
proprietor	*n.*	业主
pro-rata	*adj.*	按比例
protection	*n.*	保护
protest	*v.*	拒付,抗议
provide	*v.*	规定,提供
provision	*n.*	规定,条款,预备
proviso	*n.*	附文,限制性条款
proxy	*n.*	代理,委托书

purchase *v.*	购买
purchasing *n.*	采购
purpose *n.*	目的,用途
PVB (present value of benefits) *abbr.*	效益现值
PVC (present value of costs) *abbr.*	成本现值

Q

QC (quality control) *abbr.*	质量控制
QCP (quality control planning) *abbr.*	质量控制计划
qualification *n.*	条件,资格
qualify *v.*	合格
quality *n.*	品质
quantity *n.*	数量
quirky *adj.*	离奇的,古怪的;奇特的
quit office *v.*	退职
quit work *v.*	停工
quitclaim *v.*	放弃要求
quota *n.*	定额,定量,分配额,配额,限额
quotation *n.*	报价
quote *v.*	开价

R

radius *n.*	半径
raise *v.*	提出,提高
rate *n.*	比率,费率
ratification *n.*	批准,认可
ratio *n.*	比率
ration *n.*	配额
reapportionment *n.*	再分配
reasonable *adj.*	合理的
re-bid *v.*	再招标,重新招标
receipt *n.*	收到,收据
reckoning *n.*	结算
recognize *v.*	确认
recommend *v.*	建议,推荐
recompense *v.*	赔偿

reconciliation	*n.*	调解,和解
re-conditional	*adj.*	翻新的,重新装配的
record	*v.*	记录
recoup	*v.*	补偿,赔偿
rectify	*v.*	纠正
redeem	*v.*	偿还,弥补
redistribution	*n.*	再分配
redress	*v.*	补救,纠正
reduce	*v.*	减少,减低
reduction	*n.*	减低
re-evaluate	*v.*	重现评估
re-exportation	*n.*	再出口
refer	*v.*	参考,提及
reference	*n.*	参考,推荐书
reference sample	*n.*	参考样品
refund	*n.*	退款
refuse	*v.*	拒绝
refute	*v.*	反驳
regain	*v.*	收回
region	*n.*	地区
register	*v.*	注册
regulation	*n.*	条例,章程
rehabilitation	*n.*	修复,重建
re-hypothecate	*v.*	再抵押
reimburse	*v.*	补偿
reimbursement	*n.*	偿还,赔偿
reimbursement of customs duties	*n.*	补偿关税
reject	*v.*	拒绝
rejection	*n.*	拒绝,拒收
relationship	*n.*	关系
relative	*adj.*	相比较而言的;比较的
release	*v.*	放弃,解除
release...from	*v.*	免除
relevant to	*adj.*	有关的,相应的;与……有关的
relieve...from	*v.*	使解除
remain	*v.*	剩下,余下
remedy	*v.*	补救
remission	*n.*	减免

remit　*v.*	汇款
remittance　*n.*	汇款
remittee　*n.*	收款人
remitter　*n.*	汇款人
remuneration　*n.*	报酬
renew　*v.*	更新
rent　*n.*	出租,租金
repair　*v.*	修理
reparation　*n.*	补偿,赔偿
repatriate　*v.*	遣返,遣送回国
repay　*v.*	偿还,付还
repayment　*n.*	偿还,还款
repeal　*v.*	撤销,废止
re-pledge　*v.*	转抵押
reply　*v.*	回答
report　*v.*	报告
representation　*n.*	申述,说明
representative　*n.*	代表,代理人
representative sample　*n.*	代表性样品
repudiation　*n.*	拒付(债务)
reputation　*n.*	信誉
request　*v.*	请求,申请
requirement　*n.*	需要,需要量
requisitioning　*n.*	征用
resale　*v.*	转卖,转售
rescission　*n.*	解约
research　*v.*	研究
reservation　*n.*	储备,权益保留
reserve　*v.*	保留,库存
reservoir　*n.*	水库,蓄水池
residence　*n.*	住宅
resign　*v.*	辞职,放弃
resolution　*n.*	解决,决议
resolve　*v.*	解决
resort to	采取;诉诸于
resort to	依靠,求助于;诉诸
resource　*n.*	资源
response　*n.*	响应,应答

responsibility	*n.*	责任,职责
responsive	*adj.*	有反映的
rest	*n.*	盈余
rest-day	*n.*	休息日
restitution	*n.*	归还,赔偿
restrict	*v.*	限制,约束
restriction	*n.*	限度,限制
result	*n.*	成果,结果
retail	*v.*	零售
return	*n.*	返回,收益
revenue	*n.*	收入,税收
review	*v.*	审查
revision	*n.*	修改
reward	*n.*	酬金,奖金
right	*n.*	权利
risk[s]	*n.*	风险,危险
rival	*n.*	对手,竞争者
river regulation work	*n.*	河流整治工程
ROI (Return On Investment)	*abbr.*	投资回报率
rollback	*n.*	压价
rough	*adj.*	粗略的
rule	*n.*	惯例,规章
ruling	*n.*	裁决
rummage	*v.*	海关检查
run	*v.*	运行

S

SaaS (Software as a Service)	*abbr.*	软件即服务
safe	*adj.*	安全
safety	*n.*	安全
salary	*n.*	薪金,薪水
sale	*n.*	销售
salesman	*n.*	销售员
sample	*n.*	样品
sample	*n.*	货样,实例,样品
sanction	*n.*	法律制裁
satisfaction	*n.*	履约,满意

satisfy *v.*	使满意
saving *n.*	储蓄
scam *n.*	骗局,诡计,欺诈
scarcity *n.*	短缺,缺货
scheme *n.*	方案,计划
scrutiny *n.*	审查
SDR (special drawing right) *abbr.*	特别提款权
seal *n.*	铅封,印章
sealed sample *n.*	封样
season *n.*	季节
seconds *n.*	次品
secrecy *n.*	保密,机密
secretary *n.*	秘书
seize *v.*	扣押(财产),没收
sell *v.*	销售
seller *n.*	卖方
SEM (Search Engine Marketing) *abbr.*	搜索引擎营销
sender *n.*	发货人
sentence *n.*	判决
SEO (Search Engine Optimization) *abbr.*	搜索引擎优化
separation *n.*	解雇
sequester *n.*	查封,扣押
service *n.*	劳务,服务
settlement *n.*	结算,结账,解决
shipment *n.*	发货,发运
shipper *n.*	发货人
shipping weight *n.*	装船重量
shortage *n.*	缺乏
shower *n.*	淋浴器
shrinkage *n.*	收缩,损耗
shuttering *n.*	模板
side *n.*	侧面
side line *n.*	副业
sign *v.*	签字
sign in	注册;登记
signboard *n.*	招牌
site *n.*	现场
size *n.*	尺寸,大小,规模

SKU (Stock Keeping Unit) *abbr.*	(库存量单位)以件、盒、托盘等为单位
slump *v.*	暴跌,衰退
smuggle *v.*	走私
SNS-EC *abbr.*	社会化网络电子商务
soar *v.*	价格猛涨
solicitor *n.*	律师;法务官
SoLoMo (social media, local and mobile search) *abbr.*	社交本地移动
source *n.*	来源
specialist *n.*	专家
specification *n.*	规格;规范;明细单;说明书
specifications *n.*	规格
specify *v.*	具体指明;明确说明;详述
spell out	清楚地说出;清楚地说明
spend *v.*	花费
sponsor *n.*	担保人
spot *n.*	现货
SPPWF (single-payment present-worth factor) *abbr.*	一次支付现值系数
SRM (Supplier Relationship Management) *abbr.*	供应商关系管理
stability *n.*	稳定
staff *n.*	雇员,职员
stage *n.*	阶段
stale B/L *n.*	过期提单
standard *n.*	标准
stand-by L/C *n.*	备用信用证
statement *n.*	报表
statistic *n.*	统计数
statistician *n.*	统计人员
status *n.*	地位,身份,状况
statute *n.*	法规,法令
stay *v.*	坚持,停留
step *n.*	步骤,措施
stipend *n.*	津贴
stipulate *v.*	规定,写明
stock *n.*	存货,股份,股票
style *n.*	风格

subagent	*n.*	分代理人
sub-agents	*n.*	分代理人,副代理人
subassembly	*n.*	配件
sub-bids analyzing	*n.*	分包报价分析
sub-clause	*n.*	款(合同的第……款)
subcontract	*n.*	分包合同
sub-contracting	*n.*	分包
sub-contracting records	*n.*	分包付款的核算
subcontractor	*n.*	分包商
subdivision	*n.*	细分类住宅小区
subject	*n.*	主题
sublet	*v.*	分包,转包
submit	*v.*	提交
sub-mortgage	*n.*	二次抵押
sub-sampling	*n.*	二次抽样
subsidiary	*n.*	子公司
subsidy	*n.*	津贴
substantial	*adj.*	基本的,实质的
sub-total	*n.*	小计
successor	*n.*	后继人,继承人
suit	*v.*	控告,诉讼
suitability	*n.*	适用性
sum	*n.*	金额,总额,总和,总数
summary	*n.*	汇总表,摘要
summons	*n.*	传票
supervision	*n.*	监督
supervisor	*n.*	监督人,监理
supplement	*n.*	补充,增补
supplier	*n.*	供货商,供货者
supplies	*n.*	物料
supply	*v.*	供应
support	*v.*	证明,支持
surety	*n.*	保证,保证人
surrogate	*v.*	代理
surtax	*n.*	附加税
survey	*v.*	测量,勘察
surveyor	*n.*	测量师
syndicate	*n.*	银团

synonymous   *adj.*   相同的;近似的[+with]

system   *n.*   系统

T

T/T (telegraphic transfer)   *abbr.*   电汇

Table   *n.*   表格

take   *v.*   取得

take… into account   考虑;重视;体谅

take over   *v.*   接管,接收

take-home-pay   *n.*   实发工资

tallyman   *n.*   分期付款商

tare   *n.*   皮重

target   *n.*   目标

tariff   *n.*   关税

tax   *n.*   捐税,税,税收

tax holiday   *n.*   减税期

taxable   *adj.*   征税的

taxation   *n.*   征税

taxes   *n.*   税金,税收

tax-free   *adj.*   免税的

telex   *n.*   电传

tenant   *n.*   承租人

tendency *n.*   趋势

tender   *v.*   投标

tenderer   *n.*   投标人,投标者

term   *n.*   期限,条款

terminate   *v.*   终止

terminate a contract   *v.*   终止合同,解除合同

termination   *n.*   解雇,终止

terms   *n.*   条款

test   *v.*   检验,试验

text   *n.*   本文,文本,正文

thrift   *n.*   节约

through   *v.*   经过,通过

through B/L   *n.*   联运提单

tick   *n.*   记号

tie   *n.*   关系

till *n.*	钱柜
time-rate *n.*	计时工资
title *n.*	所有权,头衔
tolerance *n.*	公差
toll *n.*	通行税
tone *n.*	行情
tone of voice	口吻;说话的语气
tonnage *n.*	吨位
tools *n.*	工具
top *adj.*	顶部
tort *n.*	民事侵权行为
total *n.*	总计
TQC (total quality control) *abbr.*	全面质量管理
trade *n.*	贸易,商务
tradition *n.*	传统
traffic *n.*	交通,运输
training *n.*	培训
transaction *n.*	交易
transcript *n.*	副本
transfer *v.*	过户,转让
transferable L/C *n.*	可转让信用证
transit *v.*	过境,转口
transmit *v.*	传达,转达
transportation *n.*	运输
treasurer *n.*	司库
treasury *n.*	国库
treaty *n.*	合约,协定
trouble *n.*	故障,麻烦
trust *v.*	信任,信托
trustee *n.*	受托人
turnover *n.*	营业额,周转额
typewriter *n.*	打字机

U

U.S. dollar *abbr.*	美元
U.S.C. (unforeseen site conditions) *abbr.*	不可预见现场条件
UCC (Uniform Commercial Code) *abbr.*	统一商法

ultimatum *n.*	最后通牒
UN (United Nations) *abbr.*	联合国
unabsorbed cost *n.*	待摊成本
underselling *n.*	廉价出售
undersigned *adj.*	签字人
understanding *n.*	达成协议
undertake *v.*	承担
undervalue *n.*	低估价格
UNDP (United Nation Development-Program) *abbr.*	联合国开发计划署
undue debt *n.*	未到期债务
unemployment *n.*	失业
UNIDO (United Nations Industrial-Development Organization) *abbr.*	联合国工业发展组织
unilateral *adj.*	单方面的
union *n.*	工会,联合
unit *n.*	单位
unload *v.*	抛售,卸货
unofficial agreement *n.*	非正式协定
unpredictable element *n.*	不可预见因素
unreasonable *adj.*	不合理的
unreservedly acceptance *n.*	无保留验收
unsatisfactory *adj.*	不能令人满意的
unsecured loan *n.*	无担保贷款
unskilled labor *n.*	壮工
unsuccessful bidder *n.*	不中标者
unsuccessful tenderer *n.*	不中标者
up to date *adj.*	最新的
UPC (Universal Production Code) *abbr.*	通用产品编号(代码)
up-keep *n.*	维修费
urgent repairs *n.*	紧急修理
usage *n.*	用途
usance L/C (Usance Letter of Credit) *n.*	远期信用证
User *n.*	用户
User Experience *n.*	用户体验
usury *n.*	高利贷

V

vacancy *n.*	闲置率
vacation *n.*	假期,休假
validity *n.*	有效性
valorize *v.*	政府限价
valuation *n.*	估价,计价
value *n.*	价值,数值
variation *n.*	变更
vault *n.*	保险库,地下室
vehicle *n.*	车辆
venture *n.*	风险
verdict *v.*	裁决
verification *n.*	检验,验证
verify *v.*	证实
version *n.*	说明,文本,译文
vertical *adj.*	垂直的
vessel *n.*	船只
vesting *n.*	归属
veto *v.*	否决
vibrator *n.*	振动器
vindicate *v.*	辩护
violate *v.*	违犯
visit *v.*	访问
void *v.*	失效
volume *n.*	产量,容积,体积
vote *v.*	表决,投票

W

wage(s) *n.*	工资
waive *v.*	放弃
warning *n.*	警告
warrant *v.*	保证
warranty *n.*	保证,担保,保修单
waste *v.*	废弃,损耗
weight *n.*	重量

welfare　*n.*	福利
welfare expense　*n.*	福利费
wharf　*n.*	码头
wharf age　*n.*	码头费
wholesaler　*n.*	批发商
win　*v.*	成功,胜利
withdraw　*v.*	(从银行)取款,收回
withdrawal　*n.*	撤回(发盘),提款
withhold　*v.*	扣留
withholding　*n.*	扣款
witness　*n.*	见证人
woodwork　*n.*	工制品
wording　*n.*	措词,用语
workshop　*n.*	车间,工场,讲习班
writing　*adj.*	书面的

X, Y, Z

yard（yd）　*n.*	码;庭院
YC（your cable）　*abbr.*	贵方电报
yd（yard）　*n.*	码
yield　*n.*	产量,收益
yield rate　*n.*	收益率
YT（your telex）　*abbr.*	贵方电传
zero　*n.*	零点,零度
zone　*n.*	区域